# Practical Dog Breeding

# Practical Dog Breeding

D. Brian Plummer

PERRY GREEN PRESS

First published 2000
by Perry Green Press, Sudbury.



**British Library Cataloguing-in-Publication Data**
A catalogue record for this book is available from the British Library

ISBN 1 902481 06 2

Typeset by Florence Production Ltd, Stoodleigh, Devon.
Printed in Great Britain by Athenaeum Press Ltd, Gateshead, Tyne & Wear

# Contents

# Introduction

IT HAS BEEN SAID that the dog has suffered a period of domestication for over ten thousand years, changing remarkably little from its wolf or wolf-like ancestors over this period of time. What is more remarkable is the fact that dogs have survived this period of domestication, for a great deal of human stupidity and old wives' tales have always been attributed to dog breeding. This stupidity, ignorance and downright superstition exists today even among serious professional dog breeders, so one can assume these problems have existed since the dawn of time or whenever the dog entered what is euphemistically, and somewhat inaccurately referred to, as its symbiotic relationship with man.

After such a high flown introduction it now behoves me to offer my qualifications for writing this book, and I shall eschew my academic qualifications, for I have read many dog breeding manuals penned by veterinary surgeons who had little practical experience of dog breeding. Indeed few vets have actually witnessed a great many natural and normal births for only the most unworldly and inexperienced breeders call in a vet to be present at a perfectly normal parturition.

I have bred dogs virtually all my life and have experienced most of the problems attendant with the birth of puppies. I have also made most of the mistakes dog breeders make, though my scientific training has perhaps allowed me to check and dodge most of the unscientific hokum that clouds the minds of conventional dog breeders. I have also bred dogs in number, not merely a litter from Old Sal every two or three years. Indeed, at the time of writing, I make my living by producing puppies of many breeds, so perhaps the unwholesome title of dog farmer might be levied at me, for my numbers are large by any standards – though as an afterthought or perhaps defence, I must add that my kennels are both clean and well maintained.

I have also produced my own breed of dog, the Plummer Terrier, perhaps not everyone's choice of animal, but to produce any true breeding type one needs to be conversant with the problems wrought by inbreeding, or if I might use another euphemism, line breeding. Stay with me reader. Don't throw up your hands in horror, for I shall explain the more simple ramifications of genetics, free from jargon and scientific buzzwords, later in this book. Sufficient to say I have also a practical knowledge of the sundry undesirable qualities which can be produced by inbreeding, for I am no drawingroom geneticist.

I freely admit that I am not a good salesman and a truly practical dog breeder must be able to sell his wares as well as produce them. Indeed selling dogs, dealing with the most contrary and peculiar species on the face of the planet – man – is not my forte though I am learning to deal with people. Readers may choose to skip and eschew the relevant chapters concerning the sale of puppies, or read it simply because it is pock marked with accounts of personal mistakes I have made or anecdotes of peculiar people I have met.

However people seldom bother to read introductions to books so I shall bring this brief chapter to a close, and allow the reader to unravel the vagaries, complexities and problems which are likely to beset anyone engaged in the practice of professional dog breeding.

# 1

# The Reasons for Breeding Dogs

I AM SOMETIMES approached by loving owners who keep bitches and have been told that it is good policy to breed from a bitch at least once in her lifetime to ensure her longevity and good health in later life. I keep a variety of stud dogs and this explains why pet owners approach me. Now the idea that breeding once in a lifetime improves the health of an animal is bunkum, pure unscientific baloney. There is quite a lot of evidence to suggest that a maiden bitch will suffer far fewer women's problems than a bitch who has just had the one litter in her lifetime. So if one's wish is to keep the bitch in good health for her natural life span, ignore the notion that she should have one litter in her lifetime. Victorian and Edwardian dog writers were ever eager to draw analogies between dogs and man, totally unscientific analogies one must add, and often mentioned the mental condition of the village spinster – often a frosty schoolmarm who was intolerant of others and petulant about life – and likened such a woman to a bitch which was denied motherhood. Today this would be a totally unacceptable sexist comment to make, and woe betide any writer who put such a notion to print. I have never been particularly politically correct, but my objection to this analogy is a purely scientific one, based on the weighing of cause and effect in the creation of human peculiarity. It is totally unnecessary to breed from a bitch to ensure her good health. If a bitch suffers from nymphomania, a veterinary surgeon will usually suggest spaying the animal to stop it coming into season every few weeks, and not breeding from the animal, which may exacerbate rather than reduce the problem. I freely admit I dislike the modern preoccupation with sterilising every pet dog, simply because I regard this practise as a veterinary catch penny. Such operations are not only unnecessary but quite expensive, but the process of breeding from a bitch which suffers from nymphomania, which is a morbid uncontrolled sexual appetite in female animals, not to be confused with the actions of a promiscuous woman, may well perpetuate the problem among her progeny. There is little scientific evidence to prove conclusively that the disorder or disposition is inherited, but there is some indication that bitches which come into season every few years rather than twice a year may well produce bitch puppies which are also reluctant to come into season. There is also some indication that bitches which are forever giving an indication of being ready to mate, some will come into season as many as six times a year, may well suffer from a gynaecological disorder (an ovarian cyst perhaps) which prevents them from conceiving. Whatever the causes of this peculiarity, it is better to sterilise such an animal rather than to breed from it to affect a cure for the disorder.

Many people who have kept a beloved bitch believe that it is wise to breed from the animal in order to keep back a bitch puppy which has similar desirable characteristics, and in many ways this can be said to be a good practice, particularly if the bitch is the belle ideal of everything the owner desires in an animal. The logic behind such thinking is that while the male part of the equation may confer some qualities which are possibly somewhat less than desirable the bitch will stamp at least some of her desirable qualities in the progeny. This is a great way of breeding perhaps particularly if one wishes to continue a good line of exhibition or working dogs. The shortcomings of such a practice only become apparent if the owner wishes to perpetuate the bloodline of a much beloved but ageing pet animal which has no outstanding aesthetic or working qualities. Comparisons are not only odious but totally unavoidable and quotes like ‘There’ll never be another Belle, Mollie, Sal etc.’ are inevitable, for the progeny of Old Belle, Mollie, Sal etc. will seldom measure up to those of their much loved dam.

I feel such a hypocrite writing the previous passage, for over the last forty or fifty years I have deliberately bred my own strain of lurcher and a breed of terrier simply because I value the mental qualities of the sires and dams I use to produce my very inbred families. My reason for doing so is to produce animals I know and understand, for not only do I know what these animals will do but I am also aware of their shortcomings: ‘I know what they can do and what they can’t do’ is the quote I most often use in my articles in the canine press. Yet I too am all too prompt to compare – and to compare unfavourably – the qualities of a youngster produced from a particularly good bitch.

Most dog owners enter into dog breeding to experience the fun it can be to rear a litter and some of them even become addicted to dog breeding. I have met dozens of young enthusiasts who bring a bitch for mating just for the fun of producing a litter of puppies, watching the progeny develop and become characters in their own rights and then finally homing the litter and keeping in touch with the dogs and their new owners. Indeed I have made many such friends via dog breeding, However, few of these tyro dog breeders seem to wish to continue producing further litters of puppies, for the process of dog breeding is not only fascinating but also time consuming and extremely tying. True it may be fun, racing home from work every breaktime to ensure the puppies are fed four times a day, but the entertainment may begin to cloy when the process continues for five or so weeks or until the puppies are sold.

A word of caution to what I infer to as the 'fun breeder'. When such a person comes to my premises to mate a particularly beloved bitch I always ask them how they intend to home any of the puppies they may produce if the mating is successful. Every last 'fun breeder' I have ever met states 'All my friends want a puppy from Mollie, Sal, Belle etc.' Fun breeder beware! When the time comes to home some of the puppies it is amazing just how many friends decide against having one and will offer a variety of excuses as to why they are refusing to home a whelp – and the number of friends opting out of a verbal commitment increases rapidly if the puppies are to be sold rather than given away. Forthcoming holidays, social problems and an amazing number of other reasons, some so curious as to defy belief will be offered as reasons why friends can't home a puppy.

A further 'caveat' on which the fun breeder must ponder, is the production of a second litter should all one's friends prove extremely trustworthy and home the first litter. Unless the fun breeder has a huge number of friends and lives in a social whirl of people who are hell bent on homing a particular breed of dog, it may be quite difficult to find homes for a second litter.

So to the third type of breeder who decides to breed dogs, to make either pin money (a curious expression I explain below) or to make a living by dint of dog breeding. Now make no bones about it, a living, indeed a good living, can sometimes be made by breeding dogs, but once again let the would-be breeder beware. At the time of writing the majority of my younger friends are experiencing a bad attack of premature mid-life crisis and are thinking of leaving their mundane jobs to take up dog breeding or to attempt some form of similar self-sufficiency. It is not that simple I am afraid.

Pin money: a lady's allowance to buy trivia. Apparently makers of pins were only allowed to sell pins on January 1st and 2nd and ladies saved to buy them – at least that is what Brewers Dictionary of Phrase and Fable says.

A few days ago a friend of mine, a shepherd by trade, bleated (a bad pun considering the occupation in hand) that sheep breeding was the most financially perilous of occupations, for sheep seem to have one aim in life and that is to secure the extinction of all ovine creatures. So hell-bent are sheep on self-destruction that the saying 'where there is livestock there is deadstock' certainly applies. Yet despite the complaints of shepherds that there is little profit in the production of sheep, there is always a market for food even if the profit margin of the production of meat is small.

There is not always a market for dogs. Indeed, when an economic crisis threatens and that capricious creature, the man in the street, needs to pull in his belt a notch or so – the purchasing of pets is the very last item that he will consider. Furthermore, from time to time, it is virtually impossible to sell certain breeds. In 1996 it was virtually impossible to sell good Labrador Retriever puppies, for the market in this breed was totally flooded. A glance at the Yellow and Blue papers will indicate that up to thirty litters of puppies would be advertised each week. In 1998 there was little or no market for German Shepherd puppies, even well bred ones. As I write, I have a seventeen week old litter of German Shepherd puppies for sale. They are both beautiful and very well bred yet such is the glut of German Shepherds that the litter may have to be given away. A week ago I paid £400 to inoculate the batch, for it is courting disaster to keep uninoculated whelps in the kennel, particularly in a kennel the size of mine, for diseases are certainly attracted to uninoculated dogs. I must of course write off this sum of money if I am to home these whelps free of charge. If I run them on, the cost of feeding growing puppies becomes crippling, for sapling youngsters eat with gusto and should be fed only high grade expensive food.

If one is astute and able to predict the market for dogs, it is possible to make a great profit breeding the 'in breed' of the time. Shortly after Akitas – huge Spitz type animals with often voluminous coats, appeared in the country, puppies were advertised at £1000 each and were snapped up as soon as advertisements appeared in a paper. Now it is difficult to sell puppies for £200, particularly since, a large, powerful male Akita did ferocious damage to a child in 1997 and the attack received equally ferocious publicity. Shortly after the film *A Thousand and One Dalmatians* was shown there was a huge market for Dalmatians, despite the fact that about 20% of all Dalmatians are born deaf. The craze will not last, for another showing of Turner and Hooch will tempt the public to buy a delightfully ugly Dogue de Bordeaux puppies presently selling at £1000 each, for the breed is rare in Britain.

On a more macabre note, despite the bad publicity given to the Rottweiler and to a lesser extent the Doberman, a showing of the films *Damien, The Omen* and *The Boys From Brazil* will attract a fair number of near lunatic purchasers eager to own Devil Dogs which will perpetrate horrendous damage on their enemies and friends alike. I breed white GSDs yet when there is a rare showing of *White Dog* – a totally illogical film about a white GSD owned by red necked hill-billy types, which is fine with white children but attacks black people with gusto and frenzy, I deliberately withdraw my advertisement from the papers for a fortnight, lest I should be pestered with strange people with a grudge against coloured neighbours eager to own such dogs. Indeed so strange are the telephone calls that one wonders how such callers are able to dial restricted as they are by the cosy confines of their straightjackets.

I have a terrible habit of running ahead of myself in print, a habit I trust the reader will forgive or at least learn to tolerate, but might I play out my role of iconoclast demonstrated earlier in the book to dispel a myth about dog breeding. It is popularly believed that in order to prosper financially as a dog breeder one needs to show dogs regularly. The notion is perpetuated in the majority of books about dog breeding. Not only is such a statement untrue, it is totally illogical. The majority of dog buyers are would-be pet owners who are not the slightest bit concerned with how well the parents of the animal are doing in the show ring (though they do like to see the odd Champion or so in the pedigree). Shows are seldom the advertisement the would be pet breeder needs, for the majority of exhibitors already own dogs and the spectators at such shows are seldom visiting the event with a view to purchasing a puppy. True champions change hands at Crufts for incredible sums, Japanese and Chinese buyers come wishing to buy bloodstock, but these buyers will not be the bread and butter of the pet dog breeder who produces good or above average stock. Furthermore I question if many show breeders profit much from the sale of stock which has been made up to champion status (three Challenge Certificates given by three different judges). Trips to shows are decidedly expensive both in travelling expenses and entrance fees, and when one considers the time spent at shows there is seldom a great deal of money to be made from the sale of a champion dog or bitch.

Those seeking to make a modest living from dogs should perhaps visit shows from time to time to see how the fashions in particular breeds are changing but the shows are not the shop windows most breed books make them out to be. For instance, there are many thousand GSD puppies bred each year yet there are perhaps only three hundred or so regular exhibitors attending the shows. I shall deal with advertising puppies at a later stage of the book so perhaps readers will forgive this slight digression so early in the pages of this manual.

Might I conclude this chapter by writing that the would be dog breeder out to make a living from dogs should shut his ears to advice given by amateurs who have little idea of the very fickle dog trade. In 1996 a friend in the village tipped me the wink that I should get myself some more Labrador bitches as the public were crying out for more Labrador puppies. I bit my lip and said nothing but the same week I gave away a litter sired by the top British stud dog. I could not sell a single puppy despite the fact I'd spent £500 or so advertising them.

# 2

# Points to Consider before Starting up

LET US CONSIDER that the reader wishes to start up a kennel to breed dogs on a commercial basis and has decided on the breed that he or she wishes to keep. Apparently the production of a commercial breeding kennels should be just plain sailing. Reader it isn't!

Most dog breeders start out in a small way and somehow grow the business to proportions that soon take over the breeder's life. A single bitch producing a litter of puppies a year and perhaps attracting a dozen or so potential buyers to the house may convince the neighbours that the dog owner is a slightly eccentric but harmless person. A string of clients and a string of litters sold via the local newspapers will do otherwise, particularly if the breeder looks like making a success or a profit out of his or her hobby. Britain is a strange country in many ways. In America the general public greets success in any field with applause. In Britain success is met with envy and in no time the breeder will be reported to the local Council for operating a business without planning permission. Frankly I find the British mania for reporting people, usually hiding in anonymity while reporting, is quite unpleasant, but then I grew up in a very rough mining district where the only offensive four-letter word was 'nark'. If the breeder lives in a council house his business enterprise will be shut down forthwith, for the purpose of council houses is to provide living accommodation for people and not to be used as business premises. If the breeder owns his own property he will be required to apply for planning permission to run a kennels and his application will need to get the sanction of his neighbours, the very same neighbours who have probably reported him to the council.

Britain is a crowded country so such red tape is necessary and while the joyous barking of pets or the 'I am here' morning howl of kennel in-mates may delight the owner of the dogs, neighbours will be less enthusiastic about the cacophony. At the time of writing I am an expert witness (a curious and questionable title) on a case concerning noise made by a long established kennels, the proprietor of which never bothered applying for planning permission. A neighbour, a solicitor by trade, has brought an action in an effort to have the kennels closed down. The case is a messy one and has caused the owner of the dogs considerable stress and grief. Had she applied for planning permission when she considered dog breeding, much though not all of the worry she has experienced could have been alleviated. Now after twenty years of breeding and selling dogs she is faced with the prospect of having to get rid of her life's work and because the dogs are her sole source of income, face a bleak future with a retirement in penury.

A visit to one's local council offices will usually provide advice on how to apply for the necessary planning permission. A trip to one's solicitor is well worth the money paid so that loose ends concerning one's planning application might be tied up. Planning permission is essential if one is to consider starting up a breeding kennels, and for those who doubt the seriousness of failure to obtain such permission, might I suggest a month's subscription to one of the canine periodicals will do much to convince the doubter. Such magazines are often packed with tales of woe relating to the sale of dogs from long established kennels which have been forced to close because the owners were operating without planning permission when a vindictive neighbour has decided to complain. Even friends become envious if a person seems to be making a success out of business, any business, and often react in a totally unreasonable way. Indeed the more I see of men the more I like my dogs – not an original quote but a singularly apt one, I am afraid.

However important planning permission may appear, a breeder's licence is of equal importance. Prior to 1973 dog breeders often kept dogs in quite unpleasant conditions existing just beyond the reach of the 1911 Protection of Animals Act (1912 Scotland). In 1973 The Dog Breeders Act was passed which empowered the local authorities to issue a breeders licence, subject to inspection by a public health officer (see Appendix 1). If a person keeps two or more breeding bitches which are to be used for breeding, a breeder must apply for a dog breeder's licence. This licence is only issued if the dogs are satisfactorily housed and fed. It also ensures that dogs must be properly and adequately exercised. A fire extinguisher must be maintained in any building that houses dogs and the surfaces of all buildings which are in contact with dogs must be impervious, to allow the kennels to be thoroughly cleaned – wooden buildings must be painted to make them impervious to liquids. All food stuffs must be suitably stored. Meals should be kept in metal vermin proof bins and meat stuffs housed in refrigerated containers (unless fresh or cooked meat is collected and fed each day). There must also be suitable runs to allow the dogs to exercise, and it must be possible to keep these runs free of faecal and uriniferous matter – a large grass paddock is only suitable if big enough to prevent any urine build-up in the soil.

Premises must be open to inspection by environmental health officers whenever they wish, and they are entitled to shut down unsatisfactory premises at a moment's notice. This however is seldom done for the majority of these officers are reasonable men who will advise and suggest what must be done, rather than prevent a breeder from selling his or her puppies. The 1973 Dog Breeders Act is a thoroughly fair and reasonable one that has been beneficial to both the dog buying public and breeding bitches. What a shame some authorities have been lax about implementing the Act. A copy of my own breeder's licence for the reader's perusal is in Appendix 2 at the end of the book.

At the time of writing unlicensed dog farmers – usually situated in Wales – have received much adverse criticism. Horrendous tales of puppies raised in unpleasant conditions, worm ridden, pot bellied and underfed are legion. Tales of puppies reared on fallen stock (animals which have died from some injury or disease) seem to have a morbid fascination for both journalists and the newspaper-reading public. It is perfectly legal for licensed foxhound and stag hound, beagle, mink hound and harrier kennels to feed hounds and puppies on such meat – though a curious Act of Parliament passed in 1936 prevents pet keepers feeding the same provender.

Such horror stories have obviously been exaggerated by the press and, because of this, it is likely that by the time this book is published, yet another Act of Parliament will be passed to restrict the activities of puppy farmers, particularly unlicensed puppy farmers. Such an act is totally unnecessary. If the local authorities simply implemented existing regulations and implementing the powers given them under the 1973 Dog Breeders Act, unlicensed puppy farming would come to an abrupt end and the lot of puppies and puppy purchasers would improve dramatically.

Part of the problem seems to be that not only are certain authorities rather lax in implementing the Act but when an unlicensed breeder is prosecuted under the provisions of the 1973 Act the courts seem reluctant to take the issue seriously. In 1981 a large unlicensed kennels was found to be operating in the Midlands and the owner prosecuted under the provision of the Dog Breeders Act 1973. The court after some deliberation fined the owner £25, for despite the fact the owner was operating an unlicensed kennel, his stock was in excellent condition. However it does appear that public opinion may alter the attitude of both courts and local authority environmental health officers. In recent times both press and television seem to wish to fill up 'slow days' – days when there is little exciting news -with accounts of visits to unlicensed kennels in Wales. Frankly some of the photographs of dogs in kennels are puzzling and show animals housed in perfectly serviceable if rather bleak kennels, fed on perfectly adequate food, but for some reason this sight of puppies reared in concrete pens – even very clean concrete pens – seems to provoke the distaste of the general public.

It is interesting to note the price of a breeder's licence seems to vary from authority to authority – in Scotland £87 per annum seems to be a fairly average sort of fee but the licensing fee seems to be dictated by particular councils.

So having dealt with the legalities of becoming a dog breeder, let me deal with the practicalities of such an enterprise. There is little point in obtaining a breeder's licence and securing planning permission for an enterprise if there is no sale for the stock one is likely to produce – shades of Occam's Razor perhaps but I'll explain more fully. A dog breeder in the Orkney or Central Wales will find little trouble in obtaining a breeder's licence or even planning permission but would be unable to market his stock. Orkney has a population of roughly 28000 and a fairly large kennel easily saturates such a population. There was a time when such kennels were able to market their wares by sending them south to dealers in Yorkshire, Birmingham and London but now such activities are frowned on by the RSPCA, the environmental health and the Kennel Club. The reasons for this antipathy? Puppies traumatise easily during long road or rail journeys and arrive at a dealer's kennels dehydrated through vomiting and in a state of shock. It can be argued that .breeders can sedate the puppies with chemical products such as ACP's so that the whelps sleep through the trip and arrive at the dealer's kennels in a more settled state than would an unsedated puppy. However it is not really fair to subject eight week old puppies to such raw deals particularly as once they reach a dealer's kennel, within days of their arrival they will be sold to a new home. Incidentally the profits made by certain dog dealers were at one time extraordinary and it was by no means uncommon to find a three hundred per cent profit margin made by dealers. Now this tells the discerning breeder quite a lot more than one first imagines. A dealer obviously has overheads such as rates, heating and advertising etc., but I would suggest that such figures indicate a fairly high mortality rate among puppies between the time of arrival at kennels and the time the puppies are sold to new homes. It would be impossible to substantiate this statement even by subtracting the Kennel Club transfer numbers from the Kennel Club puppy registrations for many people don't bother to transfer the puppies they buy, a pedigree and a registration form are all pet buyers seem to require, but I would suspect the mortality rates in dealer's kennels even dealer's kennels regulated by the 1951 Pet Traders Act, are uncomfortably high. I shall deal with the 1951 Pet Traders Act presently and with possible forthcoming Acts of Parliament.

As I write there are already moves afoot to outlaw the practice of dealing in puppies. Indeed many breed clubs produce charters for members to sign and these charters prohibit the selling of stock to dealers. At the time of writing it is impossible to legally enforce some of the regulations contained within the charters, but an almost inevitable Act of Parliament will eventually make dog dealing a verboten practice.

To be successful as a dog breeder one needs to be situated near to a fairly large population, several towns or cities. David Hancock, the world's most successful lurcher breeder, (lurchers are hybrid collies or other breeds – mated to greyhounds or other sight hounds) has achieved his amazing success not only because of the quality of the stock he breeds, the dogs are formula bred, but also because of the situation of his kennels. Cottage Farm Kennels is situated on the outskirts of Birmingham, virtually in the centre of Britain. David has clients who come from the far north of Scotland as well as purchasers from Wales or Cornwall. His kennels are really suited to sell puppies. My own kennels, by no means as successful as David's, are situated within easy reach of both Edinburgh and Glasgow, two of the most populous cities in the far north, so I am usually able to sell puppies I breed.

Might I crave the reader's patience once more if I digress a little? The casual observer might assume that most people in Britain own cars but this is not so and potential clients will often find it quite difficult to travel to kennels in isolated districts and because of the nature of the business the noise, the smell etc. most kennels are situated in isolated districts. Hence if one advertises puppies in the local press it gives one an advantage over competitors to write 'can deliver' at the end of one's advertisement. Such deliveries can be a bit of a chore particularly if the potential client lives in the middle of a large city, (and frankly such deliveries seemed to be frowned on by more conventional breeders) but deliveries do increase one's sales considerably. I have found that if I advertise a litter and will deliver the puppies, my sales increase by at least a third.

I freely admit that I have been to some amazing places to deliver puppies and have a wealth of tales concerning deliveries. Several times I have decided not to place puppies in homes I consider unsuitable, but I must also admit that the delivery of puppies has changed my outlook on what I consider to be a good home. Hitherto I had considered the arrival of up market cars and well spoken people to be an indication that the puppy I am about to sell will go to a good home, but this is not always the case. I have known puppies lead very unhappy lives in antiseptic very tidy homes, and conversely seen dogs reared in very messy homes grow up to be delightful and happy pets. I shall deal with the homing of puppies at a later date but I cannot resist an anecdote even at this point of the book. In 1994 I was telephoned by a person with a very strong Govan accent and asked to deliver a white German Shepherd dog puppy to a district of that town. At the time of writing Govan or rather certain parts of Govan has a rather unsavoury reputation in Scotland and I was advised not to travel to the district after dark. The natives of my own village related tales of drug dealers and muggers and hence, I must admit, I made the trip with some trepidation. I confess I have an appalling sense of direction so I frequently stop passers-by to ask for directions. I also confess that my sense of trepidation was increased when virtually everyone I stopped to ask the way was either drunk or bleary eyed with cannabis. The smell of burning jute sacking seemed to linger around everyone I stopped, for jute is a type of cannabis, another useless piece of information.

To cut quite a long story short. I arrived at the house and was greeted by a couple who seemed clearly not house proud and like the Old Woman Who Lived in a Shoe, had little idea of birth control. Even if one believed that the majority of the children were neighbours who had popped in to see the puppy, it was obvious that the lady of the house had experienced a pregnancy every year of her marriage or had the fecundity of a Large White sow. I was about to make some excuse that the puppy was not really suitable for the family when I noticed that the whelp was endearing itself to one of the three year old children whose face was covered in some black syrupy liquid which the puppy had started to lick. For a while I stood there amazed that the family who were living in dire poverty had the funds to purchase and feed a £250 German Shepherd Dog puppy, but the husband paid me in single pound notes, still legal tender in Scotland, and a hundred stinking pound coins for it was painfully obvious the household had saved for some time to acquire the money to make the purchase. I confess I left the premises with some reservations about the fate of the puppy, whose fur was now sticky from the handling the children were giving the mite, but the children clearly adored their new pet and the puppy reciprocated the feeling. On arriving home I sold the litter sister to a middle aged couple who arrived in a brand new BMW and who radiated opulence and status so I was forced into an odious comparison between the fate of the two litter mates I had sold. How wrong I proved to be. Two years later I delivered another puppy to Govan to the self-same street as the Sticky family. Indeed the second whelp was sold on the recommendation of the family. The whelp had grown into a delightfully beautiful outgoing bitch, badly trained perhaps, but really loved by the Stickys, and whatever food they had fed it had allowed the animal to radiate health and vitality. I have in fact seldom seen a more happy puppy. The second puppy, the one sold to the BMW owning couple, was returned at six months of age because it shed its coat – a moulting white GSD will make a house look as though it has experienced a snow storm. The bitch was shy, nervous and obviously unloved by the antiseptic couple who returned it. I refunded the purchase price, but biting my lips at my own stupidity for selling them the puppy and immediately went to Govan to re-home the puppy (free of charge) with a cousin of the Sticky family, where it has grown into a delightfully happy and well adjusted young animal. I love this tale and make no apologies for telling it so early in the book.

Yet another consideration for the commercial dog breeder is the proximity of the kennels to a ready supply of food. For while it is easier and cleaner to feed proprietary meal to puppies and adults alike it is also a very expensive way of keeping animals. The proximity of an abattoir to the kennels or a chicken processing plant will certainly reduce the cost of feeding the inmates of a kennels though feeding such fare is messy, smelly and time consuming. However puppies rear well on raw and pungent meats and can be produced more cheaply than if fed a high class, high protein commercial feed. An abattoir will supply tripe (the stomach's of a cow – low in calcium high in fat and protein) far more cheaply than one can buy blocks of frozen tripe and frankly I find the stench of defrosting minced tripe far more sickening than the smell of fresh killed tripe. Sheep's heads are no longer readily available now that scientists have found a link between ovine scrapie, mad cow disease and that unpronounceable human equivalent ailment, CJD, and this is a pity for the puppies usually enjoy the meat of sheep heads and the large adult dogs crunch up the residual skulls with gusto, leaving not even a trace of the teeth uneaten.

On the subject of feeding raw meat it is policy to mention the feeding of fallen stock again, which the reader may remember is illegal unless one owns a registered kennel of working hounds. The legislation surrounding the 1936 Fallen Stock Act is curious until one examines the ramifications of maintaining a modern hunt kennels that really doesn't concern the pet breeder. Sufficient to say that while I have seen excellent puppies reared on fallen stock flesh, and uncooked flesh at that I must add, I would refrain from feeding such flesh to my own dogs. Sheep bloat shortly after death and this necrosis does little good for the flesh surrounding the abdomen. Furthermore there is little guarantee that the disease which has brought about the death of the farm animal isn't equally injurious to the dogs which will feed on the meat, and simply boiling the flesh does not kill all the injurious bacteria within the meat. Certain strains of salmonella and E-coli survive the death of farm animals and are readily transferred to puppies.

Fallen stock is so easy to obtain, for farmers are now required to bury dead beasts on their own land or pay a fallen stock collector to fetch the cadavers, that breeder might be tempted into feeding carcasses to the dogs. It is not a good purchase however and leaves one open to the investigation of environmental health officers who will probably be reluctant to renew a breeder's licence if such material was found on one's premises. Feeding such fare is not only illegal it is also inadvisable.

However if one decides that feeding raw flesh is wrong or the breeder is antipathetic to the sight of bloody meat bone and viscera, meal feeding is an easy option although it does increase feeding costs a little. High-class dog meal with the correct proportions of fats, carbohydrates, vitamins and trace elements is expensive particularly if the meal is pelleted rather than simply flaked. I will explain.

Flaked meal crushed cooked oats, flaked maize, fish meal, barley and meat meal powder, usually finely ground greaves or dried meat, is wolfed down by some dogs while others merely pick out the portions of meal, usually the greaves or fish meal pellets and are therefore living on a somewhat less than balanced diet. Pelleted meal which mixes all the ingredients together before pelleting the composite gives some guarantee that the meal is a more complete one, because dogs are unable to select favoured portions of the food.

Yet some of the pelleted and powdered complete meals are ridiculously expensive and simply cater for the pet owner rather than the commercial dog breeder. Nonsense advertisements extolling the virtues of a meal designed by veterinary surgeons should be ignored. Every commercial dog food producer employs a nutritionist to design the formula of a particular dog food and also a food analyst to ascertain the digestibility of the feed. In fact the Trades Description Act investigators are particularly vigilant about the quality of food of any sort. Certain vitamins start to decompose on storage and hence out of date dog foods are sold cheaply or dumped. This also explains why makers of dry foods often add twice the required quantity of certain vitamins to dog meal, to allow for this vitamin deterioration.

Complete dog foods are a relatively new notion, and now follows a fairly massive digression, so readers concerned only with the meat and two veg parts of this book would do well to skip the following passages.

Prior to the late 19th century the lot of the housedog was not enviable. Gowland Hopkin's discovery of vitamins was not published until 1908 and few people knew the role of proteins, carbohydrates, fats and vitamins in diet. Hence most dogs were fed household scraps and allowed to forage for food around the dustbins, a practice which led to the spread of disease and the risk of kidnapping pure bred dogs, a common practice in the 19th century when kidnapped dogs were frequently ransomed by distressed owners. The sale of unwanted ship's biscuits, hard tack biscuits, which acted as common seamen's fare for long voyages, was eagerly attended by owners of pet dogs who believed this fare would constitute suitable dog food. This inspired an enterprising dog biscuit manufacturer/corn chandler from Holborn, a man called James Spratt, to market a dog cake including meat in the form of greaves, dried knackers meat. The food and his business boomed as a result of this innovation. So successful was his venture that he employed an equally enterprising young salesman, Charles Cruft, who had an interest in breeding pedigree dogs, to market his products and readers can guess at what followed.

However it was not until the 1920's that nutritionists, now in receipt of Gowland Hopkin's researches concerning vitamins, attempted the first of the supposed complete dog meals. Credit of this product is laid at the feet of one Milton Seeley, a sled dog enthusiast at the Wonalancet Kennels in the U.S.A., who supposedly produced a formula for the complete dog food taken by Admiral Byrd on his Antarctic Expedition.

# 3

# Making A Start

BEFORE PROCEEDING further, might I present the reader with, what to the general public (myself included) must seem a baffling enigma. A cattle breeder with herds the size of John Chisholm would be held in great esteem, likewise the shepherd with flocks the size of those of a Patagonian farmer/rancher would be treated with great respect. However the show fraternity regards a dog breeder with a large commercially viable kennels with something a little less than esteem. The commercial breeder, no matter how good his kennels maybe, how wonderful his stockmanship, is seldom respected by the dog owning fraternity and the show fraternity is not the only group which regards commercial dog breeding as something a shade infra dig.

The world of lurcher breeding and lurcher keeping is a shadowy one, for frankly the lurcher, a crossbred greyhound which at one time enjoyed great popularity as a healthy family pet as well as a working dog, has an extremely bad deal from the public at large. So cheaply is the average lurcher purchased that lurchers are swapped, sold, bartered and frequently treated as currency by somewhat less than pleasant dog owners, and once again I am dealing in bland euphemisms to disguise the hideous fate that many lurchers must endure. The majority of lurchers are owned by people who have little knowledge of dog training, no knowledge of condition, and a dismal understanding of stockmanship. Yet when a poultry farmer from Sutton Coldfield adapted his buildings to produce what must be regarded as one of the most commercially successful dog breeding establishments ever, the lurcher world threw up its hands in horror. The sporting press was cluttered with attacks from contributors who had clearly penned their letters in purple crayons, the traditional tool of the half-witted numskull which condemned this venture. Indeed there are some amazing people in this world and some of the oddest seem to keep dogs.

Thus the commercial breeder must be prepared to face criticism, ostracism and contempt from the rest of the dog owning world no matter how spectacular and hygienic his kennels are, and how efficient his stockmanship. Now lest the would be breeder decides that he or she is able to shrug off such overt hostility let me also mention that there are other ways this spiteful attitude will be manifested and, in true British tradition, the dislike and hostility will grow if the commercial dog breeder becomes successful. So, suitably worried, the would be breeder must consider how and where to purchase stock to start his commercial kennels.

I would advise anyone starting with such a venture to begin in a small way and to start with the purchase of puppies. Puppies, providing they have been properly reared in warm kennels on a good sensible diet and properly socialised, such an important factor as I shall explain later, are virgin clay which can be shaped, moulded and trained exactly how the breeder wishes. Such dogs once used to their owners will seldom be a problem at whelping time – guarding and carrying their puppies until they are crushed to death – for they will have absolute trust in their owners. I shall deal with the purchase of adult stock presently.

If the commercial breeder wishes to stay in business and not attempt a quick killing on the market before selling up his stock and seeking pastures new, he should not only know about the breed he seeks to perpetuate but also learn where he can purchase sound stock of that particular breed. The dog world is pockmarked with pitfalls and if the breeder is to be successful at his project he must learn how to avoid them. It can be argued that as the commercial breeder is producing puppies to satisfy a not too discerning public's desire for pets, the quality of one's initial stock need not be too high. Nothing could be further from the truth. To produce defective pets which have a short and decidedly miserable life is morally reprehensible and frankly has given the production of commercially bred puppies the bad name it seems to have today.

The world of pedigree dogs is peppered with genetic defects. Breeders must be aware of the defects that beset certain breeds and take measures not to perpetuate these peculiarities. Cavalier King Charles spaniels (a delightful little dog) are prone to heart diseases (I run mine as a rabbit hunting pack to ensure my stock is sound). German Shepherd dogs have a myriad of problems including epilepsy, haemophilia and hip dysplasia. Golden Retrievers are also prone to hip dysplasia and also hereditary eye problems; I eye test mine and have still produced the odd puppy with cataracts despite the quality of my original purchase, and the testing of her progeny. West Highland White terriers are all too prone to genetic faults including the hideous lion jaw syndrome and would be breeders should be particularly careful about purchasing stock which carries undesirable traits. The fact that one's initial purchase is from the very best show line is no proof of the soundness of the stock however. Indeed some of the worst genetic problems are sometimes carried by the very best show families, and reader few breeders are prepared to divulge that they produce stock with problems from time to time. Indeed the Jewish proverb 'No fishmonger has ever been known to cry 'Stinking Fish' as an appraisal of his wares', is very true where dog breeding is concerned.

It is therefore wise for the breeder to purchase puppies from stock which has been tested for soundness – but even testing will give no absolute guarantee of the progeny bred from such stock. Some years ago I bred some particularly good white German Shepherd dogs which suddenly produced progeny which had hip scores that read like space invader figures. I'll finish the tale. I advertised the parents as free to a good homes and told the new owners of the problems their dogs had bred, only to find that the new owners promptly bred from the animals I had given away! Likewise, I have heard tales of Cavalier King Charles Spaniels which had regularly passed the annual heart checks (defects in the mitral valves and discernible by examination with a stethoscope) and produced scores of puppies only to fail the test in their sixth year. I have already explained the problems I experienced with my Golden Retrievers. Yet it is policy to purchase stock from tested rather than untested parents and to test the puppies before they too are ready for breeding.

Might I mention in passing a caveat? The latest madness in the world of pedigree dog breeding is pedigree endorsement and often the public is totally unaware of the limits these endorsements place on the puppy they have bought. It is now possible for a breeder to sell a puppy and prevent the new owner breeding registerable stock from the animal by endorsing the pedigree as 'unsuitable for breeding'. Now there is little rhyme or reason in this policy but the dog world abounds with silly behaviour and malicious pettiness. It can be argued that the breeder has knowledge of the puppy he or she is selling and should therefore be able to determine if the animal is suitable for the perpetuation of the breed or breed type, but this is seldom the case, for the purpose of endorsing the pedigree is to prevent competition in the puppy market. There is of course nothing to stop the breeder from mating a bitch and selling unregistered puppies, but sales of registered puppies are seldom easy, so disposing of stock which cannot be registered can be a serious problem, though I know of many breeders who are unable or disinclined to register puppies yet succeed in selling them.

The breeder is more likely to encounter the problem of the endorsing pedigrees if he or she wishes to purchase a stud dog, and there is often something supercilious in the attitude of the exhibition stud breeders if they are approached with a view to the purchaser of a puppy for future use as a stud dog. Frankly I find nothing more pompous than show breeders who are new to dog breeding but have experienced a brief, but sometimes very ephemeral, success in the show ring. Many have little knowledge of the subject of breeding and no knowledge of genetics, but present the would-be purchaser with what they consider to be the Wisdom of Solomon. They will often advise or pontificate that it is unwise to purchase a potential stud dog because there is a perfectly good champion male only a hundred or so miles away from the would be purchasers home, the owner of the stud dog is usually a close friend of the person advising this, one must add. Now if a breeder owns only a single bitch of a particular breed then the use of an outside stud dog is not only good policy but sound economic sense. Yet should the breeder have three or more bitches of a particular breed it is fairly essential to have ones own stud dog. Trips to and from a distant stud are time consuming, expensive and sometimes unproductive, for after a lengthy journey a bitch might be disinclined to stand to be mated though she will be very receptive to the dog in the home kennels. Yet because stud work is often fairly easy money (well sometimes, anyway, for I am often faced with some difficult bitches if I offer my dogs at public stud), there is a tendency for breeders to endorse the pedigree if any male puppy they sell to prevent its use as a stud dog.

Now this practice is not only avaricious and petty but frankly a recipe for the decline of the breed. To limit the gene pool by allowing only certain males of a breed to perpetuate their lines is a brainless, senseless attitude – but then the breeder will encounter many instances of brainless senseless and greedy attitudes when he or she enters the world of professional dog breeding. Might I add there is no indication that a particular superb specimen of a particular breed might be any more potent as a stud dog than his more plain litter mate though the aesthetically pleasing sibling will have more opportunity to prove his worth at stud for obvious reasons. Might I conclude this passage with yet another cautionary note? Exhibition breeders will on hearing that the purchaser wishes to buy a puppy for use as a stud, often push up the price of a puppy. Just recently I bought a Cavalier King Charles Spaniel puppy from successful show breeder who was selling her whelps for £280. I paid £350 for my puppy, despite his lack of his 'show potential' simply because the breeder knew she had me over a barrel, for the majority of other breeders I had approached were engaged in the destructive and greedy practice of endorsing the pedigrees of any males they were prepared to sell. I love Ping (the Cavalier) dearly but I am also aware I have been a victim of something akin to sharp practice. The would be professional dog breeder will encounter many instances of sharp practice and pettiness in the dog breeding world – as a glance at any doggy newspapers and the accounts of prosecutions of dog breeders therein will clearly indicate

There are of course other ways of starting up a breeding kennels, and now we come to that minefield of dog breeding, namely the use of animals on what is described as breeding terms. If the established breeder or exhibitor has been shocked or distressed by my forthright and frank exposé of the world of dog breeding so far, might I suggest that he or she girds up his or hers loins for there is worse to follow. Now to be perfectly honest I have put out several bitches on breeding terms, but have never benefited from this practice though I have known many breeders who have. Bitches offered on breeding terms are usually fairly well bred but substandard (or at least substandard as far as the vendor is concerned, for they might only wish for a kennel of exhibition animals) . These bitches will be sold cheaply (or given free of charge) to potential breeders on the agreement that a future date;

a. the new owner will mate the animal to a dog of the old owner's choice.
b. a certain number of puppies from that litter are returned to the person who has released the bitch on breeding terms.

The practise of taking bitches on breeding terms might be considered by those with little funds who wish to jump start kennels (breeding bitches will usually be ready for breeding within six months of their time of arrival in the kennels) but accepting such bitches on these terms is often a perilous practice. Some of the contracts I have seen issued by those putting out bitches on breeding terms are not only restrictive, but so Draconian as to defy belief. Now a further piece of advice to those considering taking bitches on breeding terms. Despite the fact that many of the contracts are so badly drafted as to be unenforceable in a court of law, many of those who issue these contracts are fiercely protective over their supposed rights. Civil litigation is prohibitively expensive, so expensive in fact that few sane people take matters as trivial as the ownership of an animal to the courts. Yet despite the down at heel appearance of many dog breeders, many of them have a Kamikaze urge where the ownership of dog or the rights concerning that dog are concerned. Some are prepared to pursue a claim in the courts despite the fact that such a court action will result in their financial ruin. Indeed many of the court cases concerned with the actions of putting bitches out on breeding terms are so bizarre as to create an air of hilarity in Chambers before and after the case. Indeed there are some very strange people in this world, and as I keep repeating, the majority of them keep dogs.

Please read contracts before signing them. My contracts involve the giving away of a bitch to a new owner free of charge, in exchange for one or two puppies from two litters, after which the new owner is given the bitch and its registration documents, for it is usual for vendors to keep registration documents while the bitch is out on terms. Indeed it is little short of madness to give registration documents away at the time of the initial agreement, for the first owner of the bitch has little control in the future of the bitch once these documents are handed over. In the days when I bred unregistered terriers I put numerous bitches out on breeding terms, and once the puppies were born I was told to go and whistle for my fee – and the reader wonders why I have little faith in dog breeders and why I take such a high moral stand point! I also include the free use of my own stud dog as part of the contractual agreement. Other peoples contracts are a shade more harsh. Some insist on half the litter for three or more litters. I know of one breeder who takes back the entire litter and gives the puppy rearer the price of a single puppy for her troubles. Some retain the breeding rights over the bitch until the death of the animal, others until the bitch is past the age of breeding. The Kennel Club is reluctant to allow the registration of puppies born to bitches above the age of eight years old, and rightly so, for there is a time beyond which bitches should be denied parenthood for their own welfare.

The use of breeding term bitches is a quick way of starting up a commercial dog breeding kennels, but in the long run quite an expensive way. It also leaves the tyro dog breeder with an often aged, quite useless and substandard bitch at the end of the contractual agreement, and these points must be considered before entering into any agreement involving the use of breeding term bitches to start up a kennels. I must confess that my own ventures into releasing bitches on breeding terms have been financially disastrous. More often or not people have joyfully taken breeding term bitches bred one litter from them, sold the litter and then made some excuse not to keep the animals returning the poor devils older, jaded, dispirited and more bewildered than before. There are so many mistakes to be made in the world of business, I know, for I've made most of them.

In 1993 I was approached by a young TV interviewer/producer who had ambitions of producing a film exposing what he described as the dog farmers of central and west Wales. I declined to help him for I dislike people who rejoice and profit from the misery and discomfiture of others. Somehow or other the general public has a notion that anyone with a large number of dogs is automatically ill-treating the creatures. This notion is accentuated still further if the public believe that the person in question is making a healthy living from breeding dogs, which is frankly ridiculous, for to make a maximum profit from dog breeding a person must look after the stock which is producing that living.

After the producer called I did some research into the dog farmers of central Wales and arrived at some interesting conclusions. Most kept their animals in reasonable conditions (contrary to popular opinion) and the allegations that they refused to let clients see their kennels, but met them on the motorway stations, was simply due to the fact that their kennels were so remote that it was difficult for potential buyers to their way to such places. More interesting still was the way most dog farmers obtained their breeding stock. Most of the breeders – I shall desist from using the term dog farmers as the expression has a derogatory note about it – perused the newspapers which circulated large towns for bargain priced, or free to good home, pedigree stock and used this stock as the foundation blood for their breeding kennels.

On the surface of it this must seem an undesirable way of starting a kennels, for it could be argued that one reason grown or half grown dogs are offered for sale is that the animals have developed undesirable characteristics and this is why the owner has decided to dispose of them. This is clearly true in some cases, but one should ask why these dogs have developed antisocial habits. The quote that 'there are no bad dogs but a great number of bad owners' is not always true, for as I have explained, certain breeds manifest innate, undesirable characteristics.

Some years ago I kept a bloodline of heavily built phlegmatic German Shepherd Dogs, white with old fashioned flat backs, so easily trained as to be a delight to own. However I found that I needed an outcross, for the line was becoming very inbred, so I sought out an unrelated stud from a German bloodline which produced the occasional white sport in litters of coloured puppies. I used one of these white sports to mate to my best bitches and produced some far from desirable results. Some of the puppies were decidedly hyperactive, so hyperactive that they were not a pleasure to own and when transferred to kennels drove the other dogs wild. Readers may not be acquainted with what psychologists call PVS or provocative victims syndrome, an unpopular premise which tactfully suggests that when battered wives sever relationships with violent husbands they immediately settle to further relationships with men who also batter and abuse them. It is possible, but only possible, I must add, to avoid reprisals from women's rights groups, that these women have some psychological or physiological quirk which invites attack from a man – a hot potato if there ever was one! Certainly the outcross bitches I kept displayed classic provocative victim syndrome and caused pure hell in the main run.

However, most peculiarities are the result of nurture rather than nature, and frankly I feel bitter resentment to the imbecile who returns a perfectly stable youngster to the kennels saying 'it won't train' which translated into realistic terms usually means 'I am a fool who has no idea of how to train a dog'. Fortunately despite the ideas once advanced by Lysenko, acquired characteristics are not inherited, so the free to a good home type stock offered for sale in the local press is unlikely to pass on the undesirable characteristics to its offspring. True most of the stock sold in these Supermart type papers will be pet bred and seldom of show quality unless, that is, the pet breeder has had the good fortune to visit a top grade stud to mate his bitch, and the bloodlines of the stud have combined with those of the bitch to produce aesthetically pleasing stock. It matters little however to the majority of dog farmers, (that term again) as trade will be conducted with buyers who want a typical healthy pet not a show dog (readers might remember that only three hundred or so exhibitors regularly show German Shepherd Dogs) and it is the legal and moral duty of any breeder to produce sound healthy stock which will give pleasure to the buyer for the rest of the dog's life.

I have never favoured the purchase of adult stock simply because I enjoy rearing puppies and watching them reach maturity, but I had the good fortune to pick up a bargain, which while not exactly free to a good home, was remarkably cheap and useful. A friend of mine noticed an advert on the 6p a week local pet shop board and passed the ad on to me. The ad simply stated 'Two German Shepherd Bitches, 2 years old £150'. I didn't really want these dogs and frankly I was pushed to find the £300, but to be polite to the lady who had gone to the trouble of copying out the advertisement I telephoned the number on the card and found that the bitches had been sired by Champion Moonwinds Golden Mahdi, so I promptly bought the pair. It transpired the owner's daughter, who exercised the pair, had taken up a position as a secretary in London, and hence the pair were unexercised. They were free from vices and have bred some splendid puppies. I was very pleased to hand over my £300 and even more delighted when I was handed back £150 for the vendor wanted just £150 for the pair. Not all cheap adult dogs sold in the trade papers are of poor quality though I confess many are.

It would be impossible to leave a chapter concerned with the acquisition of breeding bitches without a mention of David Hancock, possibly the most successful dog breeder the world has known and whose lurcher kennels in Sutton Coldfield has produced a staggering number of puppies and dogs which are used in competition and in the field.

Hancock's career as a dog breeder began in the late 1970's when his poultry farm went bankrupt after a sharp increase in maize prices. Stock feed became prohibitively expensive, and many egg producers went into liquidation. David cleared out the poultry, paid off his debts and promptly converted his poultry sheds into the world's most successful lurcher breeding kennels.

The Anglo-Saxon riddle 'which animal can become extinct today and be common next year', answer, a mule; is appropriate, for just as a mule is a cross between a horse and a donkey so a lurcher is a hybrid bred by mating a base breed (usually a collie) with a greyhound. Hancock secured the services of some collie and collie bred stud dogs and approached various greyhound kennels for bitches. The life of a greyhound bitch is curious. Several thousand are bred each year reared on the very best of diets in the very best conditions. If they are capable of racing (and not all are one must add) or coursing they are kept until their seventh year after which their speed wanes rapidly. If not, their lot is far from enviable, and once again I am using the most exquisite of euphemisms. After the seventh year a greyhound is considered not only useless but an encumbrance, and while many greyhound rescue groups attempt to home these now unwanted animals, many are put down.

There is in fact a rather sick quote from the Abbess Juliana Berner, the Prioress of Sopewell Abbey, who penned a fascinatingly, sometimes rhyming book, *The Book of St. Albans* in which pre-dating the Stratford-on-Avon bard by a hundred years or so she describes the seven ages of a greyhound – I believe Shakespeare penned the Seven Ages of Man (As You Like It) after reading the Abbess's work. However the Abbess was disinclined to let her greyhound reach the 'sere and yellow leaf stage' for 'when he hath come to the seventh year get him to a tanner so that he might be killed, skinned and the hide made into gloves or falconry equipment'.

Hancock was an excellent businessman despite the failure of his poultry farm, and sensed the potential economic value of these greyhound bitches as lurcher broods and secured a great number free of charge or very cheaply indeed. Greyhound bitches are not allowed to race before, during and immediately after they come into season hence this is the time when most greyhound trainers seek to dispose of over-the-hill greyhounds. Hancock was a great opportunist and approached a great many trainers and offered a placing, rather than a permanent home perhaps to retired or retiring bitches. It is worth mentioning that the use of these broods is not all beer and skittles for many bitches are injected with certain hormones to prevent them coming into season during their racing career, so many may be a shade reluctant to come into season in retirement. However once they do, they are regular and easy breeders – few have whelping difficulties that many other breeds seem to have.

On a more cautionary note it is worth mentioning that the late 1970s there was a huge market for lurchers, and animals of dubious origin and poor type found a ready market in a world saturated in what can best be described as 'lurcher ethos'. It was in fact quite fascinating to see demure and gentle ladies and very effete men with long thin dogs on leashes, boasting that the dam or sire of the said animal was a renowned poacher's dog. Yet the same people with poaching dogs on slips would have been horrified if their son or daughter had stolen a chocolate bar from a corner shop; such dual values are so common in society today I am afraid. Today the market for lurchers is limited for fashion in the dog world is a fickle jade, and the lurcher is no longer the 'in' dog to own. Nevertheless when Paul Florkowski and partners set up the now defunct Heartbreak Fell Bedlington/ Greyhound Kennels at Lancaster, during the kennel's brief life they were able to sell a huge number of Bedlington greyhound hybrids.

Longdog production (longdogs are bred by mating a sight hound, usually a saluki, to a greyhound) is another method of using over the hill free-of-charge greyhound bitches. Beware of breeding these fleet and brainless longdogs. True, an advertisement will attract a great many buyers to your premises. The same advert will also attract the most loathsome, foul, degenerate flotsam, social derelicts who will convince the seller that the most extreme forms of fascism are entirely justified. Many of the would be buyers who come to your house will appear to be near misses on the evolutionary tree of man, creatures the remains of which the Leaky family regularly exhume in the Olduvai Gorge. Some will be travellers but the vast majority will be thieves who will examine your stock, check your kennels security and pay you a visit the following night, stealing both stock and any valuables which are not firmly anchored down. I am not too harsh in my criticism of these clients. I suggest the reader who is contemplating the production of longdogs reads the sad little advertisements that appear in *Countryman's Weekly* and other sporting periodicals which all tell the same sad but totally predictable tale. 'I advertised a litter of longdog puppies and was visited by two men in a transit van (always a transit van – the vehicle of thieves just as a Ford Cortina was once 'the' get away car to use). They didn't buy a puppy but next night they were seen around the back of the house. All my adult dogs were taken and so were the puppies. I am offering a substantial reward for the return of these animals.' Such people who are advertising for the return of their dogs are indulging in a practise as futile as the chasing of rainbows. They will never see their dogs again. Indeed so frequent and typical are these thefts that the National Lurcher and Racing Club has set up an agency to trace dogs stolen in such a manner. Please God let this agency flourish and please let the Bench have experienced a distressing night prior to the prosecution so that the sentencing of the thieves is Draconian.

I must now fire my second barrel in a bid to advise the reader not to produce longdogs. The lot of the longdog is not a happy one. Like greyhounds, their period of usefulness ceases by the time they are seven, but unlike greyhounds these wretched creatures will have seen a great variety of homes, each one worse and more uncaring than the last until death brings a merciful end to their tragic lives. Indeed many of these ageing athletes would have been happier if, in their seventh year their current owners had 'sent them to a tanner', for the lot of a dead dog is considerably better than the fate of some of the dogs which are currently passing from hand to hand. These sad creatures change hands with a rapidity that leaves the casual onlooker amazed at the fact that the fur of these unfortunate beasts does not catch fire with the friction so generated. These are the dogs specially suited to the lout and the numbskull for the only training they receive is to take them onto a field and to slip them when a hare appears, a process which would not tax the mental ability of a good chimpanzee. They are often pitted against the greatest mammalian athlete in the world, the brown hare, and cursed, vilified, beaten, killed or sold when they fail to catch this creature.

Some of the kennels which regularly produce longdogs are far from desirable for the majority of longdog breeders are also dog dealers who specialise in the art of being purveyors of canine misery. Amazingly there seem to be few prosecutions of those who profit from the keeping of dogs in these nasty unpleasant conditions, and I suspect this is because the owners of these kennels are usually as rough, uncouth and criminally inclined as the clients they serve. I suspect the environmental health officers and RSPCA officials alike fight shy of visiting such people's premises where they will be often met with extreme violence and offensive behaviour. I know I would be reluctant to visit these kennels and request that I looked over the property, for I was never a brave man, so I cannot blame such officials.

I was present as a reporter when one owner of a notoriously bad longdog breeding kennels was brought to court. A veterinary surgeon who was brought in to testify as to what he had seen stated 'I could not believe that such a place posed as a kennels. The yard was simply a burial ground for ancient broken down cars in which a variety of ill fed dogs were quartered. The floors of these cars were covered in mummified dog faeces some of which were covered with microscopic fungal growths, and the upholstery of the cars stank of urine. Puppies had been reared in these cars and while some of them appeared well, others were in a very poor condition. An amazing number of dogs were quartered in these broken down vehicles and there was little chance any of these would have been exercised.' When asked to explain his actions the owner of the emporium stated 'The sort of clients that come to my place wouldn't buy a dog if I had posh kennels' and this tells the reader quite a lot about the clientele who are likely to frequent such kennels.

However a good living, no, a very good living awaits anyone who operates a pristine kennels which specialises in the production of well bred, properly reared longdog puppies.

# 4

# Rearing and Maintaining Breeding Stock

IN 1957 METCALF PUBLISHED an amazing paper concerning the behaviour of plants and animals which were reduced to near death conditions. Apparently groundsel, a common ephemeral garden weed will, when denied water, germinate, produce seed leaves and promptly flower in an effort to produce seeds to continue the species. Rats faced with starvation conditions apparently come into season every few days in the faint hope that they might copulate and produce perhaps only one single ratling to perpetuate the line. There is little doubt that a species not preparing for extinction – and many species give many indications of their impending and inevitable extinction – cling on to the concept of the perpetuation of genes with great tenacity.

However tenacious the life element might be, it is not good policy to deliberately deny breeding stock comfort or food if one intends to profit from the production of the stock's offspring. In short an animal destined for breeding should be in perfect health and in 'high' condition before it is mated, and no animal can achieve such condition unless it has been properly reared and fed. Hence the tales of huge profits made by Welsh puppy farmers who kept dogs in awful conditions denying them creature comfort and food, are ludicrous.

I must confess to being rather a heretic where the feeding of dogs is concerned. In an age where it is both convenient and conventional to feed a complete diet of dried processed food, I still feed a diet which includes raw and bloody meat. My method of feeding is I confess, messy and inclined to be expensive for I travel over a hundred and fifty miles to fetch the meat, but my dogs eat it with gusto. Furthermore when I have unable to get raw flesh and have been forced by necessity to feed complete dried meal, my stock has not fared well on the diet and lost condition and zest accordingly. True, many maintained weight on such diet but they lacked the sparkle and coat condition I expect from my breeding stock. It is said that complete meals lack for nothing, for they have been scientifically tested to provide all the known essential elements and proteins a dog needs. However such meals lack texture and dogs are naturally carnivores which are designed to tear and rip meat and bones and whose alimentary tracts are designed to dissolve and digest flesh, not a ready pulverised, processed and pre-digested mix of carbohydrates, fats and proteins. From time to time I board friends' dogs when the friends go on holiday or sometimes experience financial difficulties, as has been the case recently. These boarders, and I am reluctant to board for I am convinced no breeding kennels with a fixed stock should bring strangers onto the premises for reasons I shall describe presently, are usually accompanied by a small quantity of meal which is meant to be the staple diet during their stay at my kennels. The meal can be what is euphemistically described as 'rough cut' by Irish breeders, tailored merely to keep the dog alive but little more, or high grade, very expensive pelleted food of the sort which needs a house mortgage in order to purchase a 561b sack, but whatever the diet they have been fed on these dogs voraciously devour the raw and bloody meat my own dogs eat and shun the conventional processed diets during their stay at my premises.

However before attempting to feed such a diet it is wise to learn something of nutrition, for the production of a complete and adequate diet requires some considerable thought. For instance, I mentioned I fed raw flesh and achieved good results. Yet a diet of raw meat alone is decidedly deficient in essential bone forming calcium. In 1976 at the British Veterinary Association conference Dr. R.S. Anderson stated that the feeding of unsupplemented raw meat was found to be one of the main factors responsible for bone disease in young dogs, particularly the giant breeds such as Newfoundlands, St. Bernards and Great Danes, for raw meat simply doesn't provide enough calcium to produce bone in a growing whelp. Dr. Anderson stated that in order for a growing whelp of 22lb to obtain enough calcium from red muscle meat to produce bone commensurate with muscle growth, the puppy would need to ingest 112lb of red muscle meat a day. Clearly this is a preposterous amount of meat for a whelp to eat and whelps fed on raw meat, and raw meat alone, develop poor skeletal structures. Throughout my long and largely unsuccessful life I have worked part time at various hound kennels, largely to subsidise my teacher's salary, which was tailored to allow a person enough money to keep a large hamster as a pet. At one kennels a pregnant foxhound bitch was put out to whelp at a local farm where it was fed fallen stock. The puppies it produced were also fed on this diet and being unable to ingest and digest bony material which would have given the essential calcium the whelps needed, they grew thin, bent legs as a result of rickets. When the puppies were put onto a diet of oatmeal plus beef broth plus bone meal the condition rectified itself in weeks to such an extent that one of the hounds was placed at the prestigious Peterborough Hound Show.

I mentioned that I fed raw meat but the majority of the flesh I feed is minced chicken, the waste products of poultry production made by mincing the rib cages, damaged or bruised meat and wings of young poultry. This type of provender obviously contains large quantities of bony material which is a rich source of calcium for the growing puppy. It is popularly believed that the tiny fragments or chards of bone in minced whole chickens is damaging to the dog for these bony pieces are said to scar the gut and stomach of the animal. I have never found this to be the case. Many years ago manuals about the rearing of dogs advocated that no poultry products be fed lest these bony fragments damaged the dogs alimentary tracts. This was true at the time for such was the method of production of table poultry that fowls were a year or so old before they achieved killing weight and condition. By this time a fowl's bones were hard and the fragments of bone often sharp and dangerous.

These days poultry achieves the same weight in weeks, and hence the bones are soft, pliable and cause little or no harm if ingested, and minced young chicken is an excellent food for the growing youngsters and adults alike. True the cooking of this chicken does harden the bony fragments a little, but Dr. D.W. Holme (1976) suggests that the cooking of any meat reduces the risk of any digestive upsets and kills many (but not all) of the dangerous bacteria which meat is said to harbour. Raw chicken is said to be a rich source of salmonella bacteria.

Yet meat is not a complete dog food even if the flesh fed is rich in bony material. Meat with the exception of liver is deficient in Vitamin A though an excellent source of many of the B vitamins, so if a diet is high in meat is fed it needs to be supplemented with foods which are rich in Vitamin A, for instance, egg yolk, fish roe and milk. When Gowland Hopkins published his findings that certain amines were vital for health (vital amines became corrupted to vitamins) he labelled the A vitamin carotene for he found traces of vitamin A in the yellow pigment of carrots and many of the dog manuals published in World War I suggested dogs should be fed large quantities of carrots to provide Vitamin A. There are better, more suitable sources of Vitamin A available for dogs however, for a dog would need to ingest a huge quantity of carrots to obtain the necessary amount of Vitamin A to survive. Yet it must be mentioned that too much Vitamin A can be decidedly harmful.

Meat diets need cereal supplements to provide the necessary vitamins and mineral salts to allow a dog to flourish. I feed large quantities of flaked maize, cooked barley (uncooked barley is indigestible) and wheat products. I am decidedly sceptical about feeding Soya products though Soya is a rich source of vegetable protein. On digestion Soya will produce large quantities of saponins (soap like substances) which can cause bloat, and bloat is a common cause of death among German Shepherd Dogs fed on a Soya rich diet.

Feeding minced chicken has other advantages. The stools passed by dogs fed on such a diet are usually firm and easily cleaned up, an important consideration if one has a large number of dogs in the kennels. I shall deal with the subject of the disposal of waste later in the book, and the disposal of waste can be a serious problem when one keeps a great many dogs. I particularly like the rustic wisdom of my Romany friend Moses Aaron Smith who said of proprietary cheap cereal-based, meals. 'I stopped feeding them when I realised I was putting 2lb in the dog and getting 4lb out the other end. I found birds feeding on the dung if I left it in the run and this proves the dogs weren't getting much from this type of meal'. Animals fed on large quantities of bony material, and minced chicken has high levels of bony chards, will sometimes pass very solid concretions of partly digested bony materials which cause really bad constipation. For this reason I feed large quantities of flaked maize soaked in meat juices to facilitate the passing of normal stools.

It is very difficult to feed a totally balanced diet if one is feeding a variety of meats rather than a proprietary meal. For instance minced chicken has a satisfactory protein, calcium/phosphorus combination, while tripe, and green tripe is highly acceptable to most dogs, is quite high in protein, very high in fat but decidedly deficient in calcium. Beef is also high in protein and phosphorus yet very low in calcium content.

When I lived in Caithness, my only source of raw meat was green tripe which I fetched from 150 miles distance. To supplement this diet I added quantities of dicalcium phosphate to the tripe, with disastrous results. All the puppies from this litter developed a skeletal disorder called hip dysplasia, a condition where the head of the femur fitted badly into the acetabulum or hip joint, despite the fact that both parents of the litter had low hip scores. I have always attributed this problem to my unwise use of additives. I now feed a more natural bony material to my dogs together with some cereal – wheat, flaked maize etc.

The cost of high quality, high protein, complete foods is often prohibitive if one intends to make a profit from the sale of puppies. Hancock of Sutton Coldfield tells an interesting tale of his search for a fairly cheap complete diet. At first Hancock fed sheep tripes boiled in water and mixed with a cheap 'roughcut' meal. Bitches (greyhounds) were fed on sheep heads which they ate uncooked and devoured entirely – even the teeth were eaten. When the first hint of BSE occurred public health officials panicked and the sale of sheep heads was considered infra dig – despite the fact that scrapie, an ovine form of BSE, had been known for centuries and had little effect on dogs fed on sheep heads. Hancock resorted to mixing his own meal. He bought a large quantity of cheap rough cut meal produced by a local blender, roughly 18% protein, far too low for puppy rearing, and diluted it still further by mixing it with flaked maize, 10% protein, creating a mix with a protein content of 14%. To this Hancock added a quantity of high-grade fishmeal, 66% protein. By mixing three units of maize/rough cut complete meal with one part fish meal he produced a maintenance ration of over 21% protein, more than enough to maintain an at-rest greyhound or a greyhound in the early stages of pregnancy.

3 units of rough cut meal/flaked maize = 42%
1 unit of fishmeal = 66%
4 units of mixture = 108 units of protein 27% protein

A spot more fishmeal increases the protein level to 31% or 32%, a high grade puppy rearing meal. Hancock has achieved great fame as a rearer of high quality lurcher puppies fed on this diet. It can be argued that this meal mixture lacks essential vitamins and trace elements but Hancock, an ex poultry farmer who blended his own poultry feed, stated that makers of proprietary meal are over generous with both trace elements and vitamins and hence the dilution of the original roughcut meal can be justified.

A word of warning regarding supplementing dog food with fish rations. Raw or only partly cooked fish can cause all manner of dietary disorders particularly a problem known as Chastek's paralysis. When I lived in Caithness I heard of a tale of a dog breeder who specialised in producing gun dogs, who fed salmon waste to his dogs (salmon trimmings from a local salmon farm could be bought for perhaps £20 a ton – very cheap feed). Whether he fed raw salmon or the flesh was not properly cooked has yet to be ascertained, but there were instances of a type of paralysis amongst his dogs. Yet when I worked for a short spell in Greenland I found that at one time sled dogs known to the Kennel Club enthusiasts as Eskimo Dogs, were once fed on a diet of sun dried cod or rock fish (lesser spotted dog fish) and suffered little from such a diet. It is however more than possible that native dog owners simply buried their mistakes without recourse to autopsy to ascertain the cause of death.

It is however wise never to feed the same mixture to at-rest broods, pregnant and lactating bitches and puppies. Protein is an essential part of a diet but the breakdown of surplus protein produces both urea and ammonium carbonate, and the excretion of these poisonous substances puts a strain on the animal's kidneys. An at-rest brood bitch not subjected to strenuous exercise will be quite happy on a diet with a protein content as low as 18%, though 21% is a better diet to maintain breeding condition. A lactating bitch deserves and needs a higher protein diet 28–32%. The same diet rears puppies well.

In passing, it is worth mentioning the high protein greyhound feeds which are free of VAT. Such diets are very high in protein but low in fat, and terrier breeders such as Brian Nuttall of Holmes Chapel find that puppies reared on racing greyhound food develop thin coats and look rather sorry for themselves. It should be worth mentioning that most makers of greyhound mixes also produce a puppy mixture which is ideal for weaning and growing whelps. This would seem to be a better mixture for rearing puppies as well as greyhound whelps.

High class puppy food is expensive, and the loss of a single puppy from a litter can often find the breeder rearing the litter at a loss, or at the best perhaps 'breaking even'. However there are a few short cuts to the art of puppy rearing and the production of breeding stock, so the breeder must either find a cheaper but equally good alternative or else bite the financial bullet. Frankly although the use of unadulterated rough cut meal will rarely produce top flight well reared puppies or really good breeding stock, there is little to choose between any of the high grade feeds.

At the time of writing (1998) the subject of inoculation of dogs is a hot potato. Reports of puppies and older dogs falling ill after inoculation against parvo virus, distemper, leptospirosis, hepatitis and even kennel cough are popular topics in the dog press. Reaction to the various vaccines range from simple abscesses at the point of injection to anaphylactic shock (reaction to alien protein being injected into the body) and more rarely, death. In 1996 several people wrote to *Countryman's Weekly* reporting such incidents and there are now groups who refuse to inoculate dogs in the albeit mistaken belief that there is more danger from the vaccine than from the disease which the vaccine was tailored to prevent.

At the risk of sounding like a quaint old man droning on about the crispy bacon of yesteryear and supermarkets on whose car parks sheep used to graze, it would be difficult not to remember 1948 when a devastating form of distemper called hardpad swept the country. The disease known as paradistemper at the time, caused the pads of the dog's feet to harden until the dog clattered as it walked. This form of canine distemper swept Britain and many thousands of dogs died. These days distemper is rare, and is seldom encountered even in the worst run dog sanctuaries. This is simply because vaccines are now both effective and safe. Only twenty years ago in 1979 a form of feline infectious enteritis or a mink killing enteritis virus mutated until it was capable of infecting dogs, particularly young dogs and puppies. The majority of puppies were killed by this parvo virus infection, and even dog shows were postponed in order to try to prevent the spread of the virus. Hancock of Sutton Coldfield cremated a huge number of very young (six and seven week old) puppies after an outbreak of this disease and other kennels experienced similar tragedies. At the time I bred five litters of German Shepherd Dogs, a total of fifty six puppies. All reached six weeks of age in apparently perfect health but during the sixth week all sickened and died of the most horrific type of enteritis, a scouring so severe that two puppies died with their rectal passages protruding an inch or so beyond the anus, a singularly grisly death by any standards and one I will always remember. In many ways I am totally unsuitable for the role of professional dog breeder as I lack the ability to stoically accept the death of my dogs. I felt such a sense of hopelessness during this time for there was no vaccine to counter the effect of this terrible disease. For a while veterinary surgeons advocated the use of the feline infectious enteritis vaccine for canine parvo virus was so similar in type and classification to the disease which killed cats, but the vaccine was far from effective and newly inoculated puppies continued to sicken and die.

I feel that I am more than justified in relating to the reader the end of the unhappy tale. In the 1980's Smith Kline Health Ltd. obtained a licence to market a vaccine called the Snow Leopard, a strain of feline infectious enteritis, slightly different from the conventional cat vaccine which gave some protection against the disease, and two years later Wellcome Ltd. licensed an inactivated (dead) vaccine which proved effective in the control of canine parvo virus. I make no excuses for this scientific discourse or the repeated use of anecdotes to illustrate my points for if only one puppy is saved as a result of my persuading an owner of the benefits of inoculation the labour of producing this book is justified.

Perhaps an explanation of how vaccines are produced is also justified in order to persuade the reader of the benefits and the relative safety of inoculation. Inoculation against a disease is carried out with the specific purpose of stimulating the production of antibodies in the animal's system, and it is these antibodies which confer immunity to the disease in question. Vaccines can be live viruses whose virulence has been reduced, an attenuated vaccine or a dead virus or other organisms (leptospirosis is a spirochete – I'll explain later). On rare occasions a related virus is used to stimulate the production of these protective antibodies: Jenner used cowpox to create immunity against the more deadly but related virus which caused smallpox. In fact the term vaccination (vacca – a cow) is derived from the fact that Jenner used samples of tissue taken from a cow to inoculate his patients. The attenuated virus is sometimes produced by a process known as passaging, passing the organism through an animal other than the normal host species, though most attenuated viruses are obtained from chick embryos.

Live viruses are sometimes inactivated (killed rather than attenuated) by the action of phenol or carbolic acid or more commonly by bombarding the organism with ultra violet rays. The organism is killed and hence cannot revive and multiply in the new host. Such vaccines are very safe, for the organism is unable to regenerate and infect the new host. When Jenner was experimenting with cow pox as a preventative measure against smallpox he noted that other surgeons were inoculating patients with the pus from the sores of those who had recovered from smallpox. The virus in the pus was weakened (attenuated) perhaps but revived and reinfected the new patient with smallpox. It must be noted that medical science has made considerable advances since the days of Jenner. Some reaction to alien protein found in the vaccine may possibly occur. This problem, known as anaphylactic shock is however extremely rare and although I have vaccinated thousands of puppies, I have yet to encounter the problem.

However a word of warning, if a puppy or dog is known to have a particular ailment it is unwise to add to its problems by inoculating it against this infection for the puppy is already attempting to produce antibodies against the virulent strain of the disease. In fact veterinary surgeons invariably check the animal about to be vaccinated to ensure it is in good health for it is not policy to inoculate unhealthy animals.

There is some evidence that vaccination against certain viruses last for life and that further inoculation against the ravages of the specific viruses is unnecessary. However, leptospirosis is caused by a spirochete and yearly vaccination is necessary to maintain immunity against this dangerous rat borne infection. When I operated my rat pack – a pack of about sixty terriers which hunted some five nights a week, it was my practice to inoculate puppies at twelve weeks of age and while the vaccine was at its most efficacious expose the puppies to rats which possibly carried the spirochete. Monlux (1948) mentions that 55% of all healthy rats carried this terrible disease. The puppies were subjected to a dose of the real infection while the vaccine was still able to protect them. As the terriers were regularly ratted and exposed to leptospirosis, I never inoculated the puppies against the infection again. However a few kennels actually court the attentions of this spirochete in this manner and it is wise to inoculate puppies and adults every year – possibly twice a year if recent events are indicative of how widespread leptospirosis is. In times before the perfection of a vaccine to combat leptospirosis many kennels were unable to rear puppies because of leptospirosis in the stock, for even long after the dog has recovered from the disease (and most don't one must add) it is still capable of excreting the spirochete in its urine and infecting other dogs and even human beings.

However, vaccination does not only protect the animal being vaccinated. Puppies are born into a disease filled world but are not only in receipt of some antibodies passed across the placenta from the dam to the foetus but also via the first milk or colostrum, a thick yellow milk rich in antibodies which are tailored to protect the whelp for the first few weeks of its' life – and I shall deal with this subject in a later chapter.

When I left Caithness I bought a licensed greyhound kennels on the border of Scotland and England. In common with many NGRC (National Greyhound Racing Club) kennels the buildings were properly constructed and quite hygienic. However, what the sellers failed to let me know was that the premises had seen some incidence of parvo virus deaths. I realised my mistake when I sold an eight week old uninoculated puppy to a teacher in Cumbernauld and the trauma of its move to a new home triggered a parvo virus outbreak which killed the puppy within a week. I have a policy of refunding money and replacing the whelp free of charge, but this did not ease the problem of the presence of the virus on the premises. Hence a week before the bitches were due to whelp, I not only inoculated them, but kennelled them on the premises in which the whelps had died, for a fortnight before parturition. This more or less assured me that the pregnant bitches were in contact with the infection and were almost certain to pass quantities of antibodies across the placenta to their young and also via the colostrum. The whelps achieved immunity for six weeks after which I inoculated them. My parvo virus outbreak came to an abrupt end and I have not experienced further troubles from parvo virus infections.

On a more macabre note – and this is not for the squeamish. When pig breeders suffered from a particularly virulent form of swine fever in the 1970s it was common practise to take piglets which had died of the infection, liquidise the carcasses and feed the flesh, bone and tissue to sows nearing parturition, which certainly contravenes the 1973 Boiled Swill Regulations. The sows developed a high level of immunity to the disease and this was passed via the colostrum (not the placenta) to the piglets. The process smacks of ghoulishness to the average person, I suppose, but it was a method I adopted in my efforts to control the parvovirus outbreak in 1979. My friends were horrified, although my veterinary surgeon agreed with my methods. I can't leave the story half told I'm afraid. The virulence of the early outbreaks of parvo virus will not be forgotten for not even my witches brew of raw liquidised puppy flesh succeeded in curbing the disease and it was not until I adopted inoculating the whelps with a NoBIVAC parvo vaccine that I managed to curb the ravages of the disease.

Enough however of the subject of vaccination, not to vaccinate is a recipe for disaster, particularly in a large kennel of dogs. It is sufficient to say that it is not necessary to study the history and treatment of certain preventable diseases. One should simply inoculate against these infections and forget about them.

# 5

# Exercise

ONE OF THE GREAT criticisms levied against dog farmers is that the breeding stock they keep is seldom given enough exercise and if this criticism is true then it is a great pity, for subject to certain limitations, exercise is one of the finest conditioners for a breeding bitch.

Unscientific and anthropomorphic as it might first appear, I lay most of the problems of the modern dog down at the feet of lack of exercise. At the time of writing the press is filled with articles and letters concerning the incidence of heart troubles amongst Cavalier King Charles Spaniels, mitral valve problems, described none too poetically but rather accurately by Halden as the 'drop down dead syndrome', is rampant in the breed, so rampant in fact that breeders invariably advise buyers to be sparing with the amount of exercise a puppy is given. I am considered by many as an iconoclast, one who sets out to destroy commonly held notions, and in 1997 I accepted a challenge to match a team of Cavaliers against conventionally bred working terriers. In order to stimulate the hunting instinct in these diminutive spaniels I ran them daily at rabbit and rat, hunting the steep hills adjacent to the sources of the River Clyde. Some days these spaniels hunted non stop for a full six hours running at perhaps seven miles an hour and often faster when they 'sprang' and coursed a hare, thus hunting a minimum of about fifty miles in the course of a days hunting. Not one of these tiny toy spaniels showed the slightest sign of exhaustion one associates with dogs suffering from mitral valve problems. At the 1998 Edinburgh Championship Show I handled many winning exhibits some of which were groomed to perfection and whose coats shone like glass. They were shown in immaculate condition but were 'soft' muscled. I returned home and handled my own Cavaliers. All five were lighter, leaner and, I believe, happier than the wonderful spaniels I had seen at the show.

One veterinary surgeon I know is particularly interested in the whelping problems experienced by miniature breeds. On hearing I had bought a miniature dachshund, a tiny 10lb smooth coated dapple (or merle) bitch, he remarked that the miniature dachshund bitches he had encountered often led a house bound or caged existence, and needed caesarean sections to give birth to puppies but one or two of the farm reared animals he knew, who roamed around the farm hunting rabbits and mice, produced puppies on a far too regular basis perhaps, but seldom experienced any problems during parturition. One bitch somehow coupled with a border collie – the union must have been an incongruous sight – and whelped a litter of crossbred puppies unaided, under a cattle feed box trough. Amazingly the hideous offspring were easily homed and I believe, greatly loved by their owners. I saw just one – an amazing looking chimera.

I breed and train golden retrievers, admittedly the work strains not the heavier more silky coated exhibition stock, and I find that they exercise best in the River Clyde which runs only yards from my kennels. A full hour's exercise swimming in the river does wonders for their condition and they really adore this type of activity, which Hahn describes as the 'most complete exercise, (all limbs and muscles come into play when an animal or man swims), and race into the Clyde at a moments notice. They run ahead of me and stand belly-deep in the shallows waiting for me to encourage them to retrieve objects from the fast flowing river, but seemingly not everyone approves of my actions. The village in which I live is a tourist attraction and we get many visitors even in mid winter. On January 7th 1997 a particularly cold spell froze the Clyde, and that morning my seven bitches raced to the river smashing the thin layer of ice to swim into the middle of the Clyde. A lady tourist standing on the bridge camera in hand photographed the scene and became furious, threatening to report me for and I quote 'causing the dogs suffering by making them swim in freezing water'. My bitches returned to kennels dry from their exertions in the woods near the river and joyously raced to the river again later that afternoon.

How little the man in the street knows of dogs and how much damage unscientific misconceptions do to dogdom. On 5th June, 1998 I was interviewed by the behaviourist, academic and sled dog enthusiast, Professor Ray Coppinger, and I related the story of the retrievers swimming in the icy waters of the Clyde. He laughed, and said that in New England animal rights activists are active in bringing about the cessation of sled dog racing because, I quote 'it is cruel to make sled dogs run and pull a sled'. How foolish such reasoning is. Sled dogs love to pull in front of their owners and become ecstatic when a sled or a harness appears. I am almost terrified that in the near future some crank with unscientific views will lobby some equally unscientific Member of Parliament and by dint of doing so produce yet another ludicrous Bill to be debated in the House of Commons. Thank God for the Lords say I, lest we live in a country where that which is not forbidden becomes compulsory – political aside over and I shall now return to the text!

Although strenuous exercise is an excellent method of conditioning breeding stock, there are of course times when excessive exercise is inadvisable. When young dogs are growing the amount of exercise they are given should be limited and this particularly applies to giant heavy breeds such as Bull Mastiffs, Great Danes, Newfoundlands etc. If these young dogs are to be exercised it is best to allow them to exercise at liberty (preferably with other young dogs) in a large compound where they can run and play but also sleep when they become tired. Long exhausting walks, literally forced marches are inadvisable where these large breeds are concerned, for such dogs subjected to this treatment develop all manner of disorders such as dysplasia and damage to cartilage. However I am rather concerned about breeders who dissuade young dogs from climbing stairs or descending from settees unaided so that in later life these dogs can achieve low hip scores (hip scoring is done when a dog or bitch is one year old or older). I cannot but feel that scores obtained in such a manner have an element of artificiality.

It is unwise to over-exercise bitches which are near to parturition or to engage such bitches in violent and strenuous games. Bitches have been known to miscarry when subjected to such an exercise programme. The tale of the dam of a famous Waterloo Cup greyhound bitch which coursed, caught and killed a large dog fox before returning to kennels and whelping a litter of ten puppies is well known, but greyhounds are the most physically perfect members of dogdom, and despite the fact that they are considered the most blue blooded of dogs, are extraordinarily tough, tenacious and ailment free. Seldom do greyhound bitches miscarry and rarely do such bitches experience problems during parturition. Ten thousand years of the most stringent Darwinian selection programme has created the most incredibly tough and tenacious of animals. Bitches of other breeds however are seldom able to engage in strenuous exercise on the day of parturition. Yet I hunted my terrier bitches regularly until the day they began to whelp and experienced few problems when the animals began gave birth to their puppies.

In passing it is worth noting that in certain districts it is impossible to exercise bitches off the lead or to allow them to run free. Such animals need to be walked to improve their physical condition. I learned a lot about the psychology of walking dogs early in my teaching career when penury induced me to take part-time jobs, gutting rabbits, packing poultry and for three years walking a string of eight greyhounds, the property of an NGRC licensed trainer, who was crippled as a result of arthritis. Dog walking is a lot more skilful than first imagined if, that is, the dogs are to improve in condition as a result of a forty-five minute twice a day gentle exercise periods. I found that greyhounds subjected to walking the same route each day developed a jaundiced attitude towards exercise and did not improve in condition. I therefore constantly altered the route, taking them passed buildings and fields which triggered interest in the hounds. They enjoyed walking past an abattoir or a field where cattle grazed and for some reason the local Salvation Army hostel triggered great interest, possibly because of the smell of freshly cooked food which wafted from the building. Dogs which are to be walked to improve condition need to be walked on a varied route to keep their interest. I must confess I really didn't enjoy exercising the string of greyhounds I was paid to walk, particularly as the owner of these dogs insisted that I walked the dogs each day no matter what the weather. He also insisted I dried off the hounds free of charge when they were exercised in the rain. My job came to an abrupt end when the dogs' arthritic owner went into hospital to undergo a trivial operation and somehow died in surgery. He died owing me two months wages!

It is policy to test all dogs for certain genetic disorders particular breeds are known to manifest, though I have certain reservations about specific forms of testing.

The hip dysplasia testing scheme has proven to be quite a success in the control of this crippling disorder, though there is some evidence to suggest that certain environmental conditions may produce this disorder in genetically sound stock. Be that as it may the scheme has not completely eradicated hip dysplasia, but according to veterinary reports the incidence of the disorder has become less common in recent years. Briefly the scheme entails taking a dog to a licensed veterinary surgeon who anaesthetises the animal before X-raying the pelvic girdle and ascertaining how well the head of the femur fits into the acitabulum or hip socket. The X-ray plates are then sent to experts in the task of grading hip scores and these experts grade each hip separately. Scores range from 0–53 for each hip – a low score being an indication of a good hip, a high score an indication that the head of the femur is not fitting into the acetabulum. Hips are graded thus 4:4 (an excellent hip score where both hip joints are fitting well) to 40:40 a very poor hip score which indicates a very ill fitting ball and socket joint.

In passing, seemingly it is not always the case that a poor hip score invariably results in a crippled dog, although this is usually the case. Some months ago I spoke to an RAF dog handler who, during his service, was allocated a very fine German Shepherd dog of the heavy English type which I like, but does not find favour amongst the present day show fraternity. The dog performed well in the field, winning many contests including high and long jump events which sorely test the skeletal structure of any dog. When a survey was conducted by a military veterinary surgeon the dog was found to have an unacceptably high hip score . Seemingly only the hind leg muscles kept the hip joint in place during the strenuous exercise in which the dog engaged. It is however likely that in later life, when muscle tone usually declines, that the dog would experience some problems with arthritis. In passing it is also worth noting that when the otterhound was embraced by the show fraternity after the cessation of otter hunting in the 1970s, working hounds from various otter hound packs constituted the foundation of the future exhibition stock. Yet very bad hip scores were recorded in the first generation of the show stock. It can therefore be assumed that the foundation stock also had defective hips. This might be explained by the fact that the life of a working pack hound of any sort, harrier, beagle, fox hound, staghound etc. is very short, for as soon as the speed of a hound begins to wane it is 'replaced' – a euphemism for 'destroyed' – and hence might be spared the arthritic problems which clearly plague dogs with ill fitting hips in later life.

Eye testing, or rather the relevance of eye testing, breeds known to experience problems with hereditary cataracts is a bit of a moot point amongst breeders, as indeed is the heart testing of breeds such as Cavalier King Charles spaniels which are known to have a high incidence of mitral valve problems (I mentioned my own treatment of my own Cavalier King Charles spaniels earlier in this chapter). There is some evidence to suggest that few young dogs show signs of cataracts and hence might well be used for breeding. Later in life at the age of five or six some of these dogs develop obvious cataracts. It is therefore advisable that dogs are tested each year even though they may have bred several litters of puppies before a cataract becomes apparent.

Similarly the testing for heart problems might be a rather futile attempt to eradicate the mitral valve disorder amongst Cavalier King

Charles spaniels. At the 1998 Kennel Club Show in Edinburgh I met two breeders who told the story of a very prepotent stud dog. The stud had been tested for several years, each time it was taken for its vaccination booster, and found to be negative for heart disorders each year. It was used to mate a great many bitches and subsequently a huge number of puppies many of whom were show winners. In his seventh year he was found to have defective mitral valves – and it had clearly passed on many of his defective genes to his progeny. I am however, rather sceptical about tales heard at shows related by people with little knowledge of science or genetics, particularly as the show fraternity are so spiteful to anyone who is successful in any field. believe I have already mentioned that very British malaise – the dislike of anyone who is experiencing a modicum of success.

Yet there are excellent reasons why breeders should test their stock before breeding from both dogs and bitches. I am reluctant to attribute racial characteristics to any nationality, but just as the British dislike successful people so the Americans display a strong desire to sue everyone who offends or displeases them in the most trivial way. Recently the success of a cancer sufferer who sued a tobacco company for supposedly causing his affliction became news – an amazing decision, as ludicrous as a builder being responsible for a person who repeatedly beat his head against a wall and experienced blinding headaches perhaps. Nevertheless the 'vice American' is now catching on in Britain. In 1997 a woman who bred a Labrador retriever with defective hips was successfully sued by a buyer and paid a large sum in damages. Yet the parents of the defective animal had been hip scored and found to have acceptable hips – below 20 the combined scores of both hips would have been acceptable. One shudders to think what sum would have been awarded if the parents of the animal had not been tested! Testing one's animals for the defects the breed is known to carry is the very best form of insurance in a country about to embrace the American curse, suing anyone who offends, a malaise which explains the typical American's distaste for lawyers.

> Question: *Why does New Jersey have the highest incidence of pollution and New York the highest incidence of lawyers engaged in civil litigation.* Answer: *Because when God gave out desirable qualities New Jersey had first choice.*

I once met the comedian George Burns whose act consisted of tales of Vaudeville turns and one of his tales was of the perils of buying a dog from an unscrupulous breeder. The perils an honest breeder experiences in these days are seemingly many times worse. Testing one's stock guards one's back against civil litigation – but seemingly only to a certain extent! Truly a dog breeder's life is not a happy one.

It is often said that one should not breed from a bitch during her first season, but this is an extremely loose statement. Some toy breeds and even some terriers come into season at six months of age, and this is clearly too soon for a bitch to be considered for motherhood. Conversely many greyhounds do not come into season until they are four years of age and are therefore well grown and mentally mature at that age. In fact the downfall of my own strain of lurcher has been the fact that not only do my bitches come into season irregularly but they are also rarely in season before their sixth or seventh year. They have been bred since 1948 for their physical and mental prowess and it has been a monumental oversight that I have paid too little regard to their fecundity. Hence if I am able, I always mate my bitches during their first seasons, for they are usually five or six years old when they attain sexual maturity.

Might I ask the reader to indulge an ageing man in his idiosyncrasies, but I am decidedly anthropomorphic about the age when I first mate a bitch. One of my favourite quotes is from Ecclesiastes 3:1 *'There is a time to be born and a time to die'*. Might I endorse such a statement and state that there is a time when a bitch is not ready to breed – a time for growing up perhaps, a time to establish canine relationships and then and only then a time to reproduce, and I can think of no reason why a bitch should be mated before it is fifteen months old. A bitch, even a bitch intended to be used exclusively as a brood, needs and deserves a childhood. It is rather unfair to breed from any bitch before this age. It can be argued that breeding gilts should be mated as they come in season. Indeed gilts left too long before they are mated are reluctant to conceive because they lay down fatty deposits around their ovaries. However dogs are not pigs and even those who seek to become dog farmers should insure that a bitch is allowed a happy, eventful puppyhood before it is allowed to breed.

Still there are advocates of breeding from bitches before they are a year old. Many argue that toy dogs and small breeds of terrier are physically mature before they are a year old and that the pelvic bones of such an animal are soft, pliable and flexible enough at this age to allow the easy passage of puppies. This is clearly the case, for fewer young bitches experience problems during parturition. Conversely very young bitches often produce puppies easily enough but the mothering instinct, the innate disposition to clean and care for newly born puppies is sometimes absent in these animals. Indeed I have seen very young bitches horrified at the sight of puppies which have emerged from them. I have also seen very young bitches savage puppies which have suddenly emerged from their bodies, yet a year or so later clean and tend their second litters with loving care. Some years ago an illness disabled me enough to warrant having a friend to tend my terrier pack – I ran a rat hunting pack for twenty-three years. Now even friends with the very best intentions are seldom reliable in kennels, and when I returned from a lecture trip I have to steal myself for loss or damage to my stock during my absence. To cut a long story short during my spell in hospital the bitch Beltane, a puppy with tremendous potential was mated by her brother and produced a litter of puppies. I had to hand rear the fruits of this incestuous union for I found that while Beltane had given birth to them in the corner of a shed she was cowering as though terrified of the whelps in the far corner. I undertook the rearing of the litter with something akin to a bad grace, for I was still unwell and cursed my friend for his incompetence in allowing this alliance. I also viewed Beltane's future as a brood with some uncertainty and trepidation in the light of her behaviour during and after parturition. She was five years old before I decided to mate her to continue her bloodline for she was a truly amazing bitch with all the qualities I wanted in a terrier. I need not have worried. She whelped her second litter easily and was the most devoted of brood bitches. I have one of her descendants – a great, great, great, great, great, great grandchild – at my feet as I write.

I am not in favour of the system of breeding and the regulations attached to dog breeding that exists in Germany – one is offered a choice of a few stud dogs the breed club decides are suitable, and the number of whelps a bitch is allowed to rear is also determined by the breed club. I once published an article on the subject entitled 'We Have Ways of Making You Breed' which I hasten to add was not well received in Germany! However I applaud the British breed clubs such as the Northern Bullmastiff Club which advises but does not compel its members to breed from bitches only when they are over two years of age. Bullmastiffs are very babyish and immature until they are at least eighteen months old and contrary to their appearance often very benign dogs for the rest of their entire lives. My own bitch Wobbly – yes, I allow the village children to name my dogs – allows children to put their hands down her throat – its a strange child who wants to I thought at the time, but most of the village children attempt this practice and Wobbly enjoys the attention.

In passing, breeders who intend to produce many litters of puppies from a bitch should remember that the Kennel Club allows only six litters to be bred from a bitch, and will not allow a breeder to register puppies from a bitch which is over eight years old, unless the breeder obtains a special dispensation from the Kennel Club. This is a very wise decision for I have seen too many elderly bitches which have produced and reared too many litters of puppies, and by the age of eight a bitch is ready for retirement. Of course the regulation does not apply to breeders of dogs such as lurchers, long dogs and certain other 'unregistered' breeds of dog, but it is a good policy to follow breeding guidelines laid down by the Kennel Club if only for humanitarian reasons. Some breeders continue to breed from elderly worn out bitches and do not register the puppies born to these matings. I shall refrain from commenting on this subject. I shall merely leave the reader to draw his or her own conclusions on the matter.

I shall draw the chapter to a close with the mention of antibiotics in the preparation of a bitch which is intended to breed a litter, merely giving the facts and allowing the reader to once again draw his or her own conclusions, though I intend to deal with the practical aspects of the use of antibiotics in a later chapter. Sufficient to say that in the late 1970s Australian veterinary surgeons dealing with injured pregnant greyhounds which were being treated with antibiotics, noticed a significant increase in litter size and an improved survival rate of puppies born to bitches treated with antibiotics just prior and immediately after mating. It has been argued that while present breeders may reap the benefits of this type of treatment, future breeders may find that they are plagued with organisms that are resistant to certain antibiotics. Indeed at the time of writing there are moves afoot to restrict the use of antibiotics in the treatment of animal diseases – re foodstuffs etc., to prevent or at least delay the production of resistant organisms.

# 6

# Stud Dogs

WHETHER THE commercial breeder should own his own stud dogs is in many ways a debatable subject. It can be argued that the space a stud dog occupies may be more profitably filled by a brood bitch and in certain circumstances this is obviously true. In fact, if I kept only one or two breeding bitches of a particular breed, I should be reluctant to own a stud dog. Indeed while it is true that a male, even an entire male (and I have very mixed feelings about the present craze for castrating most male dogs) can be kept perfectly happy without mating a bitch. Once a stud dog's sexual appetite is whetted the animal's character changes slightly, and henceforth the dog requires more bitches. Thus unless a person has more than one or two breeding bitches and/or is prepared to offer the animal for public stud use – I shall come to this matter presently – keeping one's own stud dog is something of a mixed blessing. If an animal is regularly used at stud it is possible that he may be hostile to other males in the kennels particularly when bitches come into season and there is always a possibility of a misalliance if two or more stud dogs are kept in a poorly regulated kennels.

Most 'antique' books concerning the breeding of dogs state that there is little point in keeping one's own stud dog if one can use the best stud dog in the country for a nominal or reasonable fee, and of course there is some truth in this statement, for at the time of writing the services of a first class stud dog can be used for a fee of £100–£500 (it is curious that certain breeds seem to command a greater stud price than others – for instance £200 seems to be a fairly average price for the use of a champion German Shepherd Dog, whilst £500 is usually asked for the use of a Bullmastiff of similar quality. What causes this disparity in prices between various breeds is a subject I shall deal with shortly). Yet the initial payment of a stud fee is not the only imposition a would be breeder must face. A suitable stud dog may be stationed two or three hundred miles away and the cost of the trip to and from the stud dog may also have to be considered, and this price can be compounded by the fact that few bitches are willing to come into season at the weekends, so the cost of a day off work may also have to be taken into consideration. If a suitable stud dog can be found locally, such a dog is a treasure, providing that the owner has no social commitments which restrict the times when a bitch can be brought to the kennels. At the time of writing I am having a dreadful time getting my Bullmastiff bitch mated to a dog of my choice, because the owner of the stud dog leads a very active life and Wobbly steadfastly refuses to come into season at suitable times. In passing I must add that although the Bullmastiff received bad press in 1997, most breeds of dogs get bad press from time to time, Wobbly has the sweetest disposition and will tolerate and seemingly enjoy outrageous treatment from young children and puppies alike.

Some bitches are reluctant to stand for mating if distressed by a very long journey in a car or train, though in an age where many people have access to the use of cars and dogs are frequent passengers in these vehicles, these cases are becoming increasingly rare. True some nervous and excitable bitches are reluctant to mate if carted across country to a stud dog but they may also be equally reluctant to mate on their own turf. Still a journey of perhaps 400 miles is a great imposition for the would-be breeder – one I am having to face as I write this paragraph in fact.

If one owns more than two bitches of a particular breed the ownership of one's own stud dog is entirely justified – and once again I must welcome the reader to a veritable minefield of problems. I should be reluctant to purchase an adult stud dog, even a tried and tested adult stud dog, quite simply because I would question why the owner would wish to sell such an animal. It is possible that social problems may prompt this sale – work commitments, break up of marriage etc. It is also possible, and a great deal more likely one must add, that the stud dog has certain undesirable qualities or is passing on such qualities to his offspring and this may be prompting its owner to sell him and not all dog breeders are totally honest or truthful one must add. Yet the purchase of an eight week old puppy with the intention of running on the youngster for use as a stud dog can also present problems. It can be argued that there is no guarantee that the puppy will be sexually mature or fertile, though it is fair to say few males are indifferent to bitches or are infertile, so if possible the purchaser of a suitable youngster is preferable to taking on an old hand veteran stud dog.

A commercial breeder, I really must find a more socially acceptable term for someone who tries to make an honest living by breeding dogs, may well consider breeding from any healthy bitch which is typical of the breed despite the absence of champions in her pedigree, but I would suggest that a stud dog bought to couple with these bitches should be of superlative quality. It is often said – and I try to resist using glib aphorisms – that a stud dog is half one's kennels and of course this is perfectly true for a strong, eager, sexually active male dog will couple with as many as a hundred bitches a year. In fact during the time when I was engrossed in the production of my own breed of dog, my own stud dog Rupert – a very prepotent male by any standard – bred 2,800 litters of puppies during his long and active sex life. This of course caused many problems later on, when consanguinity and its attendant problems dogged the strain, but as Kipling says 'that is another tale'.

The would-be owner of a stud dog should seek out the best male puppy to use for breeding. Reader, welcome to the first hurdle you must leap and likewise to an absurd practise and the equally absurd people who tend to use this practise. A popular craze at the present time is for breeders to endorse the pedigrees of the stock they sell so as to prevent the purchaser of this stock from using the animal for breeding. On the surface of it this practise is commendable for it is said to limit the number of puppies produced and also to improve future breeding stock by ensuring that the only animals used for breeding are of superlative quality. However I suspect there are darker more unsavoury motives behind the practise. By endorsing pedigrees stating that the animal purchased must not be used for breeding, the breeder/vendor is effectively creating a loosely fitting monopoly by eradicating possible competition, but I suspect even darker less acceptable motives for the practise. Lorenz, that master of animal behaviour, whose researches also cast shadows on human peculiarities, states that each man wishes to become a king but as there is only a limited scope for monarchy, (there can only be one king or queen) he or she invents his own kingdom, and woe betide anyone who ventures into or seeks to invade that kingdom. Alfred Adler 1870–1937 was a follower of Freud and his work seems to suggest that one of the driving forces of human behaviour is the acquisition of power – an archetype perhaps explored in one of the earlier Arthurian legends. This system of endorsement of pedigrees gives petty, inadequate people ample opportunity to exploit this desire for power. By endorsing pedigrees the breeder also limits the gene pool and possibly creates future problems with the breed, by creating undesirable inbreeding and its attendant problems.

Be that as it may, the breeder may possibly find some difficulty purchasing a well bred puppy with an unendorsed pedigree, for the better bred the animal, the more jealously the breeder seems to guard the stock he or she produces – which knocks on the head the notion that the breeder is endorsing pedigrees for the general good of the breed just a little, doesn't it? Some may try to sell a puppy with an endorsed pedigree stating that should the puppy grow into an animal the breeder/vendor considers to be of superlative quality, he or she will lift the endorsement – and this really gives the breeder a sense of power, for pettiness and spitefulness abound in the world of dog breeding. The chances are that no matter how aesthetically pleasing the animal proves to be that endorsement will not be lifted. In fact if the animal does grow into a superlative male the breeder will view the young male as competition and will be most reluctant to see possible stud work passing to another breeder. My advice is to not to touch a puppy with an endorsed pedigree with a barge pole. Purchasing a potential stud dog with an endorsed pedigree, the endorsement of which the breeder may be (or may not be) prepared to lift, is bad practise. Stay well clear of any breeder who seeks to establish his or her superiority and power by endorsing pedigrees.

Personally my choice would be to buy a young male, 8–12 weeks of age which can be trained as a stud dog. This comment may baffle the casual observer for logically the sex act is surely innate and does not require training but this is far from the truth. I sometimes get outside stud work – I must admit I do not encourage it for reasons I shall explain more fully at a later stage of the book – and the majority of the bitches brought to me have been 'tried' with another dog, an animal with no experience of mating. The bitch is often bewildered by the experience of meeting a virginal would-be stud dog who like as not will respond to the flirtations of the bitch with something akin to bewilderment. He will mount her head, her flanks or perhaps wish to be away from the animal who is lavishing outrageous sexual attentions on him. Some dogs will be hostile with a bitch who is attempting to ravish them. Many of the bitches I have brought to me for mating have bruised vaginas as a result of the attentions of an over eager but inexperienced stud dog and will refuse the attentions of my own stud dogs simply because of the mental and physical damage brought by these inexperienced dogs.

However yet another caveat. There is a genetic disorder known as unilateral and bilateral cryptochism to consider, a condition where one or both testicles fail to descend into the scrotum. Should neither testicle descend, the dog is rendered sterile though not impotent, for the temperature of the testicles needs to be slightly lower than the rest of the dogs body in order for viable sperm to be produced. When only one testicle descends the undescended testicle tends to atrophy and become carcinomous and thus needs to be removed surgically. It is therefore unwise to breed from dogs manifesting only one descended testicle for there is every indication the condition is inherited. This alone makes the purchase of an entire working stud dog preferable to the purchase of a puppy with undescended testicles.

A young dog bought for stud work should be handled regularly, cuddled, lifted and become very use to human company. Some males of the toy and terrier breeds – I own a very precocious, sexy little Cavalier King Charles Spaniel – show an interest in bitches when they are as young as six months of age. Some of the larger breeds are bewildered by an in-season bitch when they are this age, and giant breeds such as Danes, Newfoundlands and Mastiffs show little interest in sex at a year old. However once a dog is reasonably mature and shows a marked interest in trying to ride bitches or other dogs for that matter, it is time to introduce him to his first bitch and just as Zola believes a first love, and the experiences with that first love can influence the rest of a man's life, so a stud dog can be made or ruined by his first sexual experiences. A young immature male should seldom be allowed to mate a young boisterous or nervous bitch, but if possible introduced to an older more experienced bitch who has not only mated but produced a few litters of puppies – and what is to follow does resemble a plot of a book by Emile Zola. The older bitch should be prepared to engage in the canine courtship ritual, be absolutely ready to mate and be ready to stand for the act of mating on the day the young future stud dog is to be used. The bitch should also be firmly held and prevented from pulling away and damaging or frightening the young male. Once the male has mounted the bitch and engaged in the seemingly bizarre posture known as 'a tie', the bitch must be securely held until the mating is over and the dog parts company with the bitch. At no time during coition, and I shall describe the art of coition presently, should the young stud dog be frightened or hurt by the experience, so it is best to allow matings only in a very private part of one's kennels where not even an incoming telephone call can disturb the process of mating.

In passing I suggest the reader disregards advice that a stud dog needs a special diet in order to maintain his virility – he doesn't. A good maintenance diet of 21% protein is enough to keep any stud dog happy and willing to mate. He does however need to be exercised and fit and I suspect many of the unconsummated attempts at mating a bitch are the result of the male being unfit. It is indeed a very taxing experience for a stud dog to manage to copulate with a difficult bitch and I have seen dogs experience total exhaustion when the bitch is reluctant to copulate but determined to engage in flirtatious courtship. I allow my own stud dogs to exercise freely. Indeed my Cavalier King Charles Spaniel dog runs for roughly thirteen miles a day chasing rabbits and hares.

If possible a dog's first love should be of similar size to the dog – not too big and not too small, so that a perfectly normal unaided sexual union can be achieved. Giant or tiny bitches need special handling if the new stud dog is to be successful in the coupling and the experience pleasurable and satisfying to the stud. I would have no objection to my stud dog mating a mongrel bitch providing the bitch is willing and capable of mating and easy to mate. The majority of show breeders, particularly inexperienced show breeders who have experienced a brief and possibly ephemeral success in the show ring, are usually horrified at the prospect of a pedigree stud dog serving a mongrel bitch, but the act does no harm to the stud apart from the fact that mongrel puppies may be produced in an age when even well bred pedigree puppies may be difficult to home.

Might I back-track a little concerning the supposed knowledge of some show breeders. Some are quite au fait with the scene of breeding while others who are new to the dog world are less so. Yet for some reason, a show breeder who has experienced an albeit fleeting success at Crufts immediately assumes the mantle of the authority of all things canine. This is a ghastly mistake for many Cruft winners are first time dog owners who for some reason had the good fortune to buy an animal with good show potential. Experience can only be gained by experience, and if that experience is tempered by some scientific knowledge, so much the better. Many owners of 'stars of the Big Ring' at Crufts are certainly not experts in the art of dog breeding.

If I owned an easily mated bitch, I should be inclined to allow a young stud to mate her many times during the season until she ceased to encourage the attentions of the dog. Despite popular beliefs, a young stud, providing he is healthy and willing, can be allowed to mate many bitches in his first year at stud, and the notion that there should be a six month period between the stud dog's first and second bitches should be treated as an old wives tale – and such tales abound in the world of dog breeding. The more a stud dog is used the more proficient he becomes in the act of mating but he must be kept away from bitches which are far too big or far too small until he is a proficient, competent and very eager stud dog. The reason behind the notion that a stud dog should be used once and then allowed a six month period to elapse before the second mating is easy to understand though totally illogical. It can be said that by allowing this six month period between first and second matings the breeder is able to see the progeny of the young stud dog, which will be four months old at the time of the second mating, and hence able to see if the stud dog carries certain defects. However certain defects can be the result of the union of this particular dog and this particular bitch and not really apply to other unrelated bitches. Furthermore certain undesirable qualities may be inherited from just one parent – though these defects are rather uncommon. It is a fact a very clever breeder who can ascertain the qualities a stud dog can pass on to his progeny by dint of examining just one litter.

I refer to Hancock's great kennels in Sutton Coldfield yet once more, where mating of both 'home' and visiting bitches proceeds on a virtually daily basis. Hancock breeds lurchers which are produced by mating a collie or collie hybrids with a pure bred track or coursing greyhound bitch. There is of course a marked disparity in size between a collie male and a greyhound bitch – collies are roughly twenty or so inches at the shoulder while some greyhound bitches can be a full eleven inches taller. To produce a union between the two animals Hancock arranges a series of wooden or stone steps to allow the dog to climb and then mount the bitch. I used a similar apparatus when I used my stud dog Rupert on terrier bitches in the late 1960s and 1970s. So used was Rupert to using these steps that once he observed a bitch coming for mating, he ran to the steps and waited. Once when a friend brought a Great Dane bitch to my kennels to show me, Rupert raced to the blocks and waited willing to attempt to copulate with this outsized female. Hancock says his stud dogs are now so sexually experienced that they show not the slightest interest in visiting and 'home' bitches unless these females are ready to mate and he can walk an out of season or nearly ready to mate bitch past a stud dog without even exciting the male. However a dog must be well used to mating bitches before he is tried on blocks to lift him level with an in season bitch, and the dog must always be well used to being handled before he attempts such a mating.

Devices should be made before a bitch comes for mating particularly if the dog is to be used at public stud and frankly Heath Robinson devices are often dangerous and damaging to the stud. When Rupert mated large bitches I used two concrete slabs cemented together to assist the mating, when his bitches were much smaller than he was I used a small hole in which to stand the dog. I have seen breeders use bizarre contraptions and frames to effect a mating, equipment the like of which one would find in a torture chamber used by Torquemadar and these devices have proved very successful in assisting in the mating.

In the 1960s I took a bitch, a German Shepherd Dog, to be mated to quite a useful stud dog which would only mate if the bitch was standing on a particular platform bounded by two wooden rails, and he would then only complete the act if the owner, a plump little lady, ran into the building saying 'Look what lady this man has brought you'. If the dog lost interest in mating she would take him out of the shed and bring him back and utter the same expression and the dog behaved with great enthusiasm as if he had never seen the bitch before. Yet the same male sired dozens of satisfactory litters during his stud life.

Another lady lifted the bitch's hind legs waggling the bitch's genitalia in front of the dog to excite him saying 'Just look at this lovely lady who has come to be loved' and the dog promptly obliged by mating the dog in question. It was somewhat disconcerting to notice that while the lady uttered these words of sexual encouragement her lips drooled saliva and her eyes developed an almost unwholesome gleam. Still it would be a strange world if we were all the same. Incidentally I have always copied her method of exciting a dog by moving the bitch's genitalia in front of the male and found this is a very efficacious method of encouraging a reluctant stud to mate – though the practise is a shade difficult to implement if one is attempting to mate one of the giant breeds unless, that is, the breeder is also a weight lifter.

It is now time to examine the pros and cons of allowing a stud to mate outside bitches, particularly if it is inconvenient for the bitch's owner to make a daily trip to the stud and hence has to leave the bitch to board at the kennels which houses the stud dog and his entourage.

If the stud is adept at mating bitches and of sufficient quality to attract stud work then the acquisition of stud fees can be quite profitable – though certainly not money for old rope as owners of visiting bitches may think. One client bringing an in-season bitch for mating uttered 'Fifty quid for twenty five minutes work is robbery. I only earn £4 an hour as a bricklayer (1968)', but the process of training a stud dog to mate both efficiently and quickly is a lengthy process. If the bitch needs to be kennelled near to ones own breeding stock that is another tale, and the presence of an in-season, out-of-season or simply boarding bitch can make kennel life far from pleasant, time for a scientific discourse to explain this statement.

In 1951 the behaviourist Steiniger conducted some experiments into the behaviour of rats. He gathered a variety of rats from different sources – farms, sewers, maggot factories (a rich source of rodent life) and allowed them to run in a large enclosure where he could observe them. For a while the wild rats roamed around the enclosure displaying little aggression to one and other until that is a male paired with a female. Henceforth the male sought out and killed every other male while his mate did to death every female – and the manner in which rats destroy their kind is far from pleasant. The pair then bred quite happily and such is the fecundity of rats that within months the pair had incestuously bred grandchildren which they tolerated with the patience and indulgence human grandparents show towards their own grandchildren. Steiniger then brought in a strange rat. For a while the other rats ignored him, for rats seem to rely on olfactory senses to detect the presence of strangers. Once they had scented the stranger in their midst however, they tore the helpless beast to pieces and ate it. The colony then set about trying to kill each other until a single pair remained once again. Eibl Eiblfeldt noted exactly the same behaviour in house mice which are equally ferocious to their own kind. However huntsmen and kennel huntsmen involved with scent hound packs had noticed this peculiarity for centuries and had taken measures to prevent the havoc a drafted hound may cause in kennels.

When a hound or hounds are drafted from other kennels the new hound is placed in an enclosure where the other hounds can see and scent the newcomer yet are not able to mingle with or attack the stranger. Only after several days or weeks is the pack allowed to absorb the stranger and the behaviour of the pack is watched carefully for bickering or savage kennel fights. In passing it is fair to say that the chance of kennel problems is greater when hounds are drafted than when in-season bitches are brought for mating. This is because hounds are usually drafted because they do not fit in with their own pack and may be what is known as 'provocative victims' – animals which through no fault of their own, become architects of their own destruction inviting kennel mates to kill them.

The presence of an in-season bitch left to be mated will often trigger terrible kennel fights amongst normally peaceable and pleasant permanent kennel inmates. Care must be taken for the residents not to see or worse still smell the newcomer. I am frequently asked by friends to allow dogs and bitches to stay at my kennels while their owners are on holiday. I frequently refuse for I would sooner lose a friend than one of my own dogs through a kennel fight – besides which most of my friends are au fait with canine psychology and understand the problems a visiting dog or bitch may cause.

I shall conclude this chapter with the riddle 'What is the difference between a man who makes a living from breeding dogs and a person standing on a bridge chewing a mallet'? Answer; 'The man who makes a living from dogs is a professional the other is simply an amateur (hammer chewer)'. This gives the reader some indication of the damage done to my head during my eleven successive defeats in the ring in the U.S.A.

# 7

# The Act of Mating

'BITCHES ARE ready to receive a dog when they are exactly twelve days into season in the same way that women are only fertile mid way between periods'. Reader if these facts were true, there would be a lot of pedigree dogs in the world and very few unwanted Catholic children – a statement that is certain to offend someone. There is in fact only one absolute law regarding dog breeding and that is, there are no absolute laws regarding dog breeding. Hence it is wise to temper the advice given in this chapter with 'most', 'usually' and 'typically'.

Bitches come into season at various ages. Toy breeds and some terriers show signs of sexual maturity as early as six months of age, though nine months is more usual, while giant breeds such as Great Danes, Mastiffs and Newfoundlands may not be sexually mature until they are four years of age. Greyhounds are notoriously slow at attaining sexual maturity, though I believe this could be due to an unintentional selection programme on the part of the breeder/trainer. I'll explain. A greyhound bitch is not allowed to race just before a season or just after a season as a bitch develops a fatty layer around the heart at this time and the development of this adipose tissue is not conducive to racing. Greyhound broods are seldom selected on their breeding alone, but on their performance on the track or in some cases the coursing field. Hence a bitch which has achieved a great number of wins is more likely to be used as a brood than a bitch which has fewer wins to her credit. Hence bitches which are rarely in season have a greater chance of achieving a greater number of wins on the track or field, than bitches which by coming into season regularly, are unable to compete as often. Thus an unintentional process of selection has taken place, a process which has resulted in greyhound bitches achieving sexual maturity somewhat later than a dog of similar size and weight.

❧

I just cannot resist the following digression to demonstrate just how easily a breeding cycle may be altered in a very short period of time by unintentional selection. Some years ago a breeder of table poultry hatched via an incubator several million fowl a year – the incubation of the domesticated chicken being twenty-one days. On hatching, these chicks were shipped to broiler farms and the batch that hatched a day later were held back for future breeding – for they were genetically identical to the chicks which had hatched at twenty-one days of incubation. Or were they? Within a very short period of time the incubation period required to hatch chicks of this particular strain of fowl had increased to twenty-two days. Evolution proceeds at a surprising rate if given just a little assistance! I'd loved to have invented an aphorism of this nature. In fact it was the environmentalist De Vries who explored the evolutionary pattern of the Evening Primrose, who wrote it, but I digress yet again.

❧

Bitches approaching season will display a rather typical reaction to other dogs. When a bitch is not in season she will act with indifference to a male dog's advances, and may even appear hostile to a male that seeks to investigate the sexual organs and anus. She will however be less indifferent to his advances when she approaches season. Bitches approaching breeding readiness may act in a skittish manner as though coaxing a dog to play. They may dance around the male, hindquarters held above forequarters and behave in what the casual onlooker may describe as a thoroughly silly manner. However all normal animal behaviour is purposeful and such behaviour may alert or sexually arouse the male preparing him for the act of coition at a later date. Bitches may also start to ride each other but this act alone may not be an indication that a bitch is nearing sexual readiness. In a pack situation bitches mount each other to demonstrate superiority – a dominant bitch will attempt to ride a bitch somewhat lower on the social scale.

If one owns a large breeding kennels it is wise to check on the sexual readiness of bitches three or four times a week. Every morning I tend to engage in what to the uninitiated may seem a bizarre action, for on letting my bitches out of their sleeping quarters I reach down and check their genitalia. A swelling between the actual vagina and the anus indicates the sexual tracts are swelling to facilitate future copulation and hence I separate (or watch carefully) the bitch which manifests this sexual pattern, and despite the number of bitches I keep, I have very few misalliances in the kennel.

Once this vaginal swelling has been observed it is wise to watch for further symptoms of season and these will manifest themselves by the swelling of the actual vulva. After something like five or six days the breeder will notice small drops of blood emerging from the vagina. Some bitches are meticulously clean and hence lick up any of this bloody discharge as soon as it appears. Others are less fastidious and may pass a great amount of this bloody fluid. Some German Shepherd bitches are particularly productive where the secretion of this bloody discharge is concerned and the run in which these bitches are housed will resemble a charnel house. Yet this should cause the breeder no concern as it is a perfectly normal function which will seldom debilitate the bitch.

I once read an interesting paper concerning the production of bloody fluid in domesticated bitches. The paper written by an Austrian called Stellat stated that in the wild the production of this bloody fluid would not aid the furtherance of the species – foxes are quite discreet about coming into season, as are wolves – I've researched both. Stellat believes that the production of this quantity of bloody fluid is meant to indicate breeding readiness to the owner of the bitch not to a male of the same species. Stellat suggests that once man isolated the domestic dog from its wild ancestors, (Zeuner – *History of Domestication* suggests that this is one of the essential phases of the domestication of any species), the dog needed to indicate its breeding readiness to its owners. An obvious indication of breeding readiness allowed the continuance of the bloodline, a somewhat discreet breeding readiness was less conducive to the furtherance of the line. Hence bitches developed over ten thousand or so years of domestication a means of allowing the least perspicacious of mammals – man – a way of determining that the bitch was ready for mating. There is an obvious flaw in such a theory – interesting as it is, bitches only stand for mating once this bloody discharge ceases. Still the theory is fascinating if a little flawed.

By the ninth day of season this vaginal discharge will have diminished somewhat and lost its bloody hue. A pink or serous discharge indicates the bitch is approaching mating readiness. Bitches may accept (allow) a dog to mate them from the tenth day of season and matings at this time are sometimes not always successful. There is a greater success rate if the bitch is mated between the eleventh and sixteenth day of a season. It is in fact often stated that the optimum date for mating is the twelfth or thirteenth day of season but it is unwise to rely entirely on a statement of this nature for many bitches will mate as early as the fifth day or as late as the twenty third day of season, and still produce puppies.

However few bitches seem to be willing to 'accept' a male after the sixteenth day of season and many will be decidedly hostile to any dog which pays them attention at this period of the breeding cycle. This is in fact the time when most breeders of pit fighting dogs – pit bull terriers, Tosas and any of the bulldog blooded dogs are most vigilant about introducing dogs to bitches, for bitches of these breeds will often react violently and savagely to a male who seeks to flirt with them and the temperament of pit dogs being what it is, the males will sometimes retaliate with equal ferocity. Most males will however bear the attack stoically and refrain from retaliating. In fact one the worst kennel fights I have encountered occurred when my breed bitch Beltane was just past sixteen days readiness and was accosted by her brother Warlock, a large powerful and very forceful male. Beltane reacted with great ferocity as was her wont and Warlock retaliated with equal fury. Both sustained deep bites before I managed to separate them though there was little permanent damage. This behaviour pattern is quite common amongst Plummer terriers which have bull terrier ancestry.

A strong, forceful male may sometimes be able to mate a bitch from the seventeenth to the twenty-first day of her season if the bitch shows the slightest willingness to mate. A great deal of discomfort on the part of the bitch may be experienced and the union is rarely successful, yet I have seen litters produced when dogs have mated bitches at this stage of the breeding cycle.

So to the act of coition. It was at one time common practise to lock a receptive bitch and a sexually eager dog in a room together and leave the pair for some forty-eight hours. This practise sometimes produced puppies and sometimes didn't, particularly if the dog was a young inexperienced stud dog and the female a maiden bitch. Some dogs, even experienced stud dogs, are reluctant to mate in a strange place. At the time of writing I own a Lucas terrier dog, Teddy, a prolific and eager stud dog, the sire of many puppies, who will mate virtually any bitch if I construct steps to allow this nine pound dog to be elevated to a suitable level. However he steadfastly refuses to mate any bitch in his own kennels, though this is a behaviour pattern which is not typical, for most dogs are enthusiastic about mating bitches on familiar territory in which they have sprayed with urine to mark as their own. Be that as it may I should be most reluctant to pay a stud fee for the doubtful pleasure of leaving my bitch locked up in a pen with any dog inexperienced or experienced.

The fact is that nine times out of ten the satisfactory matings need to be 'helped'. I've explained that stud dogs need to be trained to mate, and the male, even the most inexperienced male, needs little help to affect a courtship. An eager young male will, on encountering an in-season bitch, wag his tail enthusiastically and strut and dance around his intended mate. She in turn will engage in a similar ritual and turn her rear end towards him pushing her vulva into the male's face. The male will usually sniff or lick the bitch's genitalia before mounting her back and engaging a thrusting action in order that his penis might penetrate the bitch.

At this point it is perhaps good sense to explain the machinations of both the dog's and the bitch's genitalia before proceeding further, for of all the mammalian courtship and mating rituals, canine behaviour is one of the most curious. Within the dog's penis is an ossified or bony structure which aids the penetration of the penis into the bitch's vagina and at the base of the penis there is a bulbous structure which during the act of coition swells to a considerable size. The bitch's genital tracts are equally curious for there is a muscular ring at the opening of the vagina which contracts once the vagina has been penetrated by the dog's penis.

The male dog will mount the bitch and engage in a pumping action in order to penetrate her and once he does, the dog's hind legs will leave the ground momentarily. Once penetration has been achieved the muscular ring of the vagina contracts on the mass of the sensitive nerves in the penis which becomes engorged with trapped blood, and the bulbous mass at the base of the penis becomes many times its original size. Because of the reciprocal reaction of both the vagina and the penis, the dog is unable to separate from the bitch. This position is referred to as a tie and while it is sometimes possible for a bitch to be fertilised without a 'tie', conception is unlikely if a 'tie' does not take place. The pair are unable to separate until ejaculation takes place, after which the male will withdraw his still enlarged penis which may stay out of the sheath for a few minutes before it contracts and resumes its normal position.

What is most curious is that during the tie the dog's hind leg, left or right, may be lifted over the bitch's back until the pair are standing back to back often with bewildered looks on their faces. This coital position often amazes first time breeder and most will ask for an explanation for the phenomenon. I am unable to give it, for there seems to be no reason why canids, including most wild canids, also adopt this posture and mate in this way. Various explanations have been advanced to explain this peculiarity – none of which seem satisfactory. One unlikely explanation is that as the couple are now standing back to back they are able to be vigilant as to the presence of predators, but goats, which are prey species, simply mount, couple and part in seconds so as not to appear vulnerable to attack by predators. Yet another unlikely explanation for this curious mating position is that because they are tied for a considerable period of time the dog and the bitch become better acquainted, but this explanation is also totally ludicrous. Wolves, the supposed ancestors of wild dogs and domesticated dogs alike (Coppinger 1998) are monogamous and the couple often stay together for life. Yet wolves also engage, though somewhat furtively, in a tie. Furthermore the visual and olfactory sense organs (the eyes and the nose) are pointing in different directions during the 'tie' so the 'getting to know you' explanation (Lyle 1946) just does not hold water.

Breaking the tie by dint of a bucket of cold water poured over the mating couple may cause the couple to part but will not be entirely successful in the prevention of conception. How strange human behaviour must appear to any extra-terrestrial being watching us. Such was the prudery of women folk in my own village that the sight of two copulating dogs simultaneously produced a dozen or so buckets of cold water so that the tie could be broken – for decency's sake. Yet man is the most promiscuous creature on the face of the planet, the only creature which copulates without the intention of producing offspring. As a young child of perhaps nine, on the way to junior school, I stopped to watch a pair of dogs copulate, sitting next to them to observe more closely and was soaked by a deluge of water thrown by a village harridan. The lady then raced to my home to report my strange behaviour to my mother, who with an attitude endemic in Victorian times when she was born, suggested that my father take me to a doctor to discuss my peculiarities. The human race is such a curious one, I am almost glad that it has ostracised me since childhood! Enough however of philosophy and autobiography and I shall return to the subject of the tie.

During the action of mating the contraction of the ring of vaginal muscle and the swelling of the bulb at the base of the dog's penis produces considerable pain for the bitch particularly in the case of the maiden bitch and she may become hysterical and snap at the dog. Some bitches become terrified by the pain and really set about the dog from which they cannot (by nature of the act of coition) escape. I have just witnessed the most savage attack on a mating dog conducted by a merle bearded collie bitch who struck at her mate so ferociously that she drew blood on both the dog's head and on my hands, for I always hold a bitch during her mating. I'll explain.

So great is the panic of a young bitch which is experiencing the pain of the tie that she may try to escape the attentions of the dog by pulling away from him. However as the pair are locked together she succeeds only in pulling the dog around by his penis, an act which does little good to the dog subjected to this sort of abuse. At one time when I offered my terrier Rupert at public stud I observed many peculiarities in the clients who brought bitches to be mated. Several would insist on what they called a 'natural mating' which consisted of the bitch snapping, screaming and towing the dog around by his penis, for they believed this act alone ensured the mating would be a fruitful one. Two refused to pay me a stud fee because I would not allow this outrage and held the pair – despite the fact that both bitches conceived, I must add. I'll return to the subject of public stud work presently, but to allow such a caper is madness as the male might well be ruptured and injured by the practice. Hence it is policy to hold the copulating dog and bitch during coition particularly during the early stages of coition when most aggressive behaviour takes place.

One more anecdote to illustrate, if nothing else, human stupidity where dogs are concerned. More than once the owner of a bitch which has been brought for mating has, once the dog and bitch have broken the tie, seized this bitch and held her head down. I asked one why and the owner replied that the action allowed the semen to run down into the fallopian tubes .in the manner of water down a plug hole and this alone ensured conception. I glanced at his five children as he expounded his theory and concluded to produce such a family his wife must have been a contortionist or at least an acrobat – enough of human frailty however.

It is a popular belief that one good mating, including a lengthy tie, is enough to ensure the bitch is fertilised by the dog. This however is only partly true. If the bitch is ovulating at the time of the mating, and ova have only a limited life, then one mating is enough. Indeed such is the state of modern veterinary science that veterinary surgeons are able to determine, by dint of blood tests, when a bitch is most ready for mating and most likely to conceive. However a breeder who wishes to ensure that the bitch is pregnant but is unwilling or unable to allow the bitch to be tested, should mate the bitch every day during her receptive period, which may be as long as ten days.

Although the sex act is a natural one, possibly the most natural one for it ensures the continuance of the species, the mating together of two inexperienced animals is often very difficult, and the act thwart with danger. A young male may become so sexually excited that he may attempt to mount the sides or the head of the bitch or ejaculate even before he enters the bitch. Likewise he may become distressed if he was hurt during his first sexual encounter, and sometimes refuse to mate a bitch again. In the mid 1960s I saw a young terrier dog at a hunt kennels and was so impressed by his appearance, his nose (so important in a hunting dog) and his gentle persistence to ground that I decided to mate him to my very best terrier bitch. However when the dog was about two years old he was allowed to mate a very truculent maiden bitch from the nearby hunt kennels and such was the inexperience of his owner that the bitch, on tying, towed the wretched dog around the hunt yard finally pulling him around a tethering pole, and savaging him badly. He never mated again, and in those days before artificial insemination was practicable he was a great loss to the working terrier fraternity. Had I used this dog I could have shortened my breeding programme by ten years – but I am reluctant to cry over spilt milk. Some males tie for a matter of moments and still manage to fertilise a bitch. Others take an inordinately long period of time to finish mating. Some of the giant breeds tie for an hour or so, but this lengthy tie is not confined to huge animals. In 1970 I was telephoned by a very unhappy police officer who had bought a working terrier dog from me and had decided to mate it to a neighbour's bitch – but dog and bitch were newcomers to breeding. The dog took only moments to penetrate the bitch. However the tie lasted over two hours which caused the dog's owner to panic somewhat. Curiously despite the length of the tie the bitch failed to conceive, but all manner of peculiarities could have prevented conception.

A bitch once mated should be kept away from other dogs, for not only is a recently mated bitch more attractive to other dogs but there is a possibility of mixed litters resulting if she is mated by a different dog – in other words a litter of puppies may have two or more sires. In the late 1960s my passion was for exploding the many myths which plague the world of dog breeding and I attempted to deliberately produce a mixed litter. I mated a Jack Russell type bitch to a Jack Russell male and immediately remated her to a Border Terrier male of the Raisgill strain. Immediately the second mating was concluded I allowed a black fell terrier bred by Brian Nuttall to serve the bitch, and awaited the results of the unions. Curiously the fact a dog has just mated a bitch excites the next dog all the more, and apparently inspires his gonads to produce a greater concentration of live sperm. Nine weeks later the bitch produced a litter of six puppies, one of which was clearly sired by the Jack Russell dog. Four puppies were Border Terrier coloured and the third was a black self coloured dog – a tale which incidentally brings us quite neatly to the subject of telagony – a hoary old myth perhaps but a tale well worth repeating for contrary to common sense, believers in telegony still exist.

In 1948 when I worked as an underaged overworked kennel help for the springer breeder Tom Evans of Blfaengarw I met a man, who with a face like thunder gave a perfectly good springer bitch, bred in the purple, to Tom as the animal according to the visitor 'been ruined' by the fact that it had coupled with a collie and produced a cross-bred litter. The gentleman was of the opinion that forever after the litters bred from the bitch mated to a pure bred springer spaniel would carry the collie taint. Tom who was made of sharper, brighter, sterner stuff, commiserated with the man about his loss, took the bitch free of charge and bred a field trial winner from her the very next litter. In an age when stupidity and ignorance was the curse of dog breeding Tom, a refuse collector by trade, was amazingly avant garde in his thinking and practise.

Much of the blame for the popularity of the notion of telagony has to be laid at the feet of the naturalist Sir Everitt Millais who spent a great deal of time and money gathering evidence to support the theory. His beliefs were apparently triggered by a curious misapprehension and the tale is well worth repeating. It appears that a hybrid between a quagga, a now extinct zebra like creature and a particular strain of Andalusian horse, had been produced and the zebra like mule foal had been put on display. Later the Andalusian mare had been mated to another pure bred Andalusian stallion and produced a foal with a stripe across its shoulders. The breeder immediately suspected the quagga had influenced the second mating and the progeny produced. However it transpired that many of this strain of Andalusian, the only Spanish riding horse that is free of Arab blood, had regularly produced striped foals or at least foals which had a shoulder stripe at birth though the marking later moulted out.

However be that as it may, the notion of telegony is totally fallacious and is rarely mentioned these days.

# 8

# Pregnancy

PREGNANCY IS THE period of time between mating (conception) and parturition (birth), which in the case of a dog is 58–63 days. Rarely will a bitch produce puppies before fifty eight days of pregnancy or after sixty five days following a successful mating. One of my only triumphs in the field of dog breeding is that I once hand reared a litter of German Shepherd Dogs which were born fifty four days after a single mating, and succeeded in keeping eight out of the nine alive, for puppies born more than a few days premature rarely survive even the most careful nursing.

A bitch needs no special treatment during the first few weeks after mating though I am a great advocate of exercise as a general conditioner during pregnancy. All my terrier pack bitches were hunted until a day or so before parturition and during this twenty three-year period of hunting the pack I bred many puppies from bitches that had little difficulty in whelping. Others who kept the same family of terriers but refrained from engaging in the same, often furious, exercise programme experienced greater problems when the bitches whelped, and from this perhaps rather unscientific comparison I conclude that exercise, providing it is not too strenuous, must be efficacious for the pregnant bitch. I have often been accused of going 'overboard' about my beliefs regarding exercise for the pregnant bitch so perhaps I should explain further. I run my pregnant bitches for a lengthy period each day up to the day of parturition, exercising each according to its own particular interests. For instance my golden retriever bitches – I keep a working strain of golden retriever – are allowed to swim in the nearby Clyde, a clean, refuse free river at this point in its course, for at least an hour a day until the day of parturition. Bird, my main brood bitch spent the morning in the water the day she whelped, and returned from her swim carrying her retrieving dummy (a moth eaten but much loved child's toy dragon) and within an hour produced the first of ten puppies. Merab my best ever working lurcher, the twelfth generation of a family I kept from childhood onwards, worked along-side my ferrets to secure over twenty rabbits on the day she produced two of her most famous puppies. Merab was ten at the time, and is now twenty-one and still in good health. Omega, one of the pillars of the Plummer terrier breed, ratted three nights a week during her pregnancy including engaging in the now famous Thursday hunts which lasted from dusk until dawn. On the Friday morning after the hunt she returned to the kennels, received the customary swab down in a mild disinfectant, for the dogs were hunted waist deep in chicken slurry, and then produced her most famous puppy Kotian.

Lest the reader should imagine that the advice I give concerns only working dogs might I dispel this notion instantly. At the time of writing I run a small pack of Cavalier King Charles spaniels and miniature dachshunds – often described as a union made in hell, for the two breeds hunt in entirely different manners: Cavaliers are quicksilver hunters while dachshunds dwell on a scent and hence split the pack badly. Both breeds run for an hour a day at rabbits even during preg-nancy, and both have their own specific genetic problems. Dachshunds, because of their long backs, are said to be prone to slipped discs, and are quite notoriously bad whelpers. Cavaliers too are not free from physical defects, as I have described earlier. Both breeds are kept fit and in hard condition by dint of their often chaotic hunts, which while they offend my pride regarding pack control, conditions both breeds nicely. I am seldom plagued with the problems common to these breeds and have little problem when these miniature dogs start to whelp. Admittedly my Cavaliers are seldom in show condition, despite the fact that my stud dog is of an excellent type, and once when visiting a championship show with friend called Stephen Gilmore, he was heard to remark on seeing a very fine show winning Cavalier in pristine condition 'Is his the same breed as yours, Brian?' The winning male, a magnificent Blenheim (copper red and white) was the same height as my own stud – his half brother, as it happens, but was a good four pounds heavier. My own stud dog, the Amazing Mr. Ping had the day prior to the show run for nearly three hours on the fell, hunting rabbits in the bracken and had covered at least twenty miles during this exercise period. He was as lean as whipcord and muscled like a gladiator. Furthermore he has manifested none of the mitral valve problems which are the scourge of the breed.

However it is not the amount of exercise that counts but the quality of the exercise. During the time when my profligate lifestyle combined with my teaching salary to produce a state of penury which necessitated my buying newspapers on hire purchase, (a slight exaggeration) I exercised greyhounds for a lazy brute of a man who ran his dogs at a local flapping track, where sometimes the hounds ran to win and other times not – I'll not dwell too deeply on this subject as it offends me somewhat. Despite the fact I began to despise the man who paid me to exercise the dogs, I learned much about canine conditioning during this time. I found hounds which had walked the same route twice a day became dispirited and lost 'tone' both physically and mentally and I soon learned to find new places to exercise the hounds. One 'trainer' – a delightful and inaccurate euphemism for this keeper of greyhounds, tied his hounds to the back of his pedal cycle and ran them up and down the canal bank twice a day, the monotony of the exercise programme was broken only when one day a cat appeared on the towpath – with terrible results – but I digress once again. The cyclists hounds had a hangdog appearance and did not enjoy this monotonous exercise programme. They subsequently lost condition and ran badly despite their excellent breeding. The lazy brute's hounds, less well bred, but exercised by a decaying academic (me) were taken on varied trips and screamed with pleasure when I arrived at the kennels with leads in hand.

Both pregnant bitches and stock in general should be exultant at the prospect of exercise 'rejoicing as a strong man to run a race' as more poetic Biblical bards might put it. I hate the modern treadmills which are now increasingly popular and masquerade under the title 'dog exercisers'. True they may produce excellent running muscles but must destroy a dog's mind when it is forced or mentally conditioned to run mile upon mile getting nowhere and seeing nothing. My own Cavalier and dachshund pack regularly hunt on a field a half mile from my kennels and are walked there each day. As the exercise programme is about to begin they squeal with delight and jump at the rack where their leads are kept in anticipation of the fun to come. As they approach the field where the rabbits abound their excited barking becomes cacophonous long before they sight a rabbit. They truly love their exercise programme and because of this pleasure I believe their mental and physical health improves accordingly.

It is not good policy to run pregnant bitches to a state of absolute exhaustion, and the practise of doing so is counterproductive to conditioning. Greyhound breeders seem all too keen to relate the tale of a greyhound brood bitch that whelped a Waterloo Cup winner the day she coursed and killed a fox. Now although many greyhounds are reluctant to course foxes, it was a characteristic of the breed mentioned as early as the fifteenth century, those hounds who do pursue foxes do it with great enthusiasm. The pursuit of a fox is a particularly bruising, strenuous chase so it is not advised that a bitch approaching parturition should engage in such exercise. In 1982 a greyhound was brought for my half bred collie greyhound Merle to mate, for the success of some his progeny produced much stud work for him. The hound increased in girth and was clearly pregnant but in her seventh week of pregnancy she was slipped at a hare and ran a long testing two and a half mile course which did her little good. She lost her litter a day or so later and became very ill, possibly as a result of coursing so late in pregnancy.

Yet the foeti, the developing puppies, are remarkably protected from the knocks and bumps of the outside world during the pregnancy. Each foetus is covered with two membranous protective layers the chorion and the amnion, and this protection is further enhanced by the fact that there is a mass of amniotic fluid between the two layers, a fluid which .buffers the foetae from minor knocks and bumps. It is in fact at times when I contemplate the structure of mammalian reproductive tracts that I tend to believe that evolution is not the chance process scientists such as De Vries would have us believe, but is directed, stage managed, call you what you will, by some higher power. I have in fact seen pregnant bitches involved in motor car accidents, the ferocity of which smashed ribs and limbs, but somehow left the foeti intact and healthy – truly the 'Life Force' if such an entity exists, is a strong one. Yet there is some evidence to suggest that that 'Life Force' can be given a little assistance without harm to either a foetus or the brood bitch and this brings me quite neatly to the subject of antibiotics and their use during the pregnancy of the bitch. I've touched on this subject earlier and now perhaps sit is time to elaborate.

## Antibiotics

It is believed, though somewhat difficult to prove scientifically, that certain antibiotics given to a bitch five days before mating and five days after fertilisation and then five days before whelping and five days after parturition improve the chances of good sound healthy puppies being produced. Certain veterinary scientists argue that the uterus of a bitch is seldom free from bacterial infection, if the bitch has been mated or produced puppies. Many of the bacteria are harmless but some are far from benign. Thus a dose of antibiotics given at the times mentioned tends to improve the quality of the litter (which grows in an uterus which is free of harmful bacteria) and perhaps even increases the size of the litter, for foeti which might have died of some infection and been reabsorbed by the bitch are allowed to live and perhaps flourish.

There are certain veterinary surgeons who are against the practise of injecting or simply giving antibiotics orally during pregnancy because there are some bacteria which may enter into a symbiotic relationship in the foetus and are therefore beneficial to the puppy and as antibiotics are not selective in the bacteria they control, these beneficial bacteria may also die. Most veterinary surgeons are reluctant to prescribe antibiotics to bitches which are maiden or have not produced a litter as they sometimes consider that the treatment has little value under these circumstances.

So to the practicalities of the use of antibiotics during pregnancy. Hancock uses ampicillin – a semi-synthetic antibiotic given orally each day a week before and a week after mating and the same treatment a week before and a week after parturition, and has achieved excellent results. Ampicillin is one of the cheapest and safest antibiotics and seldom manifests side effects.

I prefer the use of amoxycillin – a similar semi synthetic antibiotic – which is more readily absorbed orally than ampicillin. Both these antibiotics are not penicillanase resistant and are inactivated (made less than useful) by the presence of penicillinase enzymes secreted by Gram positive bacteria such as Staphylococcus aureus (a microbe that causes mastitis) and Gram negative bacteria such as the more common strains of Escherichia Coli. To make these simple antibiotics more effective, scientists have augmented them with clavulanic acid or potassium clarulanate as these substances have a mild antiseptic effect, but are effective against penicillinase producing bacteria. These augmented antibiotics, augmentin and synulox are however very expensive but in all fairness, very effective and if administered as prescribed, totally safe to use on pregnant or recently mated bitches. Just recently the sporting press has featured articles which denounce the use of such antibiotics. I have found only benefits from their use and by dint of using them I have produced some very healthy, lusty, disease free puppies.

## Diet

The best diet for the pregnant bitch is often hotly debated and there are special patent complete diets for both pregnant bitches and pregnant queens available in both Britain and America. However the would be breeder would do well to desist from the practice known in agriculture as 'sweating' or feeding the bitch large quantities of food during her early and late pregnancy. There are many logical reasons for not over feeding, the most logical of which is the fact that wild bitches – wolves, jackals, dholes etc. – are encumbered later in pregnancy by the weight and volume of the whelps and hence are less effective as hunters. It is believed that when a bitch is in the later stages of pregnancy the alimentary tracts become more efficient at absorbing essential proteins and other nutrients to compensate for a somewhat less than adequate food supply.

Yet pregnant bitches need to be fed well if they are to produce live healthy puppies. During the early stages of pregnancy an adequate maintenance ration of roughly 21% protein will suffice, for until the bitch is five weeks pregnant the foeti are so tiny as to not merit extra food in the bitch's diet. However from the sixth or seventh week onwards the bitch will need better quality if not more food. Some breeders add a late pregnancy diet, specially prepared for the bitch nearing parturition, to the normal maintenance rations of the bitch increasing the protein content of the diet to perhaps 30–32% protein. Hancock whose days of poultry farming have made him a wizard at manipulating animal feed adds extra quantities of high grade fishmeal (66% protein) to the maintenance rations of the bitch. I tend to feed extra raw flesh augmented with bony material either in the form of stock feed bonemeal (not horticultural bone meal which is treated with substances which are not conducive to absorption by a pregnant bitch), or minced chicken with finely macerated chards of poultry ribs etc. It is not wise to increase the quality of the red meat or tripe in the diet without heed to the calcium/phosphorus ratio in the feed – I will explain why presently.

There is also evidence to suggest that bitches which are heavily in whelp should be fed several small meals a day rather than one large meal, for the growth of the foeti puts some pressure on the stomach so that it is unable to take in the amount of food the bitch requires at a single sitting. I am reluctant to draw an analogy between tame and wild dogs in this matter, but pariah dogs, which both plague and sanitise the villages of the Far East, during pregnancy will forage the day long, and engage in a non stop eating spree, ingesting both garbage and human faecal matter (the human digestive tract is very inefficient and many useful nutrients pass through the average man).

## Signs of Pregnancy

Another aside I'm afraid, but bear with me a little. I am always amazed at the practise of taking bitches which are possibly five weeks pregnant to a veterinary surgeon to ascertain if the bitch is actually in whelp, for the life of me I cannot see why people waste money doing this. I suppose a first time breeder excited by the prospect of producing a litter, may well consider a vets opinion. Ascertaining pregnancy is done by a process known as palpation or literally feeling for the presence of foeti which may be the size of a lentil or pea at five weeks of age. I've met some shepherds who were quite dextrous at the process, and quite a few fancy rabbit breeders who were expert at palpating does, but I know very few veterinary surgeons who lay claim to such dexterity. I must confess that I seldom attempt the process for I am not proficient at the act neither do I find it necessary, for the symptoms which are typical of pregnancy manifest themselves soon enough.

Four weeks after the mating few bitches will show few obvious signs of pregnancy, but five weeks into pregnancy the signs the bitch will manifest are fairly obvious. Most but not all, for the 'invariable' rules seldom apply in dog breeding, will display enlarged pinky nipples and a slight rounding of the abdomen, and six weeks after the successful mating the bitch's abdomen will have extended in size, and the bitch will show signs which are typical of mammalian pregnancy.

## Worming and Deinfesting

During the seventh week of pregnancy hormonal changes will alert roundworm larvae to the presence of a new host and these unpleasant parasites will leave the muscle tissue of the host bitch to move across the placenta to infect the foeti. Virtually all dogs, even dogs which are subjected to a regular worming programme, harbour these parasites and in recent times it has become common practice to attempt to reduce the number of worms migrating across the placental tissue, so that the developing foeti are able to flourish, for badly infected puppies are certainly given a bad start in life. A bitch should be wormed during her seventh week of pregnancy in order to reduce the number of roundworm larvae.

Not all anthelmintics (worming medicines) are effective against the larval form of the roundworm. Older remedies like the purgative santonin had no effect on the larval stages of the roundworm, and neither does the more modern piperazine based drugs (piperazinecitrate or piperazine hydrate) though piperazine is very effective against the adult roundworm – it is said to kill 97% of all adult roundworms. However the more modern remedies such as Panacur, a trade name for the drug fenbendazole, is effective against both the adult roundworm and the migrating larval forms. The pregnant bitch should be dosed for three consecutive days with fenbendazole to achieve the best results for neither the adult worm nor the larval forms of the worm feed every day. A more ambitious but certainly more costly worming programme involves dosing the pregnant bitch every day from the seventh week of pregnancy to parturition with Panacur, which is said to give new-born puppies a flying start in life by rendering them virtually free of active roundworms – though not totally free of these parasites. Puppies will still need to be wormed regularly. Worming is so important particularly as public opinion seems to be very much against dogs and the presence of dog faeces in public places is not desirable, for these faeces are usually a rich source of roundworm eggs. There have been reports of children becoming infected with roundworms and the migrating larva causing blindness although such cases are very rare.

During the seventh week of pregnancy I endeavour to dip the bitches in a multipurpose insecticide to rid them of fleas, sarcoptic mange mites, ticks and lice, and as my dogs are regularly exercised in areas where such parasites are harboured this is a good practice. Mange mites become very active when a bitch's condition is reduced slightly through the process of parturition and rearing puppies and it is wise to control an infection before it becomes active. There are various mangecides on the market some more effective than others – and dear reader yet another digression I'm afraid.

I deeply regret the fact that the good old gamma benzene hexachloride (Gamma BHC) is no longer available as an agricultural dip for it was so effective against a great variety of biting and sucking parasites. Despite the fact that there was a report of a woman who treated calves with gamma BHC and convulsed after using it, I have never even had the slightest problem with the chemical. At one time I dipped the bitches twice a year in the substance and seldom encountered any problem with skin parasites or ear mites for the chemical is very effective against the mites which cause one of ear cankers. Sadly the dip was withdrawn for the treatment of agricultural animals for minute traces of gamma BHC were found in meat taken from animals which had been in contact with this insecticide. As it is not financially viable for manufacturers to produce gamma BHC dips which are used exclusively for dogs the agricultural dips were withdrawn from the market.

Hancock uses the avermectide, Ivomec as a mange, tic and roundworm control, and has achieved good results with this substance. A single injection of the substance will effectively control lice, sarcoptic mange, lungworm and roundworms in dogs. Once hailed as a wonder drug this chemical anthelmitic/pesticide was discovered in 1975 and is obtained from microscopic fungus found growing in Japan after the Merk Sharp and Dohme international screening programme. A word of caution however, the veterinary surgeon, Stuart M. Easby, published a paper concerning the treatment of a collie with Ivomec. The bitch on receiving an injection lapsed into a coma for seven weeks and was kept alive by dint of feeding an oral solution of glucose and hydrolysed protein, for the swallowing mechanism was still present in the animal. Although the bitch was blind for seven weeks she later recovered her sight and after extensive treatment recovered her mobility. Ivomec should not be used on collies for this type of dog is extremely susceptible to the drug. I once attended a talk given by a research scientist with an interest in the use of avermactides and he suggested that no collie hybrid – lurchers are frequently collie bred dogs – should be treated with Ivomec and stated that in the U.S.A. a laboratory strain of collie with extreme susceptibility to avermactide poisoning has been produced in order to test the drug and other related substances.

## Pregnancy Problems

Squalls may be encountered in the latter half of the pregnancy particularly if the bitch is carrying a large litter. Pregnancy toxaemia is said to occur when the bitch is unable to excrete the poisonous breakdown products produced by herself and the foeti. Symptoms include lassitude, discomfort and a reluctance to stand. Expert veterinary advice should be sought immediately these symptoms are noticed for the bitch will die if untreated. Once the puppies are born the bitch will recover quite quickly. If I might break my rule and expound a theory the validity of which I am unable to prove scientifically, I am of the opinion that exercise during pregnancy reduces the incidence of pregnancy toxaemia in bitches, and I exercise my bitches to the day of parturition in order to reduce the possibility of this disorder. However problems during pregnancy are quite rare, and as Steppen (1936) once remarked that the pregnancy of any mammal should be the most healthy time of the animal's life – a statement which is not exactly true but will give the first time breeder a little comfort perhaps.

## Whelping Quarters

It is time now for the breeder to consider moving the bitch into permanent quarters in order that she may whelp in a familiar environment, for few bitches take kindly to being moved into a new kennel on the day of parturition. I move my bitches to new quarters in the seventh week of pregnancy, shortly after I have wormed and dipped them, and this allows them time to acclimatise to their new environment. I have always found that bitches which whelp in a strange environment – moved into a new shed the day they whelp – are more likely to bruise and damage puppies by holding them in their mouths as soon as they are born as if to protect them from possibly hostile surroundings, and puppies treated in this manner are seldom as lusty as whelps born to a bitch which feels secure in her environment. This carrying of puppies is more common if the bitches whelps next to other dogs and bitches, for the commercial breeder will have specially built whelping units to cater for newly born puppies.

Unless the bitch whelps in one of those freak heat waves which occasionally hit Britain, she will need some source of heat when her puppies are born. Puppies born in cold surroundings rarely thrive, and are subject to an unacceptably high mortality rate. I use heat lamps suspended above the bitch which, because of the nature of the lamp, throws heat directly onto the puppies. Insulation of the pens is also a must. In 1996 I had a specially constructed whelping pen built and experienced disastrous results. Three consecutive litters of puppies died yet autopsies of the cadavers revealed nothing. What killed these mites was the poor insulation of the pen. Once reinsulated the death rate in the pen ceased.

It is unwise to keep any bitch in a concrete pen that has not been insulated to prevent heat loss, for it takes a great deal of time for concrete to warm up enough to allow a bitch to whelp in comfort. The cost of heating such a pen is also prohibitive, as I found to my cost the first winter I attempted to whelp puppies in that ill-fated unit.

In order to illustrate the importance of insulation I include a diagram of the most recently built whelping unit.

The cost of insulating such a building is high, but is more than justified by the saving in electricity to heat the building. At one time

**Roof Design:**

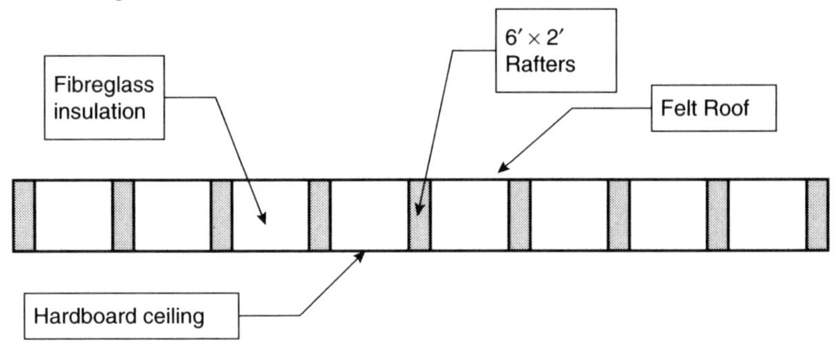


**Walls:**

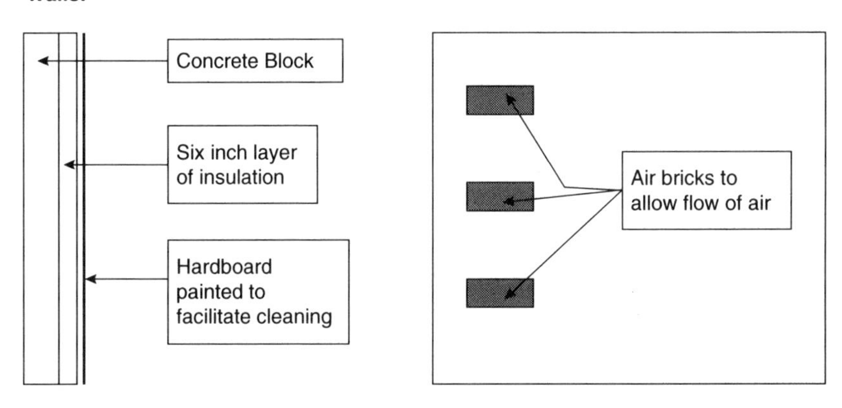


**Rear Wall/Front Wall:**

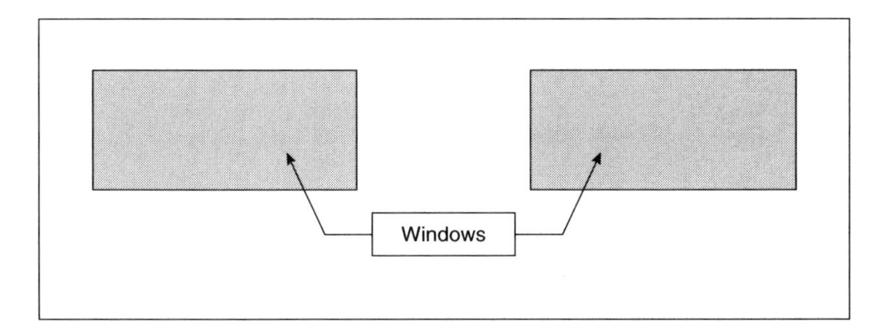


Construction of a whelping unit

I cut corners to save money and used other forms of insulation such as straw and woodchips but these proved to be very unsatisfactory. The straw became damp and decayed to produce peat like compost which attracted vermin, while the woodchips and shavings consolidated to form a solid block and an air space above the block leaked heat. Fibreglass is expensive but does not decay or allow vermin to breed and is well worth the extra expense.

Underfloor insulation is also well worthwhile. In my days of penury I used egg boxes sunk below an inch or so of concrete to insulate my whelping pen floors and this Heath Robinson device worked moderately well.

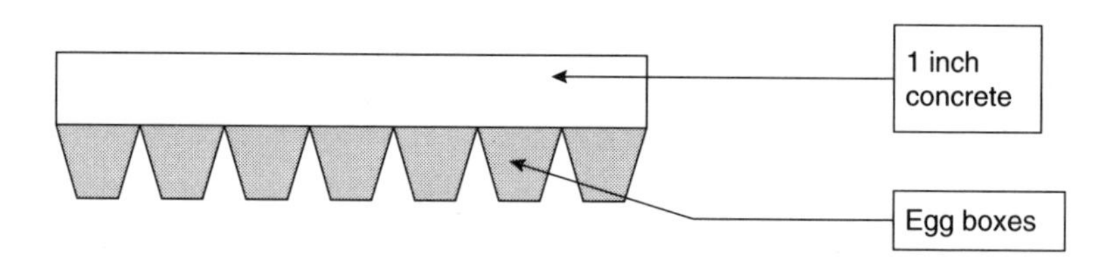


However the egg boxes are made of cardboard which decays all too readily and a better form of insulation is a two inch thick layer of industrial strength polystyrene which is resistant to decay and lasts a life time – expensive, but worth the price. Money spent insulating a pen properly is easily recouped if one extra puppy per litter survives.

All hardboard or absorbent surfaces must be painted to allow proper cleaning and the 1973 Dog Breeders Act states that absorbent surfaces must be painted or filled. Unpainted surfaces not only absorb water and allow the boards to decay, but also harbour diseases.

I am quite fastidious about disinfecting whelping units every few weeks, and I use the very cheapest most efficient disinfectant – sodium hypochlorite which is available at all farm shops. This is the principle ingredient of a quite expensive disinfectant that kills 'all known germs dead', but while it is caustic it is effective and leaves few undesirable by-products in its wake.

By far the best method of thoroughly cleaning a whelping pen is fumigation, and I fumigate as soon as there is a lull in the breeding programme which allows the whelping shed to be vacant. Fumigation is efficient simply because the gases produced will circulate to every nook and cranny of the building and kill every living organism in the whelping area. Some years ago a particularly cold winter drove mice into my main whelping pen, and try as I might, I failed to poison the mice because of their tiny appetites. In the warm conditions found in the whelping quarters their breeding cycle took on a new lease of life and I was soon plagued with them. Mice carry a spirochete leptospirosis and despite the fact all my dogs are inoculated I was decidedly worried about the prospect of disease in the kennels. I therefore fumigated the pen and resolved the problem in a brief twenty four hour period.

Before fumigation can proceed effectively the building should be degreased. I'll explain. All animals and birds produce a grease which lubricates skins and feathers and performs other functions as well. When these animals and birds rub against walls or furniture some of this grease is removed and adheres to objects. This grease also provides excellent protection for any microscopic life that can live in and under this oily layer. Thus before fumigation, all walls, floors and ceilings need to be degreased. This is done by scrubbing the kennels with a hot washing soda solution, just as effective and not nearly as costly as caustic soda, which causes the grease to saponify or change to a soapy substance which can be washed away with cold water. The walls of the kennels are left wet for fumigation to be effective and it is also wise to block all air vents to ensure the process is thorough.

An old fashioned but highly effective fumigant is formaldehyde, dangerous perhaps and quite unpleasant, but cheap and easy to use. Obviously no dog must be left in kennels while fumigation proceeds and neither must the handler stay there. The volume of the building must now be calculated, length × breadth × height, and the correct amount of fumigant used, or a little more to be on safe side. Formaldehyde gas is generated by adding 250 grams of potassium permanganate to 500ml of formalin and this is enough fumigant to generate poisonous gases to cleanse 1000 cubic feet of air space. More simply, my own whelping bays are 30ft. × 10ft. × 8ft. = 2400 cubic feet and I need roughly 750 grams of potassium permanganate and 1500mls of formalin to complete the fumigation programme. I use a steel bucket for the process and add the formaldehyde to the potassium permanganate before beating a hasty retreat and locking the shed door behind me. The reaction takes about ten seconds to start and then clouds of vapour are emitted by the mixture. The doors and windows are left closed for roughly twenty-four hours after which the shed can be considered sterilised.

Some years ago an outbreak of a particularly virulent strain of Escherichia Coli affected the production of puppies in my kennels in Caithness. Within hours of the whelps being born they began to look sickly and were dead in four days. I cleaned each pen meticulously using a strong solution of sodium hypochlorite but to no avail. In despair I turned to Virkon and some of the other omnicidal disinfectants that were popular at the time, but still the puppy deaths continued. Finally I drew up an entirely different plan of attack. I scrubbed the walls, floor and ceiling, firstly with hot soda solution to degrease the kennels, then cleaned out every portion of the shed with bleach (sodium hypochlorite). This in turn was washed away with water (formaldehyde and bleach react to form a powerful carcinogen) and finally fumigated the building. Next day I whelped a litter in the sterile shed hoping and praying that as the E.Coli infection built up again the puppies would develop immunity to the bacteria. Henceforth I embarked on this massive cleaning programme each time a bitch was about to whelp and not only did I have no more deaths but the puppies I reared were the best I'd ever seen. Clearly the massive cleaning programme had wiped out other infections as well as the dreaded E.Coli bacterium. I hasten to add that if the surfaces of the kennel had not been sealed and painted I would not have broken this dreaded infection. I passed on my advice to several fox hound kennels that were troubled by leptospirosis, and were also unable to rear puppies. They too adopted this mode of attack and with some success, though leptospirosis which is passed in the urine of animals which have recovered from the infection, is a difficult spirochete to get rid of.

It is possible merely to layer the sterilised kennel with straw and have the bitch whelp on the floor of the pen but the mortality rate one would expect using this method would be unacceptable. Thus to improve one's success rate it is necessary to construct a suitable whelping box, and allow the bitch to whelp in it. A properly constructed whelping box not only 'gathers up' the puppies, preventing them from straying from the heat, but also insulates them from the cold floor of the whelping kennel. There are some very elaborate whelping boxes offered for sale in the 'doggy' press, but these are a little too grand for someone who intends to breed puppies on a regular basis, for bitches are often destructive and chew pieces from their whelping boxes. It is in fact quite a simple matter to construct a whelping box out of wood that is equally as suitable as some of the most expensive whelping crates. It is also much better to throw the old whelping boxes away once they become stained, chewed or unsightly, particularly if these boxes have been in contact with some infection which may possibly be passed on to the next litter. I construct all my own whelping boxes and once they become soiled I burn them and construct others.

A properly constructed whelping box is easily made from plywood:

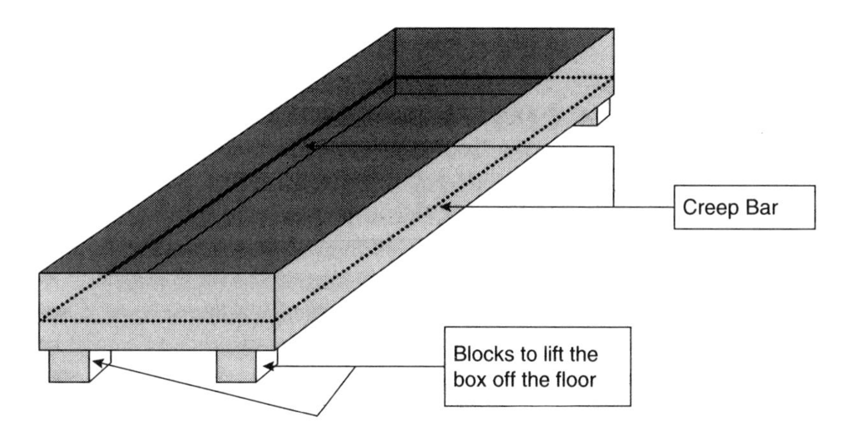


It is wise to set a 2 to 3' creep bar around the pen to allow the puppies to crawl out of the way of clumsy bitches – and some of the larger bitches can be very clumsy and crush their puppies. The bar allows the puppies to crawl away from the dam and hence survive. Paint the box with cheap non-lead paint which prevents the box absorbing foetal fluid or the urine that the puppies will produce. As the whelping approaches the box should be cleaned with a strong solution of sodium hypochlorite to render it sterile, allowed to dry and store it away in a clean, dry place. Nothing is more irritating and profit-eating than to have to clean and dry a whelping box while a bitch is engaged in whelping on the concrete floor of a whelping pen.

# 9

# Parturition or the Process of Whelping

IT ALWAYS AMAZES me that many of the dog books describe the process of whelping as though the action was as immutable and unchangeable as a Catholic mass. In point of fact each bitch will behave in a different manner while whelping and some adopt the most peculiar mannerisms while giving birth to puppies. May I cite examples which testify to the truth of this statement the case of two identical terrier bitches, Bunty and Pearly I bred in 1970, one of which became one of the cornerstones of the Plummer terrier. Both were identical in type, size and colour and I suspect that they were one of the few examples of monozygotic twins (two animals derived from the self same zygote). I spent my life with my terrier pack, yet to the day they died I could not tell Bunty and Pearly apart. However when it came to whelping their behaviour could not have been more different. Amazingly both came into season on the same day and when the pair were twenty-five months old they were mated on the same day to that scion of the Plummer terrier breed, Vampire. Some fifty-eight days later both began to whelp within minutes of each other. Pearly appeared somewhat distressed while out at exercise that morning so I hurried her home. She began to scream and tear up the bedding in her whelping box and was clearly in distress. I took her to the vet and after a series of procedures had failed to produce a litter – I'll explain the procedures presently – the vet resorted to a caesarean section. Sadly Pearly and her litter died under the anaesthetic, don't panic reader such deaths are very rare, and I buried the bitch and her six puppies, three dogs and three bitches in my garden near the kennels. On returning home I found that Bunty had torn up the crazy paving near the rockery and had dug a lair in which she produced six puppies (I shall assume with ease for she greeted me happily when I found her) three dogs and three bitches – identical in every way to the sad little litter I had just buried. One of Bunty's descendants was Omega. I'll finish the tale. For once in my teaching career my absence caused me no problem, for that morning my headmaster, a fire breathing tyrant who terrified me, had died and in the confusion no one noticed my absence. Later in my career no one noticed my absence anyway but that, dear reader is another tale.

I always watch for the onset of labour about the 56th day of pregnancy and keep an close check on the bitch from that time forth. It is invariably stated that bitches which are due to whelp are reluctant to eat and this is one of the first signs that parturition .is due, but this is not always the case. I once owned a bitch called Blackface – her sister was one of the bitches that introduced some of the spectacular black masks into the Plummer terrier – and Blackface was a voracious trencher. She wolfed down her food and her litter mate's food until the day she whelped, and as she was producing puppies she jumped up and snatched food from my hand while she was in the process of delivering a puppy.

However a bitch that is whelping, particularly a bitch that is whelping for the first time, will become very restless and show signs of anxiety as she nears her time of parturition. Many will seek out a dark secluded place other than the prepared whelping box and show an inclination to make a nest in such a place. Some will actively seek out a place to dig out a lair, a sort of miniature cave in which to produce puppies, for despite some 10,000 years of domestication, dogs still show a propensity to whelp in holes in the ground. When I lived in Caithness and my cottage was adjacent to a vast heather moor, pockmarked with peat cuts, I had to be very vigilant when exercising some of my working strain of bearded collie when they neared parturition, for they showed a marked inclination to wander off and dig lairs in rockpiles and produce puppies. One bitch regularly sought out a cairn to produce her puppies and I had to take measures to prevent her straying near that pile. I eventually remedied this family of beardies desire to nest in lairs by whelping them in enclosed boxes.

I try to whelp all my puppies on out-of-date newspapers for the paper absorbs foetal fluid and is easy to obtain. To date I have experienced no problem from print being transferred to the puppies though I have heard of people who have. Thus the bitch is bedded on a thick layer of newspaper and awaits the time when she will whelp. A peculiarity of bitches nearing parturition is that the animal's temperature drops sharply as it approaches the time when it will whelp. Ordinarily the bitch's temperature is roughly 101.5°F (a half a degree either way is not uncommon) and when the temperature drops as low as 98°F (temperature is taken by inserting a greased thermometer into the bitch's anus) it is a sure indication she is ready to whelp. Charles Needham (1962) states that he has encountered bitches whose temperature has dropped to 96°F as parturition approaches, but frankly I have not heard of this sort of temperature fall and would be a little worried if one of my bitches experienced such a temperature drop during whelping. Cermek (1984) states that he believes that this temperature fall is due to the fact that the bitch is preparing her foeti for the colder temperature of the world outside her body, but I feel this is a little too simplistic a theory to be realistic.

It has suddenly dawned on me that some readers may not be acquainted with the structure of a bitch's reproductive tracts. While the process of parturition is certainly a messy affair it is impossible to deny that the bitch's reproductive tract is a marvellously simple piece of divine construction.

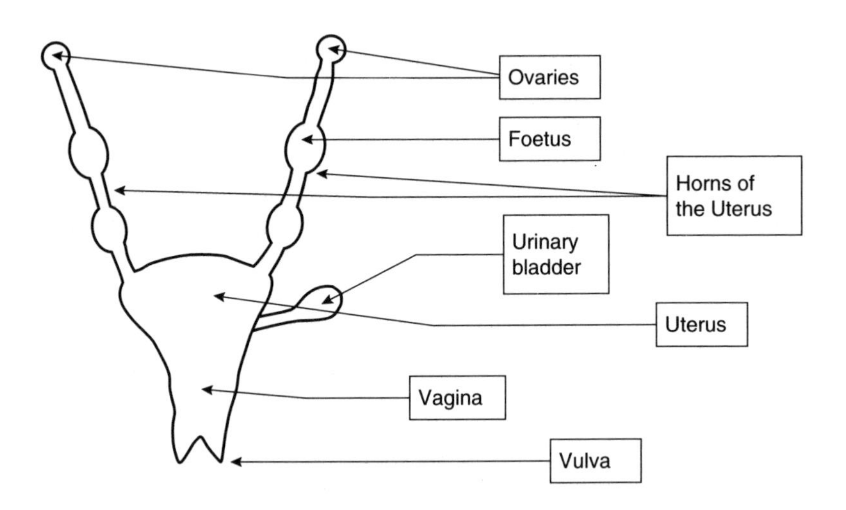


At this stage just prior to parturition, the foeti are anchored in the horns of the uterus by the placenta, a complex network of blood vessels which is able to filter off some of the less pleasant bacteria which may have infected the mother. The placenta however allows the passage of a certain number of protective antibodies from the bitch's blood to pass to the puppies so that the young might have at least some immunity to the infections of the outside world when they are born. Some antibodies find their way to the puppy across the placenta although the whelp will obtain most of its essential protective antibodies by suckling the first milk or colostrum.

During the pregnancy of the bitch, the foetus is protected and buffered from the knocks of the outside world by two sacs called the amnion and the chorion and sandwiched between the amnion and the chorion is a mass of fluid called the amniotic fluid.

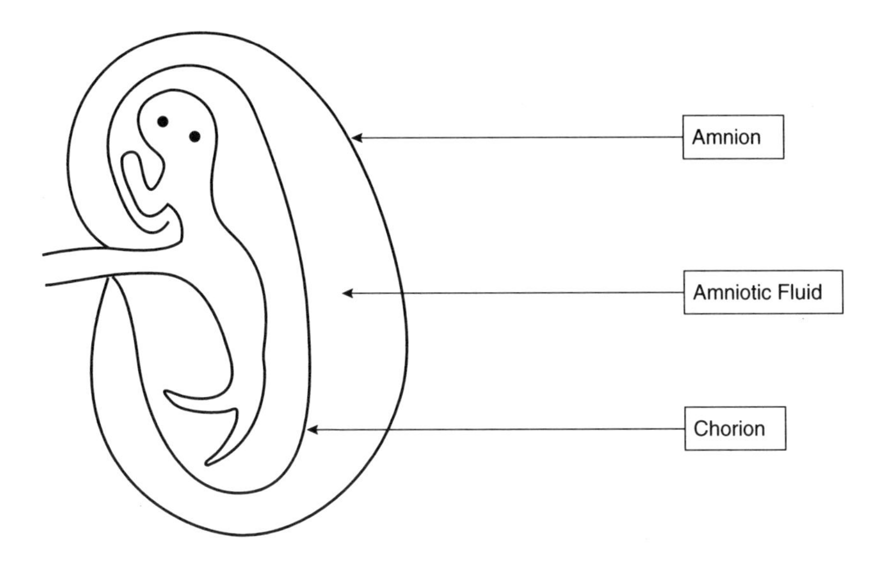


Various hormonal substances trigger the process of whelping and contractions will commence immediately those hormones are released. The bitch will strain and bear down, having periods of rest between contractions. As birth becomes imminent the bitch will lift her tail and the vagina will become distended to facilitate the passage of the puppy. Periodically the bitch will scratch the whelping box and shred the newspaper to pieces. This action is said to stimulate the hormones which allow parturition to take place, and bitches denied this activity certainly become distressed. I suspect the scratching action has other effects. Wild dogs, wolves, foxes and dholes nest in underground lairs and also perform the scratching action prior to whelping. Earth and even rock dust is dislodged by the action and this absorbs the large quantities of amniotic fluid which are released at birth. In 1969 I bred many red foxes in captivity and observed their breeding den floors had absorbed a large quantity of amniotic fluid before caking to produce an impervious layer.

Within two hours of the onset of labour, the first foetus still within the sac (the water bag) will emerge, though frequently the pressure of the contractions will cause the water bag to burst as it passes down the body of the uterus. Should this water bag burst releasing the amniotic fluid and the birth of the puppy be delayed for some time, the puppy will be denied the lubricating action of the foetal fluids. This dry delivery is not desirable although most puppies survive this mild trauma.

Some whelps are born within the sacs and the bitch must not only bite the puppy free of the placental trappings but also burst the twin sacs to allow the puppy to breathe. Some bitches, particularly maiden bitches or bitches which produce puppies too rapidly may fail to tear up the sacs which surround the puppies, and it is left to the breeder to complete the task and give the whelps enclosed within the bags a gentle shake (to facilitate breathing) as the sac is broken. There is a curious legend that animals born with unbroken sacs or cauls will never drown, possibly because they came into the world within a water filled bag. Whatever the legend, unless the bag is broken the puppy will drown, for oxygen carrying blood supplies from the bitch to the puppy via the placenta has been stopped and the puppy must breathe or die of anoxia. This is perhaps the best reason for sitting with a whelping bitch and not leaving the animal to its own devices as it whelps. An astute and alert breeder can save many puppies if he or she sits up with the whelping bitch.

Most puppies are born free of the sacs however, and once they emerge most bitches will set to vigorously cleaning them with their tongues. This often apparently rough treatment is certainly purposeful for it stimulates the action of the puppies lungs in the same way as does a shake or a smack on new-born baby's bottom. A puppy freed from its bag will usually gasp to expel the foetal fluid and then inhale air.

Bitches will usually chew off the placental trappings and ingest them and this process apparently is beneficial as it is said to increase the flow of milk which is available to the puppies. Most mammals ingest their afterbirths of their young for it is said by ingesting the afterbirth the female is preventing predators which will prey on the new-born offspring from being attacked.

Sometimes puppies are born, in or out of the foetal sacs, but refuse to move and take that first all-important gasp of air. Sometimes these puppies can be animated or revived by dipping them firstly in warm water and then into ice cold water. To be perfectly honest in forty-five years of breeding dogs I can only remember reviving five puppies in this way though I give every puppy a sporting chance to survive. I have had better success, well slightly better success, furiously massaging the apparently lifeless puppy's rib cage.

The temperature into which puppies are born is all-important and most breeders attempt to whelp puppies in a room or shed where the temperature is around 75°–85°F. J.M. Evans MRCVS (Kennel and Cattery, The Management Magazine 1991) says that a state of hypothermia exists in temperature of 79°F if the puppy is isolated from its dam. Curiously Evans also states that there are instances of a puppy, admittedly a previously healthy puppy, surviving up to twelve hours in a state of deep hypothermia. This evidence should encourage the breeder to work on any live puppy even if in a state of deep hypothermia and attempt to revive it. The majority of breeders carry an apparently lifeless puppy in their pockets in an attempt to revive it, for the secret of treating hypothermia in a puppy seems to be to revive it slowly, for too rapid reheating causes the dilation of the puppy's blood vessels, haemorrhages and cardiovascular problems. Chilling certainly does not help the future development of the puppy for it has been found (Clark 1964) that puppies which have been chilled at birth, or in the first few days after birth, seem to be more susceptible to infections to which litter mates seem to be immune. Nevertheless I persist with puppies which have been chilled and have adapted an electric blanket which gives gradual gentle heat to cope with new-born apparently chilled puppies. I must add that I have achieved considerable success using this method of reviving chilled puppies.

Anxious and nervous bitches will often attempt to carry new-born puppies in their mouths and as a result of this practice, crush and bruise the whelps. If possible the breeder must curb this behaviour pattern for bitches which attempt to carry them often damage puppies. This behaviour problem can be reduced if the bitch is kept in a quiet warm and possibly dark place away from people and other, dogs. Some years back a neighbour whelping a litter of Labradors, telephoned to say his bitch on whelping, persisted in wandering around the pen, carrying her first puppy in her mouth. I walked to his cottage some six hundred yards from my own, and found his entire extended family in the pen watching the bitch whelp, and not to be outdone, a springer spaniel standing on hind legs staring over the wall. Once I advised him (I sarcastically suggested that he sold tickets to watch the next whelping) to send the family and the family dog into the house, the bitch desisted from carrying the puppies.

On the subject of telephone calls from distressed owners of first time whelping bitches, I once received a call from a terrier breeder who panic stricken said that his puppy was emerging feet first and he had read the puppies are always born head first. I have seen dozens of puppies born feet first that were none the worse for entering into the world in this manner.

So far I have discussed normal birth patterns but not all bitches will produce live puppies unaided. From time to time the breeder will encounter a bitch which needs help to produce her puppies. Ordinarily a bitch will produce puppies at half hourly intervals, but should the bitch be found to be desperately straining (to produce her puppy) for more than an hour, it is time to seek veterinary advice. It may transpire that the puppy is too large for the bitch to pass or more likely still the bitch's uterus is 'tired' – a state known as uterine inertia – and she lacks the inclination or energy to pass the puppy. There is some indication that uterine inertia can be remedied by an injection of a calcium salt, normally calcium oleate, which will give the uterus the necessary boost to pass the puppy. Should this fail the veterinary surgeon may use a remedy to encourage the muscles of the uterus to contract and expel the puppy. The majority of veterinary surgeons now use a substance called Oxytocsin, a hormone secreted by the post pituitary gland and also by the corpus luteum which not only stimulates contraction of the muscles of the uterus but actuates the milk let down mechanism promoting lactation in the bitch. When I first began serious dog breeding a substance called Ergometrin was employed to facilitate whelping but it was dangerous to use and could cause a bitch to suffer, its use was, to quote a veterinary surgeon friend of mine, 'a little like using a sledgehammer to adjust one's carburettor'. There is a simply horrendous tale of a young veterinary surgeon that injected a bitch that was unable to pass a particularly large puppy with ergometrine only to find that the bitch's uterus contracted so violently that the womb was split asunder and the puppies forced into the abdominal cavity. Amazingly surgery saved the bitch but not the puppies. Oxytocsin is a much kinder substance to use.

Just occasionally neither the injection of calcium oleate or oxytocain succeeds in getting the bitch to pass her puppies and the veterinary surgeon will then be forced to resort to a caesarean section to remove the puppies (apparently one of the Caesar's was born in the manner hence the name of the surgical operation). Frankly I ask veterinary surgeons to resort to this operation sooner rather than later for if the section saves just one extra puppy it will pay for the operation. The operation is quite a simple one, and consists of an anaesthetising the bitch before making a surgical incision firstly through the wall of the abdomen and then the uterus to extract the puppies. Once the puppies are extracted and revived the veterinary surgeon will stitch up first the uterus and then the wall of the abdomen. It is a relatively simple operation. Indeed it is the operation most newly graduated vets first attempt but it is not a job for the stockman however adept he may be. Not only does the operation require surgical precision it also requires to be performed in a sterile situation to be successful. It is also highly illegal for a layman to attempt the operation (Protection of Animals Act 1911, 1912 Scotland).

On the subject of caesarean sections I feel I must mention the fact that some brachycephalic (broadheaded) breeds of dog are commonly produced by caesarean sections rather than by natural birth. Breeds such as English bulldogs, Boston terriers and sadly, even miniature bull terriers are usually unable to produce puppies unaided, and hence puppies are surgically removed from their dams. I cannot but voice my distaste for those who breed these canine blasphemies in order to produce the exaggerated features required by the breed standards and for once I am not alone in my views. There are moves afoot in Europe to outlaw the breeding of creatures, which because of fashion are bred with unnaturally grotesque and often crippling physical peculiarities. While I detest laws which restrict human liberty I feel there is a point where legislation should dictate that the breeding of such monstrosities should be prohibited. It will be a pity to lose such historically interesting breeds as the bulldog, once the most game and tenacious of breeds but now a wheezing asthmatic travesty of an animal, but frankly I can see no logical reason why such monster should be bred when their very shape prohibits and restricts natural birth.

## Culling

The question of whether or not to cull puppies in a large litter is a debatable one. In Germany where some of the breed clubs have more power over the breeder than does the British Kennel Club some clubs insist that a bitch is only allowed to rear six of her puppies and even if a foster bitch is used to mother the rest of the litter, the use of the foster bitch is carefully monitored by the breed clubs. This is a shade restrictive by British standards and certainly would not be tolerated here (please God let me be right), but rearing a huge litter is certainly likely to reduce the condition of the mother of the puppies. Admittedly bitches only have full control of the feeding of their whelps for roughly three weeks, after which the puppies are able to ingest solid food, which eases the strain on the bitch a little. I own a terrific brood bitch, a white German Shepherd Dog called Asa that has three times produced and reared thirteen healthy lusty puppies. Yet despite the amount of food Asa eats, and she devours a terrific amount of food both during pregnancy and during the rearing of her puppies, she looks terribly jaded after the litter is weaned. Her actual body weight does not drop a great deal if at all, but her coat has a lack lustre appearance, and she moults in fits and starts after she has reared such a huge litter. She also looks a little hang dogish on the weaning of her puppies and takes several weeks to recover her old vitality. At the time of writing the British Kennel Club refuses to register more than six litters from a bitch and restricts the breeding age of a bitch to eight years .of age. This is an excellent practise and I applaud the forthcoming legislation that will prevent breeders breeding from a bitch twice a year. Animals that have been over bred look so terribly jaded and long before the onset of old age, resemble geriatrics.

Past experience has made me check the roofs of mouths of newly born puppies, for in 1964 I was plagued with a high incidence of cleft palates in the puppies I was breeding. Deliberate inbreeding to produce a type has also produced some undesirable characteristics including cleft palate and a high incidence of hydrocephally: I hasten to add that I have long since bred out these peculiarities. Cleft palate or the absence of a roof to the mouth prevents the animal from suckling and hence the whelp dies a lingering miserable death at the end of two or three days dehydration. Bitches are usually reluctant to allow such whelps to suckle and tend to push the whelp to the corner of the box, but the bleating of a dying puppy distresses both the bitch and the breeder. I cull any cleft palated puppy at birth and do not allow the puppy to experience further distress.

I also cull out any obviously crippled puppies and unlike some American breeders I also cull out swimmers i.e. puppies which have an obvious turtle like appearance, where the rib cage is abnormally large and the rear and fore legs stick out on either side. Black's explains the condition as being due to a manifestation of juvenile femoral rotation syndrome. Such puppies are unable to rise onto their hind legs at the usual age because the heads and necks of the femurs are wrongly positioned in the shaft. The condition is also known as flat puppy syndrome. Some American breeders try to correct swimmers by hobbling the puppy, in an attempt to get the whelp to rise and walk; I am disinclined to do this, for the puppies I rear are offered for sale, and even a fit and healthy puppy may not please some buyers so a defective puppy is most unlikely to satisfy a client.

I am however very much against cosmetic culling and don't particularly favour culling certain sexes for economic reasons – I'll explain. Certain breed standards dictate that only certain colours and specific markings are acceptable, for instance a white German Shepherd Dog (in a litter of coloured puppies) is not favoured by the show fraternity, likewise a white boxer is also unshowable and unfashionable, as is a parti-coloured Cavalier King Charles with nearly blanket markings. Hence some breeders cull otherwise healthy puppies simply because they are the wrong colour or have the wrong markings. Frankly I find this practise distasteful particularly as these mismarked puppies are not the slightest bit physically or mentally inferior to those specimens which are show quality. Mismarks and undesirable coloured puppies should only be culled if the litter is so oversized that some of the whelps need to be removed. Few dog owners actually show dogs anyway, and surely pet homes can be found for unshowable but healthy animals. The ignorance of some of the show dog fraternity sometimes defies belief, particularly if the first dog such a person purchases is, by the merest chance, a show animal. The ownership of such an animal immediately elevates the owner to the level of instant expert and dolts and near idiots take to dispensing wisdom like a New York doctor dispenses Valium. Once while giving a demonstration of the all round working ability of my white German Shepherd Dog, Polly, who not only worked with a gun, herded sheep, hunted, guarded but also worked from my fishing boat, I was approached by an angry middle aged lady, who uttered 'Why on earth do you breed those animals, they are recessives' (the good lady had no idea what recessive meant) 'and should be put to sleep'. I said nothing, for by nature I am a coward and the lady looked as though she was about to add physical abuse to rhetoric. Hence I simply bit my tongue and moved away from her.

However nowhere is brainlessness encountered more than in the lurcher fraternity and where ignorance is bliss it is certainly folly to be wise. White or gay pied (more white than coloured markings) do not find favour because most lurcher owners poach and white or pied dogs are said to be conspicuous in the countryside where green and brown colours prevail. The fact is that most lurcher owners lamp, shining a brilliant one million candle power beam across the countryside. Such a beam illuminates churches, houses, multi-storey blocks of flats and alerts the world to the presence of the would be poacher, but such a poacher avoids a white or coloured dog because the dog makes the poacher conspicuous! Truly it is wise when talking to a lurcher enthusiast not to take the advice of anyone whose I.Q is exceeded by his hat size!

Culling certain sexes for economic reasons is offensive to me but I am prepared to consider that such practices can be justified. Nearly thirty years ago, I met a woman who bred miniature pinchers, cute, rather neat little dogs that make fine pets. She bred several litters of puppies a year but destroyed the male puppies at birth because they were difficult to sell. I had deplored the practice for several years until this year when there is a glut of German Shepherd Dogs (GSD), particularly white GSD puppies on the market. It is difficult to sell large powerful males and doubly difficult to sell small females, but I have persisted and repeatedly advertised in order to sell the bitch puppies. The pet dog market is a fickle jade, in 1997 it was virtually impossible to sell top quality Labrador retrievers so I stopped breeding them. This year I have been approached by many clients eager to buy a Labrador puppy of either sex. Murphy's law certainly applies to professional dog breeding, for at the time of writing nearly every white GSD puppy born at my kennels seems to be a bitch.

I believe the following tale to be apocryphal. It is the story regarding the cosmetic culling of a litter. A newcomer to Dalmatian breeding supposedly whelped his first litter of puppies and finding them all white was disappointed for his bitch was of show quality and the sire of the litter a champion. Hence, not finding a single puppy marked with the plum pudding type spots that are typical of the breed he destroyed the entire litter. Later while talking to an experienced Dalmatian breeder he discovered that all Dalmatians puppies are born white and the plum pudding markings only appear as the puppy gets older. There are some daft people in this world and many of them breed dogs.

I just have to include the following tale of trying to rear a puppy that the bitch has decided to reject. In 1980 my terrier bitch Pagan produced a litter of five puppies one of which she decided to reject, pushing the whelp to the opposite side of the whelping box and refraining from allowing it to suckle. I could see no reason for the rejection and put the puppy to her four or five times a day to allow it to feed, yet the condition of the whelp continued to decline. One day a fellow dog breeder, Terry Aherne, arrived and offered to hand rear the whelp as his wife was a particularly good stock person who had achieved great success rearing orphan animals. Jennie, Terry's wife, spent the next eight weeks carefully rearing the whelp, which, while it grew to full size, had a lopsided appearance, and found locomotion difficult. Was the bitch able to sense this peculiarity when the whelp was born and because of this rejected it, or more likely still did the suckling of the puppy give Pagan no pleasure, and because of this the bitch was unwilling to allow the puppy to feed? A hedonistic explanation perhaps but I can think of no other reason to explain the rejection of the whelp.

On the subject of daft people, and tales of such would surely fill a large book, I am often asked 'what price the runt' when potential buyers come to view a litter, a member of which is smaller than the rest of its siblings. There are possibly two reasons why people ask about a smaller puppy: first the fact that a breeder might be prepared to part with the smaller puppy for less; second the mistaken conception that the runt will grow into a better animal than its larger litter mates. Personally I am reluctant to part with a smaller puppy for less simply because those seeking cut-price dogs will usually offer the puppy a cut price lifestyle, feeding it cut price food and not inoculating the whelp. However it is the notion that a runty puppy will grow into a more tenacious, tougher, more intelligent dog than its siblings that intrigues me. This theory is believed in the Black Country and when I talked to elderly keepers of fighting dogs during my teaching spell in Bloxwich, the majority of them believed that if a small puppy had the courage to survive in the somewhat Darwinian selection programme its litter mates might mete out, it must have some indefinable but good qualities. This is rather silly reasoning, runts are smaller, less lusty and more puny simply because they have some innate deficit or have been checked during the rearing programme. Frankly the purchase of a more lusty, up to size, litter mate is a better prospect for when a disease sweeps ones kennels, even a minor infection, the more lusty puppies tend to survive, while the runts usually succumb to the disease.

I was always interested in the way strange stories and canine legends originate and I am inclined to lay the blame for the theory that runts make the best dog at the feet of one Sir Percy Fitzpatrick. Sir Percy, who incidentally was responsible for initiating the custom of observing two minutes silence on Armistice Day, lived at the time of the great empire builders such as Cecil Rhodes and spent some of his life in the South African goldfields. As a result of his experiences he penned perhaps one of the best selling doggy novels of all time, the picaresque and meandering *Jock of the Bushveld*, the tale of a bull terrier dog which became Fitzpatrick's companion during his days in the goldfields. Jock had every canine virtue (and perhaps human virtue, for the tale is woefully anthropomorphic) but had been the last choice, the runt of the litter into which he was born. *Jock* was published in 1907 and sold many copies. It was also used as a school text book in the jingoistic days between the world wars and influenced many generations of boys and girls, myself included I confess.

It would be impossible to leave the subject of parturition without mentioning the use of foster bitches. During the halcyon days of dog breeding which preceded World War II the production of foster bitches, healthy mongrel bitches which had recovered from distemper, was quite big business. These bitches were mated and allowed to rear one or two mongrel puppies. They were then advertised in the doggy press and anyone who had a litter the dam of which had died or produced too large a litter or too little milk, eagerly sought the use of these bitches, which were either hired or sold. One of the great aficionados of the production of these distemper free foster bitches was the fabulous Metcalf of Newcastle, the Airedale breeder whose advertisements were seldom accurate or politically correct for that matter. Metcalf however could lay his hands on foster bitches any day of the year and a great many excellent pedigree dogs were reared by the mongrel bitches he secured. Metcalf, who gave himself the appellation of *The Northern Government Contractor For Dogs* (a rather grandiose title perhaps) operated out of Harbottle Street, Newcastle and was once described by Sir Jocelyn Lucas as 'one of the truly remarkable entrepreneurs of our time'.

Proprietary puppy milks balanced to allow hand rearing of puppies – I shall deal with the subject presently – now rather reduce the need for foster bitches. If a bitch can be persuaded to accept another bitch's puppies, the whelps are much better reared than similar puppies that have been reared by hand. Some bitches will readily accept any bleating whelp while others are more reluctant to do so. I own an elderly bearded collie call Tilly who will mother any small animal and readily comes into milk, mid season, when she is put with a young puppy and such bitches are treasures indeed. Foster bitches are best if they are rearing puppies which are roughly the same age as those they are to foster and if the foster whelps are roughly the same size as their own, although I have seen quite tiny dogs rear giant 'cuckoo in the nest puppies' as if they were their own. It is however not only a little unfair but very unwise to allow a terrier sized bitch to attempt to rear a litter of giant sized puppies, for the smaller bitch can only produce a certain amount of milk to suckle the whelps.

Fostering a litter of puppies with an inexperienced foster mother should be done with great care. It should be remembered that bitches seldom recognise their own puppies by sight but by scent. My method is to ensure the pen is very warm and then to remove the bitch from her puppies. I then mingle the would-be foster puppies with the bitch's litter and allow them to mix and absorb the scent of the would-be mother's litter. After a period of two or so hours I allow the bitch back to her litter and the changeling whelps I have introduced. After such a period the puppies are eager to suckle and the bitch is eager to suckle them because of the pressure of the milk in her mammary glands. I watch the bitch carefully and if she readily accepts them, I leave her with them, if she shows some concern about the recently enlarged litter, I stay with her until she accepts them and if she doesn't I remove them and prepare for the nightmare ordeal of rearing the litter by hand. Few bitches reject puppies if this method of fostering is adopted though I have had a bitch that apparently accepted the foster whelps only to savage them when I left the pen. It is worth noting that some bitches that have had their puppies delivered by caesarean section are reluctant to accept the puppies as their own and will often display hostility towards them. I am perhaps fortunate in that as I own a great many bitches I am rarely without a bitch on which puppies can be fostered.

So we shall assume the puppies have been born either naturally or with help from the breeder/veterinary surgeon, now for the rearing of the puppies from a day old to the sale of the whelps.

# 10

# Rearing Puppies

READER, I PRAY YOU, gird up your loins for I am about to bombard you with doom and statistical gloom before I allow Hope to seep upwards out of the bottom of Pandora's box.

J M Evans MRCVS, in *A Practical Look at Fading Puppies* (1991) suggests that 20–30 percent of all live puppies born will die before weaning age. For further gloom the survey carried out by the Animal Health Trust in the early 1990s suggests that the death rate is as high as 32 percent – one third of all puppies will therefore die before reaching weaning age. Frankly this is not only an appalling indication of bad stockmanship and would certainly not be tolerated amongst pig breeders, as it is financially ruinous death rate. In more practical terms let us assume that a litter of nine bull mastiff puppies selling at £500 a piece might reasonably be expected to fetch £4500. However, if the Animal Health Trust figures are correct £1500 worth of puppies will die before reaching selling age (eight weeks). So, what are the causes of such a high mortality rate and what can the breeder possibly do to remedy this terrible death rate?

It is, perhaps, wise to start with the subject of puppies which die before they are fourteen days old, a condition known as Fading Puppy Complex, or FPC. There are many ailments, diseases, conditions, call them what you will, that contribute to this neonatal death rate but the puppies which die are inclined to show virtually the same symptoms regardless of the malaise that brings about their deaths. Typical fading puppy complex victims manifest the following symptoms. The puppies are born, live, lusty, and apparently healthy and for the first twenty-four hours suckle the colostrum (the yellow, first milk) lustily. The whelps then become progressively weaker and cease suckling, losing weight rapidly as a result of malnutrition and dehydration. Evans suggests that whelps so afflicted may display swaying head movements and will paddle aimlessly at the mammary glands yet be disinclined to suckle. Periods of rigidity with the straightening of the forelimbs may follow shortly before death. Death occurs after respiration becomes laboured, with periods of what appears to be breath holding and more rarely, the puppy may pass blood in their faeces and urine. A characteristic of FPC is that not all the litter may be affected and some of the litter may appear lusty and lively. Evans suggests there are five reasons why puppies may develop fading puppy complex. I shall deal with each reason in turn with suggestions how this problem can be solved or the death rate of the puppies reduced.

## Infections by Micro-organisms

A great many types of bacteria can produce fading puppy complex including the all to common haemolytic streptococci, a bacterium which causes the destruction of red blood cells and the loss of oxygen carrying haemoglobin. Certain strains of E.Coli are also very damaging to some puppies. I believe I mentioned the terrible problems I encountered in Caithness and how I dealt with these problems. Certain strains of brucilla are also very damaging to puppies, indeed American dog periodicals frequently mention the ravages of Brucella Canis, which causes great losses in America's commercial breeding kennels. Evans mentions that the disease now exists in Britain, for in 1980 a report indicated that Brucella Canis antibodies were found in two Dobermann bitches with American ancestry.

It has been suggested that treating bitches with a broad spectrum antibiotic some five days before mating and five days after mating and again five days before parturition and five days after whelping may well reduce the incidence of death due to bacterial infection. My own experience indicates that sterilisation and fumigation of the whelping pens just prior to the bitch whelping may also help reduce the death rate attributable to bacterial infections.

## The Incidence of Parasites

Evans suggests that as many as 3–5 percent of neonatal puppy deaths (death within the fourteenth day after parturition) are due to infections by parasites, the principle culprit being the roundworm Toxicara canis. Apparently some 90 percent of all puppies are infected before birth and as the larval forms of this serious parasite migrate through the lungs, pneumonia is a common cause of puppy deaths. Often the bile ducts are blocked by the migration of the roundworm larvae and this prevents the bile pigments, bilverdin and biluridin, entering the gut. Jaundice is a common symptom of puppies that have died because of roundworm infestation.

Clearly regular worming of pregnant and suckling bitches with an appropriate roundworm medicine will help reduce the incidence of death through Toxicara canis infections though it will not totally eradicate this parasite. Not all unthelmintics are effective against the larval form of the roundworm, piperazine derivatives readily kill the adult worm but have little effect on the larval form of the roundworm. Hancock injects his greyhound bitches with 2mls of Iromic a week or so prior to mating and this does much to reduce roundworm infection in his puppies but this practice cannot be adopted with collies of any sort as I have explained earlier.

## Hypothermia

Hypothermia, or the chilling of new-born puppies, is the cause of a large percentage of neonatal puppy deaths. It appears that research has indicated that a new-born puppy behaves in the manner of a cold or variably blooded animal that adapts it body temperature to that of its immediate environment. Young puppies are unable to shiver to generate heat until they are over seven days old and have little subcutaneous fat to provide insulation against low temperatures. A puppy's surface area is proportionally greater than that of a mature dog so heat is lost more easily and further more, the puppy has a low glycogen (a type of heat giving animal starch) reserves in the liver so food reserves are low.

Evans argues that if surrounding ambient temperatures are allowed to drop in the first few days of a puppy's life a disastrous irreversible chain reaction can be set up. A newly born puppy has a body temperature of 98.6°F some three degrees below that of an adult dog and it takes up to four weeks to rectify this disparity in temperature, so a newly born puppy is very susceptible to chilling. A well insulated whelping quarter with an equally insulated floor will reduce the incidence of death through hypothermia, but the breeder must be vigilant about allowing a puppy to stray too far from the dam. A bitch leaving a whelping box can easily take away a puppy attached to her nipple from the area that is kept warm by the heat lamp. Thus there is a lower mortality rate amongst puppies reared in the home where the litter is easily monitored. Some bitches are bad at scattering litters around the whelping pen and allowing them to get chilled, and these bitches can often do the same when rearing subsequent litters. I once owned a terrier called Battle, possibly the best all round working terrier I have ever owned, but a notoriously bad whelper. She insisted on moving her puppies away from the heated area to the corner of the pen where of course the whelps died. Even in mid summer during the heatwave of 1976 she lost puppies, and continued to do so until her dotage. Her bloodline was priceless but I never managed to breed a good litter from her. Battle's problems brings me quite neatly to the next cause of neo-natal deaths, bad mothering, or to use a more technical expression dystokia.

## Bad Mothering or Dystokia

It is always a surprise to me when I hear of first time breeders who are amazed when a bitch shows little inclination to mother her puppies, for they assume the desire to look after one's offspring is the most important of innate dispositions, but to believe that nature is infallible is ludicrous though the notion has prompted many clergymen to oppose genetic engineering. The truth is that nature makes many many mistakes – as any long term breeder can attest, I'm afraid.

I have already mentioned that immature bitches often display little inclination to mother the puppies they have produced. Indeed some bitches seem horrified and terrified of the whelps that have emerged from their bodies. Yet once mature, many of these bitches will become loving and caring mothers. Some bitches however are very poor mothers and extremely destructive to the puppies they produce. I have already mentioned the tendency that some bitches have to carry puppies in their mouths and how this tendency can sometimes be prevented by isolating the bitch and keeping her in a darkened but warm room, but some bitches will carry puppies no matter how secluded their whelping quarters are. Such puppies squeal piteously but this action only serves to make the bitch more possessive of the whelp they are carrying. Bruised puppies seldom recover from such treatment and although some might recover from the bruising, they seldom grow as well as they might.

Cannibalism is also a characteristic of bad mothering – or is it? Lorenz mentions the instance of a black jaguar, the most caring of mothers, which ate her ailing cub. Lorenz explains the incident thus; the ailing cub cries and the only way the bitch has of comforting her whelp is to clean it – the cub continues to cry and the jaguar in despair licks the soft belly of the cub even more, which causes the cub to continue to cry so the female, now desperate to comfort the cub continues to lick her offspring furiously and eventually eats the bowels of the stricken cub. Cannibalism is in fact triggered by the fact the puppies are sickly and the bitch, in order to comfort them licks them until the umbilicus and the abdomen bleeds. Yet some bitches will devour their puppies seemingly without reason. As I have mentioned before, I have known bitches come out of anaesthetic after a caesarean section and kill their young, probably because they did not realise that the puppies were their own.

Puppies may also die because the bitch does not produce a suitable supply of milk, or because the milk produced is of poor quality. As bitches get older their nipples often become enlarged, so enlarged in fact that puppies are unable to suckle and thus die. This is particularly so in the case of 'past their prime' German Shepherd Dog bitches. Indeed the Kennel Club edict that bitches above the age of eight should not be used for breeding unless there are exceptional reasons for breeding from such an animal, is a wise one.

## Nutrition

The last of the causes of high neonatal death amongst puppies is inadequate nutrition, for the bitch must be well fed during pregnancy particularly during the last three weeks when the growth of the foeti is greatest. An adequate supply of good quality proteinous food is essential during that time, as is a good source of vitamins particularly Vitamin A, a deficiency of which is blamed for poor viability of new-born puppies. An adequate supply of Vitamin K is also essential to guarantee the viability of new-born puppies, though the action of Vitamin K is not fully understood. It is known however to assist the formation of the blood clotting agent pro thrombrin and puppies born to bitches fed a diet which is deficient in Vitamin K often lose a large quantity of essential blood when the placenta has been severed.

The Animal Health Foundation researchers indicate that bitches fed less than 15 percent fat in their diet during pregnancy are likely to produce puppies which experience a higher neonatal death rate. Hence suitable fats should be fed to bitches in late pregnancy.

At one time it was common practice to feed bitches an inadequate diet during late pregnancy so that the puppies were small enough for the bitch to pass easily during parturition but such a practice smacks of bad kennel management, if not madness. Evans states that puppies which are less than 75 percent of the average birth weight for the breed are unlikely to survive to adulthood. Tiny immature puppies should be given a 5 percent glucose solution every three hours and kept in a temperature of 90°F if they are to survive.

Certain congenital disorders and defects will also produce a high mortality rate amongst new-born puppies. I have already mentioned the subject of cleft palate and hydrocephally which plagued the early Plummer terriers. Evans lists the absence of anus, obstruction of the urethra, neonatal jaundice or inhalation pneumonia although he also suggests that a high incidence of cleft palates in puppies may not be entirely due to inbreeding, as I found in the creation of my own strain, but could be due to feeding excessive amounts of Vitamin A.

At this point I feel I must lightly touch on the subject of inbreeding, and its influence on the health and vigour of the offspring born as a result of consanguine mating. There is every indication that during the early stages of an inbreeding programme, losses and deformities amongst one's litters will be unacceptably high. However, if one has the courage to cull and to continue this inbreeding programme, adopting a careful but vigorous selection system, losses will decrease until one's strain is just as lusty and vigorous as puppies born to unrelated parents. I feel this should not concern the commercial dog breeder who is rarely interested in creating a new strain of dog but simply concerned with the production of healthy vigorous saleable puppies. To produce such puppies, an inbreeding or line breeding programme would be ill advised. The majority of commercial dog breeders usually obtain quite ordinary brood bitches and mate them to a totally unrelated or only distantly related stud dog, possibly from a show winning strain, to obtain puppies. This is a fairly unscientific breeding scheme to those concerned with the production of a good show winning strain, but such a programme does tend to produce lusty puppies which are suitable for the pet market, for if the breeder can show a pedigree with possibly a few championships sprinkled in the tail end of the line, most pet buyers are satisfied.

Hope is now ready to flutter out of Pandora's box, for we are about to leave the gloom and doom of fading puppies and neonatal death and discuss the normal development of the healthy puppy and its needs and requirements. I am going to relate how puppies develop using the Scott and Fuller and Dunbar classifications of stages of development.

- Neonatal (new-born period) Birth.
- Transitional – eyes open (two weeks).
- Socialisation – ears open (three weeks).
- Juvenile period – weaning (ten weeks).
- Adult period – puberty (six months).

Once a puppy is born it will gasp for breath thereby clearing its nasal passages of foetal fluid. The bitch will then lick certain areas of the puppy's body mainly the muzzle and the umbilical area. This is worth noting if one is attempting to revive an apparently lifeless puppy. Gentle friction around the muzzle can stimulate the puppy's breathing.

New-born puppies live in a sensory void. They can neither see nor hear but are able to locate the dam by touch, and the strongest and most lusty puppy will feed best and most frequently. At this stage of the puppy's development the breeder would be wise to keep a close eye on the bitch but not pay too much attention to the whelps. Some bitches welcome the examination of their puppies. Pippin my Lucas terrier – Lucas terriers are cross between Norfolk and Sealyham terriers – is only too delighted if I handle and stroke her new-born whelps, whereas Apple, her sister, is decidedly unhappy if anyone attempts to peer into her whelping box. So it is good policy to expect the worst and to keep strangers away from the whelping unit until the bitch has time to accept her new litter. In fact I never so much as bother to check for congenital defects in the puppies until the whelps are two days old. Neither do I bother to sex the litter for there is little I can do to alter the ratio of dogs and bitches in the nest.

Old dog books written in Edwardian times, which saw a glut of badly written, ill advised books on dog breeding and management, advise leaving a litter until it is ten days old before the breeder considers removing dew claws and – this is a highly controversial subject – docking the tails.

Cue for a discourse on the morality and practise of tail docking, I'm afraid reader this subject is an important one. Docking or the surgical removal of tails is a debatable subject. Originally the practise was adopted to allow farm dogs or curs to go untaxed, hence the term to curtail or step short an activity. These days the practise of docking is a questionable one, though many believe that working dogs which are required to work in deep cover, springers, cockers etc. still need to be docked to prevent the caudal appendage bleeding when the dog works in thorny conditions. However the majority of veterinary surgeons seem to disagree with the practise of docking tails on moral grounds. This belief and objection has been compounded by the fact that in recent years it has been made illegal for an unqualified lay person to dock puppies. The expression unqualified has been hotly debated in courts throughout Britain, and it is uncertain as to whether much practise at tail docking justifies a person being referred to as qualified. Personally I believe practise qualifies a person to dock tails. I have docked possibly thousands of puppies and consider myself a damned sight more qualified to dock than a vet who probably has docked only one or two litters and makes a pig's ear of the job – as alas many vets do. However, should a person be convicted of illegal docking under the 1911 Protection of Animals Act Section I (1)a, the Breeders licence authorities would be perfectly within their rights to forbid the convicted person a Breeder's Licence. The Act of Parliament which prohibits an unqualified person docking puppies was hastily drawn up and passed, and frankly the Act is badly worded and ill defined. To combat the vagaries of this Act, the Council of Docked Breeds has been formed and those seeking to breed puppies the breed standards of which suggest that a puppy should have a shortened tail, should seek advice from and join the Council of Docked Breeds as to the legality of the practise.

To return to the practise rather than the morality and legality of docking. Docking is best done when the puppies are three days old, particularly if the puppies to be docked are less lusty than one might expect or wish. Leaving unthrifty whelps for ten days before attempting to dock them is bad practice, for at ten days of age the puppy has developed a sophisticated network of blood vessels and nerves in its tail and the pain and shock experienced at this age may well be traumatic for the puppy. Conversely if the operation is conducted when the whelp is two or three days old the operation is simple and relatively painless. I must confess I dislike docking puppies despite my experience of performing this operation, and I am rather relieved that the law now prohibits me from conducting this task.

When the puppy is ten days of age its eyes will open but might take a few more days before it is able to respond to visual stimuli. At about this age the puppy also develops the ability to shiver to generate heat, which brings me quite neatly to the subject of how long should puppies be kept under a heat lamp. Of course new-born puppies must be whelped in very warm conditions – I've explained why earlier in the book – but as soon as the whelp begins to be able to regulate its own body temperature, the temperature in the whelping pen should be reduced slightly. In summer conditions a puppy which is still with its dam or an orphan puppy which needs special treatment can be 'off heat' by the time it is two weeks old. In winter, particularly in conditions found in the Scottish borders where my present kennels are situated, the puppy must be kept in warm conditions for far longer – a puppy is four weeks old before its body temperature reaches that of an adult at 101.5°F. It is bad policy to suddenly switch off the heat lamp and it is far better to lift it an inch a day and gradually reduce the heat given to a puppy. It is false economy to stint the amount of heat a puppy gets during the first month of its life.

When puppies are two weeks old it is time to worm them with a gentle wormer. At one time the usual wormer was santonin, a fierce purgative, a derivative of bitter wormwood, which made the puppy's alimentary tracts red and raw and caused considerable illness and discomfort for days afterwards. I can remember the time when owners of village puppies took six week old whelps to Ffaldan Square where miners sat on their haunches chewing tobacco and waiting for the next shift. A wade of finely macerated tobacco was thrust down the puppy's throat and the whelp's muzzle held tight to prevent vomiting. If the puppy lived after such treatment, and many did not, it passed a writhing ball of roundworms later in the day but the puppy was always desperately ill for days after being subjected to such treatment.

How things have changed and I shake my head in despair at the supposed wisdom of those who seek to go back to the herbal wormers of yesterday. These days piperazina citrate or hydrate based anthelmetics are safe and effective against the adult worm though ineffective against the larval stages of this parasite. Puppies as young as two weeks old can be wormed with piperazine, which is obtained from virtually any pet shop but worming every two weeks until the puppy is six months of age is necessary if the whelps are to be kept free of roundworms. My kennels is always frequented by armies of village children who come to play with the puppies and these children are taught not to handle the puppies until the whelps have been wormed at least twice. I have yet to encounter the dreaded viceral migrans which is apparently the scourge of Central Park, New York but I am ever vigilant where roundworms are concerned. If the owner has wormed the dam of the puppies during the last weeks of pregnancy or adopted the one dose a day Panacur treatment, the puppies will void few roundworms in their faeces. Incidentally the faecal matter passed by young puppies is invariably ingested by the dam, who in turn will – once the puppies have been wormed – pass dead round worms in her own stools. It is good policy to be particularly vigilant about disposing of stools infected with roundworms particularly after a bitch and her puppies have been given a worming medicine, and I intend to write a chapter on waste disposal later in this book. At one time I composted the faecal matter from the kennels in the mistaken belief that the heat generated by the decay of the matter – up to 180°F over six or so weeks – would destroy all roundworm eggs. To cut a long story short the eggs survived in huge numbers. I now make a point of burning refuse from the puppy pens. Virtually no known organisms survive in temperatures of 400°F, the temperature of burning straw and shavings.

For the first few days of the whelps life the puppy suckles a thick yellow first milk or colostrum, which is its principal source of antibodies. Puppies reared without ingesting this colostrum are usually deficient in antibodies and are a potential prey to a variety of diseases. As I have mentioned, puppies obtain some antibodies via the placenta which is fortunate if the puppies have to be hand reared or if they are fostered onto a bitch which is past the time when her mammary glands secrete its rich source of antibodies, but the quality of the antibodies varies greatly. If a bitch is affected with some organism immediately before or during pregnancy she will secrete a great many antibodies against that particular infection in her colostrum. Likewise if a bitch is inoculated against a particular disease (leptospirosis, distemper, hepatitis, parvo virus etc.) shortly before mating (or sometimes during pregnancy, though this is a questionable practise at the time of writing when a variety of ills have been reported after the vaccination of pregnant bitches) then the puppies will usually have a high $$titer factor to combat by the onset of that specific infection. Yet these infantile antibodies are quite short lived and by the time the puppy is three weeks old the level of antibodies falls sharply, until by twelve weeks the puppy is a possible target for canine infections and should be given a complete set of vaccinations.

I'm afraid I am a belt and braces man where the subject of parvo virus is concerned, possibly because I both saw and suffered from the privations of the first onset of the disease in 1979 when dog breeding literally stood still until a suitable vaccine against this dreadful infection could be developed. Hence as soon as I believe the antibody level of my puppies is beginning to wane – usually at about three week of age – I inoculate them against the parvo virus. It is highly likely that the puppy will still have some of the antibodies it has obtained from its dam at this age, and these may combat the weakened virus introduced by the vaccine and effectively nullify the effect of the inoculation. Hence I reinoculate my puppies at the age of six weeks ready for selling when the puppies at eight weeks old. I make no apologies for my vigilance regarding parvo virus infections. I have no wish to experience the horror of the disease again.

Puppies are usually ready to start feeding on solid food at about three weeks though there is a present trend to wean puppies as early as two weeks of age. I find this a rather pointless exercise as a heavily lactating bitch is providing ample nutrition for her whelps some fourteen days after whelping. Current theories regarding the diet and weaning are a little like buses – there's usually another one along every few minutes. However by the time the whelp approaches three weeks it will display an interest in food the bitch often carries into the whelping box and attempt to smell and suck at the food, particularly if it is raw or cooked meat.

Caveat – some bitches are very protective of their food – greyhounds and other sight hounds are notoriously possessive and will often snap at any puppy which approaches a coveted piece of meat. In fact it is not unknown for greyhound bitches to snap and kill puppies which attempt to explore the food the bitch has brought to the box, but greyhounds are not alone with regards to this desire to protect food. In 1967 I befriended a young man who worked a particularly good Border terrier. The animal was not only sired by a Cruft's winner but was also a fine worker to rat, fox, badger and otter (badger and otter became protected species during the 1970s). In due course he mated the bitch to a very fine young male and with both care and pride produced a fine litter of puppies. The bitch adored the whelps and the youngsters grew at a phenomenal rate. All went well until the puppies were three and half weeks old when the young man found a very good bitch puppy stone dead in the corner of the whelping box. A post-mortem and a culture derived from the cadaver's tissues revealed nothing, but another two puppies died before the autopsy report was sent to the breeder. One evening I called in at the young man's home on my way to earth stopping, for I supplemented my teacher's salary in a number of ways, one of which was blocking the fox earths and badger setts the evening before the hunt drew country adjacent to those lairs. The youth bemoaned the sad fate of his whelps as he stroked the Border terrier bitch's ears. She was a delightful creature without a mean streak in her body – or so I believed. Quite suddenly I saw the bitch becoming tense as a puppy approached the food bowl. Suddenly the bitch erupted and shot across the room and struck at the whelp savagely – and the mysterious deaths were no longer a mystery. The bitch was mated to another top dog and once again produced a beautiful litter. My friend was more vigilant about feeding the bitch in the presence of her puppies this time, but in an unguarded moment, a telephone call or something else and he left the bitch with a dish of food. She promptly slew her five puppies quickly and silently. She was never again mated.

To return to the subject of weaning. It is common practice for breeders to introduce puppies to soaked proprietary food that has been pulverised by pressing the whelps' noses into the mush. If the whelps are roughly three weeks old they will probably lick the food pulp from their muzzle and then wade into the meal. Puppies just starting to eat make a fearsome mess but the bitch will clean up the waste food. Puppies from large litters or whelps feeding from a bitch who is a poor lactater will feed earlier than normal, whereas puppies from small litters or puppies suckling a heavily lactating bitch will be disinclined to feed at three weeks for obvious reasons. I have in fact known of puppies of four weeks old that were disinclined to try solid food until the dams were removed from them for two or three hours and hunger forced them to explore the food dish.

I am a shade old fashioned about the way I start to wean puppies onto solid food, for I believe the most natural and suitable starter diet to be red raw meat, beef, lamb or horse flesh liquidised or 'scraped'. Scraped meat means I take a piece of bloody raw flesh and scrape a blunt knife across the flesh removing the bloody tissue, but leaving the fibrous cell walls behind. This finely macerated flesh is the most suitable diet for starting puppies off on solid food though a tiny quantity of liquidised or pulverised liver or kidney is nearly as inviting. I feed this food to my hand-reared puppies for even well fed whelps seldom refrain from sucking at scraped meat. Once started on this scraped meat the whelps should not be fed on it exclusively because it may be deficient in calcium.

May I now add in the inevitable sprinkling of doom and gloom that the reader has learnt to expect. When whelps are about seventeen days old their dam is producing a lot of milk to feed them. This heavy lactation puts a great strain on the bitch's mineral reserves and her body sometimes becomes depleted of calcium. This is known as hypocalcaemia (below the level of required calcium) and she may stagger and appear uncertain on her legs. The bitch may lapse into a deep fit and death. I have found that many bitches about to fall prey to this problem develop a lustrous coat immediately prior to the symptoms I have described. There is some evidence to suggest that bitches fed a high calcium rich diet during pregnancy are more likely to develop the symptoms of hypcalcaemia than bitches fed a less calcium rich diet. I have encountered this condition, erroneously referred to as eclampsia, a malaise which manifests similar symptoms but for very different reasons, in bitches with three day old puppies but the majority of afflicted bitches succumb to the malaise later, when they are lactating heavily. A tyro dog breeder may be terrified at the sight of the thrashing, paddling fit manifested by the bitch but the treatment of this ailment is simplicity itself. An injection of calcium boroglutinate obtained easily and cheaply from any agricultural store will rectify the matter in minutes. Veterinary surgeons inject this substance into the veins of the bitch's foreleg with startling results, most recover immediately. I am reluctant to administer calcium so rapidly and much prefer to inject the calcium subcutaneously into the loose skin of the neck and to allow the calcium to be absorbed slowly. Bitches treated this way recover slowly and not so dramatically. At one time many of my terriers developed hypocalcaemia fits, for my bitches were heavy lactaters. Later when I introduced bullterrier blood into the strain they ceased to milk as heavily and the incidence of hypocalcaemia lessened. Any professional dog breeder who does not keep a store of this chemical on the premises is acting unwisely.

At the end of the fourth week the puppy's life it is only obtaining about half its sustenance from its dam, for by this time it should be eating solid food. It is fairly common practice to overfeed puppies at this age. It is advisable to feed the quantity of food that can be eaten in five minutes and then remove the food and allow the bitch to eat it. It is best to remove the dam while the puppies feed.

The constant suckling of the whelps can cause the bitch's mammary glands to become raw. My bitches exercise with the main kennel dogs during this time of the litter's development, preparing them for their return when the puppies are sold. Breeders should watch out for puppies pestering the bitch at this age and the bitch snapping at them when they approach her. Often bitches will attempt to escape the constant pestering from the litter and it is advisable to place a bench in the kennel for her to retire to. Most bitches are tolerant of their whelps but some have to be watched carefully. Wild bitches such as wolves, jackals etc. spend a long time away at this time in the life of the litter thereby easing the irritation of the puppies. Domesticated bitches should also be allowed time away.

Some bitches eat their food and then regurgitate it for the puppies to eat. First time breeders are often horrified when their bitch vomits up her food for the puppies which eagerly eat it. Many people are totally out of touch with the habits of the animal world. A dog will carry her food in the most convenient way possible – her stomach. Here the food is sanitised by hydrochloric acid secreted by the stomach's oxycetic glands and partially digested by stomach pepsin that changes protein to peptone. When the bitch returns to the litter they nuzzle the dam's lips causing her to regurgitate her food on which the whelps eagerly feed. The process of digestion produces smelly gases but regurgitating food is perfectly natural. I regularly get telephoned by first time breeders horrified at this sight. One lady asked me how she could break her bitch of this habit. Rarely does the bitch need to be broken of the habit of regurgitating food, and the practise normally stops when the whelps are six or eight weeks old. In 1970 Bill Brockley of Etwall, Derbyshire, who owned a show winning bitch called Teazle, bred from a Whadon Chase terrier bloodline, very typy, if a little small in size, after weaning her litter she refused to gain weight and remained very ribby and lacklustre for about four months. One day I found her pawing at the kennel door which housed a litter of puppies – not her own – and attempting to regurgitate her food through the wires of the door. Brockley separated the bitch from the other dogs and she returned to good health. Truly some bitches take their maternal duties to the extreme. Pippin, a Lucas terrier bitch I own, starts lactating when she hears the kittens produced by our house cat bleating and she reared the grandmother of our present queen when she found an abandoned day old kitten in the hedgerow near the house and came into milk.

Once more the subject of worming I'm afraid – boring perhaps but so important. It is important to worm puppies every fourteen days from two weeks old until they are six months of age. It is also policy to vary the worming remedy used at each worming. At fourteen days old I use piperazine citrate or hydrate to worm whelps, a treatment which kills perhaps 97 percent of all adult worms but has little or no effect on the larval form of the parasite. For the second worming I use another brand of anthelmintic for I try not to let the roundworms, which are endemic in any dog, get immune to any vermifuge – cue for another tale I am afraid. About six years ago I was given a packet of Panacur horse wormer by a friend, a sachet which was sufficient to worm a large horse. I split the packet and used it to worm some eight week old puppies with excellent results, for Panacur is an excellent, safe wormer – so safe in fact that an overdose of two thousand times the advised dosage has little harmful effect. So delighted was I with the result that despite my supposed scientific training I went a shade overboard. In 1997 I dosed a bitch which was carrying a particularly valuable litter with Panacur every day of her pregnancy from the fortieth day to parturition to give my litter a worm-free flying start. At three weeks old my litter looked dreadful and at six weeks of age I lost a puppy. The autopsy revealed a massive worm infestation and further tests revealed that this strain of roundworm was now immune to Panacur because of my over use of the substance. I am well qualified to write a book of this nature – I've made all the mistakes! Since then I have varied my worming treatment using nitroscanate alternating with piperazine and no doubt in time I shall go back to using Panacur again.

## Socialisation

It is extremely important to socialise puppies. In 1962 two scientists, Scott and Fuller, stationed at Bar Harbour, Maine, USA came up with some important research on socialising puppies. Their project revealed that if puppies were not handled regularly from three weeks onwards until weaning they frequently remained nervous and shy for the rest of their days. Dunbar, *Dog Behavior* suggests the process is reversible, though socialising older animals is tedious and a difficult process. I believe Dunbar is wrong for I have found unsocialised puppies, really unsocialised puppies, very difficult to train and they remain remote and unsociable for life. Gott (1967) suggests that puppies taken from the dam too young, weaned at perhaps three weeks old and reared apart from dogs, are well socialised where humans are concerned, were apparently happy in human company but became terribly agitated when introduced to other dogs. Some became hysterical if another dog approached them and most refused to mate, though the act of procreation must be one of the most instinctive of all behaviour patterns. I believe Gott's findings actually stopped the big city American market for very young dogs (three or four weeks of age when separated from their mothers) and reared in superb isolation in high rise flats.

It is important to socialise and handle puppies regularly because no potential client will want to purchase a nervous puppy who hides away when introduced to strangers. To illustrate my point, when the parvovirus epidemic struck in 1979 such was the panic that major dog shows were cancelled because of the possibility of spreading the disease. Some breeder became paranoid about puppies contacting the disease and did not allow strangers into the whelping kennels. Puppies and dams were watched on close circuit television until they were old enough to sell, and this resulted in many of the whelps becoming peculiar and remote because of their isolation. I sympathise with those breeders who tried to curb the disease by isolating their whelps from the public but I would avoid purchasing a puppy reared in this way.

I admit I make shameless use of the village children where socialising is concerned, for droves come to my kennels to play with the puppies once they have been wormed. True my puppies suffer the indignity of being dressed in dolls clothing and being pushed around in prams but nevertheless as a result of such socialising they greet potential clients effusively and virtually sell themselves.

Time now to suggest the actual selling of the puppies. I worm for the last time when they are six weeks old with the idea of selling them at eight weeks, and if I can I use an entirely different worming remedy from the ones I used for the two and four week worming programme. It is feasible to sell six week old puppies but not good practise. The trauma of separation from the dam at this early age hinders both the physical and mental development of the puppies. Another two weeks in kennels separate from the dam but still with litter mates will increase both the size and the mental tenacity of the whelps and fewer are returned by clients if they are sold at eight weeks.

# 11

# Selling One's Wares

'INVENT A BETTER mousetrap than your neighbour and the world will beat a path to your door' so said Ralph Waldo Emmerson 1803–1882, who judging from my Oxford Dictionary of Quotations was a master of epigrams. Yet I suspect that Emmerson would not have been able to sell a single mousetrap if his product had not been advertised and marketed properly, which brings me quite nicely to the subject of where and how to advertise one's puppies.

I know one or two breeders who claim that such is their success in the show world that they don't need to advertise and sell all their puppies by word of mouth. Frankly I believe such people fall into two categories: first, the very small breeder who touts a single bitch or dog around the shows and experiences an unprecedented level of success; and second, downright liars. The general public who are seeking to buy a sound, healthy pet typical of the breed but perhaps not of show quality, seldom frequent the dog shows and are blissfully unaware that certain breeders are experiencing a wonderful run of success. True such shows will attract foreign buyers who are prepared to pay Space Invader scores for certain top winning animals to export to other countries as breeding stock. I heard of a German Shepherd Dog which was sold for £25,000 after winning a major show, but the run-of-the-mill dog breeder will not sell many puppies by attending shows. The type of people who attend the shows are usually enthusiasts who already have specimens of a certain breed and are out to improve the quality of their show stock and are certainly not interested in buying a pet quality puppy.

It certainly pays to advertise one's wares but where and how to advertise is debatable and needs considerable thought and planning if the breeder is to be successful in marketing his puppies. For instance, I doubt if even the most carefully worded advertisement for Chihuahuas placed in the *Fish Farmers Times* will attract a great number of buyers, though I once heard of a breeder who advertised in *The Times* – hardly a doggy paper – with amazing results.

Certain magazines are taken and read by certain people – a trite comment but a true one. For instance the only place to buy lurchers and longdogs prior to 1980 was *Exchange & Mart* which once boasted an amazing number of interesting advertisements all eulogising on the virtues of poachers dogs capable of making some slightly dishonest artisan hunter a very dishonest living. These days *Countryman's Weekly* is the place to advertise one's lurchers. Likewise a litter of working Labrador retrievers of working stock, (lighter and more athletic than the show bred Labradors) would be better advertised in the *Shooting Times* than, let's say, *Knitters Monthly*.

Unless one advertises in national magazines such as *Exchange & Mart*, which has an enormous circulation and is taken and read by people who live as far away as the Falkland Islands, most of ones sales will be within fifty miles of one's kennels, for pet dog buyers seem reluctant to travel any distance to purchase a puppy. My mind instantly races back to the somewhat abortive time I spent trying to breed dogs in Caithness and my name and kennel address appeared in Yellow Pages. I spent many days banging my head against a wall after telephone calls from parochial hayseeds who said 'I want to buy a Mexican hairless dog, but I don't want to go down the line (south) to get one' and 'I don't want to pay too much for it either'. Only a handful of people in Britain breed these curious and affectionate little dogs and not one of them lives in Caithness. Yet would-be buyers expected to travel only a dozen or so miles to purchase a knock down price, hairless dog.

When about to advertise puppies it is wise to find out which papers are the most suitable for selling dogs and the best place to seek that advice is at the kennels of another breeder – one who isn't attempting to sell the same breed as you. Some papers, for instance the *Scottish Daily Record*, have a massive circulation and sometimes attract readers from quite a distance away. I live in the Scottish Borders and most of my trade comes from Glasgow and Edinburgh. Yet an advertisement placed in the *Daily Record* – the newspaper to advertise dogs if one lives in Scotland – attracted a buyer for working bearded collies who came from Bolton in Lancashire. Likewise an advertisement in newspapers such as the *Express* and *Star* or *The Birmingham Mail* will attract clients far outside what one normally considers to be the catchment areas for their newspapers. The advertising rates for these papers are high but the money is well worth spending.

Most commercial dog breeders use the Yellow and Blue newspapers which are known by different names in different areas. In Scotland these papers are known as the *Supermart* (the Yellow edition comes out on Wednesday and the Blue on Saturday). These papers are reasonably cheap to advertise in. They offer terrific value if one is selling one of the less popular breeds of dog, but not perhaps if one is advertising some of the more popular breeds such as German Shepherd Dogs and Labradors where one's advertisement becomes lost amongst similar ones.

Certain types of breed of dogs tend to be advertised in certain magazines. I have already mentioned that prior to 1980 the only place to advertise lurchers was in the *Exchange and Mart*. Now they hardly ever appear there but an amazing number of mastiffs of all sorts are now advertised there. More interesting still are the number of mastiff hybrids advertised. Some of these puppies are clearly the result of accidental matings, though mastiffs are notoriously hard to get to mate, but some are deliberate attempts to create new breeds, and frankly, though I wouldn't want one of these hybrids, I find the process of breeding new breeds fascinating. I suspect the practise of attempting to breed new types of mastiff originated in America, where breeders were attempting to produce replicas of the medieval mastiff or ban dog, by mating pit bullterriers to Neapolitan mastiffs to produce a mastiff type without the defects one associates with these dogs. Anyway anyone wishing to engage in this type of experiment finds a ready market for the stock if puppies are advertised in the *Exchange and Mart*.

*Exchange and Mart* has a coded method of allowing readers to ascertain as to whether an advertiser is a regular breeder or merely produces the odd litter for fun. Is this an indication that the man in the street is becoming increasingly hostile to the bête noir, the professional dog breeder, no matter how well maintained that breeder's kennel may be?

If the advertising rates for a particular magazine are cheap it is good policy to use quite a 'wordy' advertisement to sell one's wares. which providing the eulogy is accurate and doesn't violate the Trades Description Act, will certainly attract a larger range of would-be buyers. I'll explain. I've just reached for my copy of *SuperMart* in which I have placed an advertisement. The ad above mine reads 'German Shepherd Dog puppies – telephone number'. Mine reads – 'White German Shepherd Dog Puppies like miniature polar bears, insured, inoculated against parvo virus, licensed breeder, can deliver – telephone number'. I feel my advertisement which is slightly more costly would attract more people than would the terse one above my own. Stating that the puppies had been inoculated against parvo gives the potential buyer a sense of security and stating I was a licensed breeder assures people that the kennels are regularly inspected. The advertisement above mine gave no indication of the quality of the stock and who the breeder was. I also had my advertisement inserted in a printers box, set in bold print to make it stand out, and invites the reader to read the advertisement.

Eulogies of one's stock are excellent as long as the stock deserve the praise. For instance an advertisement for lurcher puppies stating 'These dogs will catch every hare in the country' would repel and alienate any experienced lurcher owner who is aware that hares are very difficult to catch. These advertisements insults one's intelligence leaving the seller open to prosecution under the Trades Description Act.

To write this chapter I decided to consult several professional breeders about the way they advertised their wares and received some surprising replies. Miss Eve Smail of the Toybox toy dogs who runs an impeccable hotel-type kennels in Dalkeith – an establishment that puts my own emporium to shame – believes that the very best form of advertising and by far the cheapest where sales/advertising costs are calculated, is an advertisement in the Telephone Directory Yellow Pages. I quote Miss Smail on the subject:

> Some people don't take newspapers – they get their up to date news from the television – but virtually everyone owns and telephone and hence a telephone book. An advert placed in a strategic position in Yellow Pages is the first place people will look in order to buy a dog (sic). I get at least two telephone calls a day as a result of my advertisement in Yellow Pages and while many are simply enquiring as to where they can get certain breeds of dogs I don't breed – I pass these enquiries onto other breeders – some are for the stock I keep.

I was so impressed by Miss Smail's logic that I placed an advert in the telephone book and British Telecom sent a representative to advise on the advertisement and assess the cost of advertising. A medium sized advertisement costs roughly a pound a day or about three hundred pounds a year. On the advice of the representative my own advertisement reads thus:

**RAGGENGILL KENNELS**
**Breeding German Shepherd Dogs.**
**Working Bearded Collies**
**Golden Retrievers and Toy Dogs**
**Telephone No ———**

I await the results of this advert with interest. Incidentally a standing order at one's bank allows the payments for the Yellow Pages advertisement to be spread out over a year.

Advertisements for puppies placed in the *Kennel Club Gazette* seem to produce some response, but it can be argued that the people who regularly subscribe to this magazine usually have the dogs they require anyway. Yet several breeders claim to have achieved excellent results from a mention of a litter in this Gazette. I must confess I have never advertised puppies in it.

The merits of placing an unchanging advertisement on a regular basis in any magazine is debatable. David Hancock of Sutton Coldfield places a regular weekly advertisement in *Countryman's Weekly*, and once questioned how effective the same advertisement was if seen week after week (I believe G.K. Chesterton once said that no-one ever notices the presence of a postman for he is so commonly seen). However Hancock's opinion changed somewhat when he omitted to place his customary advert one week and was inundated with telephone calls from clients enquiring as to whether he was still breeding lurchers. Personally I seldom read what are called 'persistent advertisements', but seemingly people regard a regular advertisement as a sign of stability in much the same way as clients will buy from firms which claim to have been in business from the year 1800 or Established 1867 etc.

Dog agencies are booming, and I'll be damned if I can understand why. It is possible that modern man is becoming so lazy that he is no longer prepared to glance through newspaper advertisements in an attempt to buy a puppy, and now seeks out an agent to do the perusal of advertisement columns for him? One of the earliest agencies I can remember was Glencannon Contacts which operated from a tiny council house property in Holmes Rotherham. The owner kept no dogs – though his garden was once filled with kennels – but simply kept a register of who was breeding what. The advertisement for the agency appeared in the Rotherham Advertiser for about two years 1964–66, if I remember correctly, and then the agency ceased to function. Briefly, agencies take what industrialists call a 'double bite of the cherry' for they charge the breeder to register the puppies with them and also charge the would-be purchaser a search fee for revealing the breeder's name and address -as much as £40 for registration and a further £40 for revealing the name of the breeder. Suprisingly our researchers reveal that these agencies are amazingly effective at selling puppies. Graham Nicholson of Essex bred a litter of bullmastiffs which were registered with a certain agency which was also based in Essex.

'I sold all my puppies quickly – within a week of registering with the agency and continued to receive enquiries for months after I had sold the litter. Whenever I breed another litter I shall use the same agency to sell them'.

So the advertisements have been placed and the world is set to beat a path to the door of the advertiser. Now one must deal with potential clients and I frankly admit I am not very good at dealing with people. I also admit that the next chapter is packed with anecdotes, now read on!

# 12

# Dealing With Clients

READER, THERE ARE some strange people in this world and you are about to invite some of them to visit your home. Some will be bone fide clients, really pleasant people with whom you will establish a lasting friendship. Some will waste your time and test your patience. Some will become absolute pests. Some will spend each and every weekend travelling around kennels examining dogs and puppies without the slightest intention of buying. These the breeder must learn to tolerate and above all learn to recognise and distinguish these people from genuine buyers.

A variety of people will telephone in response to the advertisement. Some will have recently lost a beloved pet and are seeking to replace it. These are often good clients, for if they have managed to keep their last dog to its dotage it is likely they will look after the puppy they buy from you. True the seller will often listen to an endless monologue about the merits of Old Ben and some of the tales will test your patience. Bite the bullet, reader, for listening to such talk is part and parcel of dog breeding and selling. Some buyers will even bring photographs of the deceased dog to show the breeder, and it is one's duty to commiserate with the clients no matter how tiring their eulogies may be. It is often wise to guide such buyers in their purchase and advise them not to buy a replica of their old dog, for comparisons are not only odious but rather inevitable and the new look alike will be unfavourably compared. One buyer once approached me to buy a black and tan German Shepherd Dog with specific markings as a replacement for his late dog. As luck or rather ill fortune would have it, I had exactly the right puppy in the kennels – except that it wasn't the right puppy for it didn't resemble Old Ben in character. Two days later the puppy was returned as the couple 'Couldn't take to it', for it simply wasn't Old Ben. I bit the bullet, refunded the money and bade them farewell but was disinclined to show them more puppies or allow another puppy on approval. There is a time to draw the line over transactions where animals are concerned and some clients are only too keen to swap and change puppies until they get one that fits in or perhaps shows some semblance of being Old Ben. Puppies just can't take this chop and change 'Can I have it on approval' life style, and suffer badly if subjected to such treatment. When someone has lost a beloved pet it is often best to suggest a totally different type of dog the replace the animal. It is fairer on the puppy anyway for nothing is likely to replace Old Ben.

On the subject of replacing pets, I am extremely chary about selling a puppy to replace an animal which has been passed on to another owner for some reason or other. I'll explain. Clients who are seeking another puppy after they had to give the last whelp away for some reason must be considered carefully. My child has asthma is the most common reason that people give for parting with their dog. Dollars to doughnuts when these people have tired of the puppy you will sell them, the child will suddenly develop the self same allergy.

I am always careful about selling a puppy to a couple who parted a few months ago and had to sell the dog, but now happily are back together again. The chances are that they will part again shortly, and you the breeder will have to rehome the whelp – no mean task, for few people want an untrained, half grown young dog which may have acquired a number of undesirable characteristics during its stay with the temporary owners.

I can't resist telling the following tale, which has a hint of sadness, about the whole macabre business. When I lived in Caithness I advertised for kennel help on a live-in basis. We had a variety of rather sad applicants and finally decided not to employ. One of the most sad people was a young man of twenty-seven who had spent several years in a mental institution on account of the fact that he kept seeing birds fluttering around the room and ducked and dived to avoid them. During his stay he met a girl friend whom he later married. We sympathised with the poor chap's plight but he really wasn't suitable for the post of kennelman. However he did form an attachment to our lurchers which literally doted on him. He later returned and asked us to sell him a puppy, but on questioning, the young man revealed that he had had several lurchers but every time he spent any time away from the house, even for a few brief hours, his wife retaliated by taking the dogs to the vet to be destroyed, need I add, that I declined to sell him a puppy!

First time dog owners, usually young couples who are on the brink of starting a family, are common buyers of puppies and often make the best of clients. Indeed we have made many friends simply by selling such couples suitable dogs. Such people need careful help about how to rear and train puppies if they are to be happy with their purchase, and it is wise to give not only a diet sheet but also a written instruction document about how to settle in a puppy and how to give it rudimentary training. This after-care service is well worth while for it facilitates the bond between the owner and the dog and helps the owner to avoid the obvious squalls which go hand in hand with puppy rearing. It is in fact amazing to note how little most buyers know about dogs and how to raise and train them.

On the subject of allowing puppies to bond with future owners, I allow any person who has booked a puppy which is not ready to leave its dam, to come each week to visit the puppy. Many bring their children and photograph them holding the whelp. I find this a particularly good way of bonding puppies to new owners and while the inevitable Saturday/Sunday family visits are sometimes tedious I have yet to have a puppy sold by this process returned as unsuitable.

First time buyers will also need guidance on the purchase of a puppy if the puppy is to integrate into the buyer's household. For instance I should be most reluctant to sell a bossy slightly aggressive Rottweiler puppy to a man who has little in the way of personality and charisma. Such a union results in squalls with an alpha male dog crushing and subduing the character of an epsilon type man. It will be only a matter of time, a year perhaps before the puppy challenges, and challenges successfully one must add, its owner for the position, at the risk of a very apt expression and a bad pun, of 'top dog' of the house. Thus a furiously aggressive, hard biting, all too dominant dog has been created in the shortest period of time. If the would-be client is set on buying a Rottweiler, the breeder would do well to suggest tactfully that a small rather shy bitch would be a better prospect as a family dog, though men with little personality and self esteem are usually set on buying a very dominant animal that is totally unsuitable for that particular person.

Yet another tale I am afraid dear reader. Caithness is famous for its sheep and also because there is an American servicemen's base on the coast. For some reason or other many of the servicemen seek out husky type dogs as pets possibly because the breed may remind them of the U.S.A. though I cannot see the connection. No more unsuitable breed exists than a husky domiciled in sheep country, for the husky types Siberians, Malamutes and Eskimo dogs are decidedly antipathetic to sheep and show their disapproval of things ovine in the bloodiest possible manner. Yet despite many well-publicised tragedies these servicemen persist in going south and buying these very recalcitrant dogs. Breeders of this type of dog must be especially vigilant about where they sell their puppies and should not only try to dissuade buyers who live in sheep country but tell the would-be purchaser that this type of dog is very difficult to get to return to hand. It is also policy to advise purchasers to take out third party insurance when they purchase such an animal. The Kennel Club or Pet Plan operate such an insurance system, as do many others. One such husky escaped and killed fifty sheep in an afternoon. The owner was not insured and left the country without paying for the damage his dog had caused.

It is not only a matter of integrity not to push sales to a doubtful buyer, but good economic sense since the chances are that a bad placement will be returned with the owner howling for the return of his or her purchase price, for just as a dyed in the wool dog breeder is aware that there are few bad dogs but many bad owners, so the client who fails with a dog is convinced there are very few bad owners, but many bad dogs -which brings us quite neatly to the subject of refunding money if the 'sale goes sour'.

I make a point of a full refund if a client returns a puppy for any reason whatsoever – and that includes the pathetic bleat of 'we can't take to it' and 'it wont house train' (not 'we can't house train it', which is closer to the truth). This is not because I am Mr Nice Guy, neither do I have the moral integrity one reads about only in books. Indeed most of my life would not stand up to close scrutiny. I refund money – all the purchase price – simply because it finalises the deal, leaving no loose ends about which dissatisfied clients can complain. I've never been able to understand the logic of breeders who insist on returning half or a third of the price when a puppy is returned or the purchase price minus the cost of readvertising the puppy, for the dissatisfied client goes away with a sour taste in his or her mouth and often considers himself cheated when he is refunded only a fraction (however large the fraction) of the purchase price. Reprisals often follow and the most common sort of reprisal is to report the breeder to the RSPCA or, north of the border, the SSPCA These organisations don't have any statutory right to search one's premise's regardless of the fact that their uniform is similar to that worn by the police, but a visit from these people often leaves the kennel owner upset for a day or so, and it is best to avoid any sort of unpleasantness. I simply smile and grit my teeth and refund the full purchase price and hope to rehome the unhappy whelp into a happier home. Over the years I have refunded the full purchase price for a variety of reasons – once because the German Shepherd Dog's ears had not gone up at sixteen weeks of age – they did the week the couple returned the whelp. The bitch was never resold and now resides in pensioners' row at my kennel – a spot where retired veterans live out their last years, for I am quite a coward when it comes to 'putting down' old dogs. I once refunded fully – and gladly I must add – the purchase price to a man who returned a puppy which would not come back when it was called – 'no matter how hard I whacked him'. The sad little mite was terrified of its owner and took months to rehabilitate. I gave the youngster away to a friend who dotes on the now ageing animal. I would have refunded ten times the purchase price just to relieve my guilt at selling the puppy to such a brute. Another returned the puppy – a beautiful blue bearded collie – because it barked when he shut it in a dark shed below the pigeon loft, where surprisingly it wasn't happy! I also paid this idiot's travelling expenses to return the whelp. He left quite satisfied with the deal uttering 'You are a gentleman sir', the stock in trade term for those who believe they've pulled a fast one on a sucker – as he probably had – but I slept better that night knowing I could end the misery the puppy had experienced. Indeed I repeat, the more I see of people, the more I love my dogs.

However I shall now return to the subject of sales techniques rather than bitter diatribes about unsuitable clients. I never push a sale no matter how much I need the money, and in many ways I am rather gauche over dealing with people. Hancock is a master salesman. He is always polite even when he has to deal with the most unpleasant, and I have yet to see him upset or rattled. He takes every client around every inch of his kennels at Sutton Coldfield and answers every question asked no matter how imbecilic it may be. Not once does he pressure the client but rarely does the client come away without purchasing a puppy. The world of the lurcher keeper is a shadowy one, and many of Hancock' s clients are decidedly seedy and unsavoury. Yet he deals with those who wear Romany dicklos (a neckscarf) in the same way as he does with clients who sport Etonian ties. Hancock's technique is both effortless and flawless and he is prepared to allow the all too obvious time wasters to visit his kennels every weekend. 'Everyone who comes is a potential client' is his motto.

Eve Smail deals with an entirely different segment of society – the more fastidious, more careful toy dog purchasers. Unlike David, Eve believes that the sale of a toy dog is best conducted over coffee in her immaculate living room, for the type of person who buys a toy dog is unlikely to be impressed by a cold walk around the kennels. Hence Eve brings puppies into the house to sell them and she is very successful both on the show bench and as a sales person. Indeed I do wish I possessed either David's or Eve's sales techniques. Sadly I do not, and I feel I must lose many sales because of my impatience and gaucherie.

I do try to be polite to would-be buyer's, but somehow I invariably fail when faced with that anathema – the bidder. I'll explain. Despite the fact that my advertisement always states the price of the puppy I am trying to sell there are those who are never happy unless they haggle over prices. Some will pretend they didn't read the advertisement properly and offer a hundred pounds less than the price advertised. These will usually have selected the puppy they want and are apparently ready to leave before they start their ploy – handing over £150 rather than £250. Bidder's pretend to have misunderstood the advertisement in the hopes the seller will relent and reduce the price. Others are a little more forthright in their approach and utter 'Will you take a bit less'. Should such people clutter up the checkout till at Sainsbury's bidding for each tin of beans, the general public would consider them stark staring mad, but such people think little of bidding for a puppy; I detest this sort of buyer and won't deal with them. People who haggle over the price of the whelp will be none too generous about giving the puppy the correct food, and will be a shade reluctant to inoculate it. Hence no matter how much I need the money, I will not sell a puppy should a would-be client attempt to bid for it.

By far the worst bidders are farmers who seem hell bent on getting cut price puppies and as I breed working bearded collies, I encounter quite a few farmers. The majority plead poverty when asked to pay full price for a working dog or puppy even though they arrive in a brand new Mercedes or BMW car. A common form of bidding amongst farmers is to ask for 'luck money'. I'll explain. Let us assume the price asked for a working bearded collie puppy is £180, which is about the price expected at the time of writing. Some will ask for £50 luck money (with the money return's the luck) to be returned to them, so effectively they are paying only £130 for the whelp. I don't do this and don't budge from the price asked – and neither do any other reputable breeders, I may add.

I really must relate the tale of one bidder – a farmer – who arrived to buy a puppy in May 1996. This man had his party piece worked out before he arrived and chose a particularly splendid puppy from the litter. When I asked for my £180 the man stated 'I thought it was only £150' and held out £150 stating that it was all he had brought with him. I dislike people who believe I am recovering from a lobotomy and reached forward to take back the puppy. The bidder seemed to relent, well almost, and uttered. 'I live three hundred miles away from you', as if this justified his behaviour, and added 'I'll just run to Lanark to get the rest of the money from the bank', still clutching the puppy which he intended to take with him. I knew I would never have seen the money or the puppy again, but I gently took the puppy away from him knowing that he certainly had the full £180 on his person. My bidder/conman resolved to go to Lanark – a return trip of an hour, if he hurried. Fifteen minutes later he returned with the £30 plus his £150 – he could not have possibly driven to Lanark in that time – but in the intervening quarter of an hour I had sold his puppy to another client who arrived shortly after his departure. The farmer ranted and raved, fulminating about my lack of trust in him – curious behaviour under the circumstances perhaps – and finally left to drive three hundred miles home, I do hope he learned from his experiments in mendacity, for it really was a lovely puppy that I sold to a lady from Motherwell, who is now winning in obedience trials with the dog.

I cannot resist the next tale, if only to illustrate just how illogical people can be, and if the reader believes I have a phobia about farmers, well perhaps I have. I am often approached by shepherds who suggest that I should be selling dogs to those who work them for less than the price I sell to pet owners because, 'the dogs will be doing a job'. Now I just cannot follow such logic, if logic is the correct term for this line of thought, for my first concern is for the future welfare of the pup and I've seen shepherds at field trials who keep their dogs in wretched conditions. Likewise lurcher breeders, whose advertisements for their puppies are offered with 'For Sale to working homes only'. The lot of many 'working' lurchers is simply frightful, one must add.

The vast majority of clients will be scrupulously honest however and thankfully bidders are rare. Most will be satisfied with their purchase, if the puppy is healthy and well reared and few will make a pig's ear of rearing and training the whelp. I've made some good friends from selling puppies, friends who still visit me long after the puppy has aged and died, and I am godfather to the children of some of these clients. However there are some oddities wanting to buy puppies, and tales of these people are worth relating if only from the entertainment value they gave me – though at the time their attentions were far from entertaining. One character called Anthony had a distinctive squeaky voice that was instantly recognisable. He telephoned repeatedly about a variety of advertisements giving a different name each time he called, and even though he promised to come and see the puppies and me, I never met him. His antics continued for nearly five years and once he called himself Professor Moriaty though one did not need to be Holmes to decide Anthony was, to put it mildly, a little strange. Eventually I became a little worried about Anthony, particularly after I read an account of one of the American mass murderer who regularly telephoned his victims re advertisements before visiting them and chopping them to pieces. My worries ceased when I spoke to another breeder about this strange character who kept phoning although I neglected to mention the man's name. 'Oh that's probably Anthony', she laughed, 'we have had him calling for nearly ten years. We have never met him but I believe he is quite harmless' she added thereby setting my mind at ease.

A slightly less pleasant character was an English woman who telephoned one evening about an advertisement I had placed to sell White German Shepherd Dogs. I related all the ancestors of the stock I had for sale, and how I had had the stock tested for haemophilia and hip dysplasia, while she chatted happily about her own life. Finally on a more sombre note she added 'I lost my own dog a few weeks ago and my mother just last week and the trouble is I haven't got a bean (sic)'. Politely I concluded the telephone call saying 'Well if you have no money to buy another GSD you would not have the money to keep one', and politely replaced the receiver. I had forgotten about the good lady until a month later when I advertised a litter of bearded collie puppies and the same lady telephoned with the same tale of woe finishing the lament with 'but I haven't got a bean'. By now anyone would have smelt a rat and my fears were confirmed when she telephoned again regarding Lucas terrier puppies with the same reply. What motivated these telephone calls will always be a puzzle. Was the lady incredibly lonely and running up a huge telephone bill and simply phoning anyone who had a telephone? Or had she a more sinister motive seeking out free puppies to sell on to, horror of horrors – vivisectionists!

For sheer cheek one would be hard pressed to beat the Glaswegian who telephoned in 1996 and came out with 'I am an old aged pensioner, will you give me a White GSD puppy – a good one?' he added compounding his sheer gall. I explained politely that rearing a GSD was an expensive business but he rang off petulantly calling me 'a mean bastard!'.

Just now and again a particular person becomes a pest after purchasing a puppy from the breeder, and my own particular Nemesis was a Mrs. Hamilton. Mrs. Hamilton sent her daughter to choose a puppy from a litter of GSD's and the good lady chose a fine very large male. Two months later Mrs. Hamilton telephoned to say the puppy's coat wasn't what she really wanted and would there be compensation for this. Apparently the coat was quite short and Mrs. Hamilton wanted a long coated puppy. I offered to refund the lady's money without question but Mrs. Hamilton wanted some form of compensation for the absence of long guard hairs on her puppy. A month later she telephoned again to say the tips of the puppy's ears were tinged with yellow – most white German Shepherd puppies sport these yellow tipped ears – and this I explained to her, but she was adamant the puppy was a crossbred Labrador for 'the man on the Glaswegian market – who knew dogs' (savants of this nature seemingly abound) had told her it was. Once again I offered to refund the money and mentally I worked out how to rehome the puppy, which by now was probably a disturbed animal, but Mrs. Hamilton wanted to keep the puppy but once again insisted I paid her compensation. Another week passed and once again Mrs. Hamilton was on the telephone asking for compensation as one of the puppy's ears was pricked but the other dropped – eventually both ears would become erect, and this time I asked to speak to Mr. Hamilton. He came on the telephone and In a world-weary voice said 'Before you start mate, I sympathise with you. She tries this game with everyone even when she buys a pair of shoes and frankly I'm so fed up that I am leaving her'. I never heard from Mrs. Hamilton again.

There will be times when no matter how good the quality of the stock and how cleverly worded the advertisement, the breeder will be unable to sell his puppies. Puppies which are ready for selling in midsummer, when many people are contemplating going on holiday and a dog would not be practicable until they return home, are difficult to sell. The threat of recession has equally adverse effects for a time at least. Again I refer to Hancock's diaries during the miners strike in the 1980s. Hancock found that at the threat of a strike sales of lurchers dropped dramatically 'but as the strike progressed and the miners had spare time on their hands, sales rose to record levels, perhaps despair coupled with the notion of owning a pot filling dog explains the increase in sales during the middle of the strike. As I write the prospect of an economic slump coupled with summer holidays is having a serious effect on my puppy sales and I am not alone in experiencing a drop in sales. It is at times like this that despair and the prospect of buying in an incredible amount of extra puppy food, causes many breeders thoughts to turn to the use of a dog dealer.

## Dealers

A dog dealer will, to quote Mark Twain, attempt to 'buy cheap and sell dear', which is perfectly sound economic sense, on the part of the dealer that is, for the prices offered by most puppy dealers are so small as to barely cover the cost of the rearing and registration of the whelps. For instance, a London based dealer telephoned me ten or twelve days ago and offered me £25 a piece for white GSD puppies I normally sell for £250 in Scotland. I believe the self same stock sells for £400 in the London area. Quite a large profit margin by any standards I thought at the time. Needless to say I didn't deal with him.

Yet dealers have in the past been an important sales outlet for breeders who live in remote areas of Scotland and Wales where land is cheap but there is not the population to buy up the puppies breeders produce. Frankly I am reluctant to treat such dog dealers with the contempt that certain doggy magazines advise. Some of these dealers are fairly honest though the prices they are prepared to pay for puppies is ludicrous. Still dealers kennels would not be in existence if there were not breeders who were prepared to sell puppies at the prices dealers offer. Some dealers are somewhat less than honest however, and I know of a story of breeders who are owed a great deal of money by some of the London based dealers, and what is worse the prospect of recovering the money owed to these breeders looks decidedly remote. I shan't comment, on the condition of some of these dealers kennels for that is the role of' the environmental health officers, besides which I knew very little of the life style of these dealers for I have only dealt with one. Cue for another tale I am afraid.

Shortly after I arrived in Caithness I was approached by a London based dealer – there is an enormous market for pedigree puppies in London – with a view to buying a whole litter – ten puppies in all - of white GSD's. I had just retired from teaching and frankly I needed the money, and he offered a reasonable deal – about a third of the price I normally ask for puppies. However my part of the deal was to deliver the puppies to his kennels in London. A trip which made Marco Polo seem a little like a stay-at-home. However as I've stated I needed the money and hence set out south calling at Perth, Glasgow, Preston and Birmingham on the way, in order to feed and water the puppies.

On arriving at the kennels in London, a lavish spacious place and so up-market as to be a little bewildering to a man from the sticks, a vet awaited me and on examining each and every whelp pronounced they were one of the best litters he had ever seen. He did in fact compliment me on the way the puppies had been reared. I was paid promptly and set out immediately to Caithness thankful that the transaction had been honoured and I was able to go home again.

I heard nothing from the dealer for nearly two years but on Christmas Eve he telephoned to say that he had sold one puppy to a rich Arab called Mr. Saleem and the puppy now had a defective mouth – one tooth was apparently out of line. Despite the age of the dog I immediately volunteered to refund Mr. Saleem's money but my dealer now adopted a voice change which clearly indicated that he had once been a very junior police officer – ex policemen usually speak quickly and adopt a staccato way of enunciating phrases – a habit which irritates rather than intimidates me. 'Oh that it was that simple' he uttered. 'Mr. Saleem has been to an orthodontist – and expensive orthodontist' he elaborated, 'and this expensive orthodontist' he repeated to impress me, 'has said the damage. to the tooth had been done in the in the nest during its rearing with you' he added. Again I repeated my offer to refund the money but my dealer now added 'and Mr. Saleem expects a 'sweetener', he paused a moment to gather financial momentum, 'of several thousand pounds, for Mr Saleem is a perfectionist – a rich perfectionist' he stated to lend force and weight to his demands. I repeated the offer to refund the money and replaced the receiver. A few days later I received a letter sent recorded delivery stating that my dealer intended taking me to court to retrieve several thousand pounds and he added, the publicity would ruin me. This would not have taken very much for, as usual, I was financially on my uppers. Hence once more I made the offer of refunding the purchase price of the whelp, this time putting my offer in print.

A year later I received another letter stating that the dealer had been abroad for a year and had returned to find that I had not paid Mr. Saleem the several thousand pounds for selling him a puppy with one tooth out of alignment and then repeated his threat of taking me to court. This time I ignored his letter.

A month later I received a telephone call from a man with a distinctive Asian accent who announced that he was Mr. Saleem. I waited for the complaint but none came for Mr. Saleem simply wanted me to sign the Kennel Club transfer forms. 'But the dog is defective, isn't it Mr. Saleem?'. A puzzled voice replied 'No of course not, I paid (he mentioned a sum some eight times the price the dealer had paid for the dog) he is a most excellent dog'. It transpired that despite the apparent opulence of the kennels and house, my dealer was in financial difficulties and hence to use an appropriate Damon Runyon expression, was 'putting the bite on me'. How on earth he expected a medically discharged teacher living on a very tiny pension to finance his ventures I really don't know, but the caper made me intensely suspicious of dealers in general.

## Returned Puppies

At this point it is perhaps advisable to mention the homing of returned puppies and if 'Hercules' evil uncle decided to attempt to devise a thirteenth labour to break the man/god's athletic back, this would be to rehome a wild, unruly untrained dog which had, to use a colloquial expression, 'got the better of its owner'.

Some of these animals are not only untrained but slightly deranged by mishandling and take some time to resettle and rehome. I am often amazed at just how inept the general public are at handling and training the most gentle of dogs. Just recently a very gorgeous merle bearded collie was returned to us by a young lady who had no time to train him. It refused to come to her and blinked like a horse at the Calgary Stampede when placed on a leash. How the owner managed to exercise poor bewildered Max is a puzzle, and at the time of writing he is still being trained in order that he might be rehomed.

To try and rehome a wild, untrained dog of this type without retraining the animal is utter madness, for not only would a future owner be disturbed at the sight of a wild eyed and apparently crazy animal bucking on a lead but anyone with the stupidity to take on such a dog would almost certainly return the dog crazier and more disturbed than before in days after rehoming it. It is therefore important to retrain a whelp or young dog before offering it to someone who is prepared to give it a home.

People are blissfully unaware that a £250 whelp which has been allowed to grow totally untrained is psychologically damaged and has lost rather than gained value during its spell of neglect. Yet another tale I am afraid.

In 1987 I sold a really sweet GSD male puppy to a Mr. Edmunds who richly deserves the appellation 'a drip', and who made me intensely suspicious of any man who referred to his wife as 'mother'. When the puppy was seven months old, Edmunds telephoned to say that it had refused to be lead trained, and anyone who can't lead train a GSD of eight weeks old richly deserves the title I gave Edmunds. As is my way, I offered to return his purchase price, an offer which Edmunds all too gladly accepted. However an hour later a cowering terrified dog reared and bucked his way out of the car followed by very rotund little 'mother'. To cut a long story short Mr. Edmunds presented me with a bill which included not only the purchase price which I had agreed to refund but also the cost of rearing the whelp, the price of inoculation and also a fifty pound bill from a man 'who knew everything about dogs', clever fellow, and had undertaken to train the GSD. I hasten to add that the man who knew 'everything about dogs' was a neighbour who didn't actually own a dog but was very, very knowledgeable and stated the whelp could not be trained. Once again I felt my head for the lobotomy scar and refused to pay the extras which amounted to over £700 and Mr. Edmunds left with a very irate 'mother'.

One of my schoolgirl helpers lead trained the puppy in a few days and I rehomed the whelp free of charge with an ex schoolmistress from Thurso. It is now a happy dog, albeit an old and tired looking dog at the time of writing.

❧

To advertise and sell an older puppy, even a retrained one, is never easy and certainly not cheap and frankly I can't blame anyone who is cautious about homing an older animal, particularly an older animal which has a history of misuse. I certainly wouldn't visit an animal shelter to get an older whelp as a pet when I could get a happy healthy puppy for the same price, so I cannot blame people who are reluctant to rehome an older puppy – even though offered free to a good home as mine are. Some newspapers will publish a 'free to a good home' ad free of charge and if this sort of advertising can be done it cuts the costs of rehoming the displaced puppy.

It is often impossible to rehome some badly mishandled youngsters and these tend to stay in my kennels for life – and the cost of keeping these dogs is financially ruinous, I must add. At the time of writing my kennels house, Mad Mollie, Mad Max and Mad Jeannie all of whom were delightful puppies but were mishandled. To add insult to injury I didn't breed Mad Max and Mad Jeannie but agreed to house them for a week or so – both are three years old and I haven't seen hide nor hair of the owners of these animals.

I have always taken care about how I home puppies and will be specially careful in the future. I've known breeders who actually resell 'displaced' dogs at a profit but to be very honest I know a lot more who groan aloud when a badly trained dog is returned to be rehomed. It has in fact always puzzled me why an owner doesn't try to rehome a whelp himself by advertising it, but then I suspect it is easier to seek out a sucker, collect one's purchase price and vanish leaving the poor devil all the trouble of sorting out and rehoming a half mad animal.

Quite a few of the problems which cause people to return young animals to the breeder can be avoided if the breeder gives advice on how to train a whelp during the formative days of its life. Most puppies are virgin clay when they leave the breeder and vices of most sorts only manifest themselves as a result of mishandling. By far the most common fault that brings about the return of a young adult dog is the animal's attempt to elevate itself up the social scale in the household. Early manifestations of this desire will be seen when the puppy attempts to cover its food tray, growling at its owner in the way it had growled at its litter mates. Later the puppy will push ahead of its owner in a bid to get out of the door and later still will growl when a person approaches its favourite chair or sleeping basket, and it is usually at this time that the puppy is returned to the breeder.

I always advise first time buyers to punish a puppy which guards its food bowl as soon as the mannerism is noticed and this prevents further attempts of assertion from the whelp. A sudden smack on the muzzle, not a furious attack from the owner, will usually convince any puppy that it is foolish to try any other tactic with its owner, but somehow my words of wisdom are often disregarded and the advice of a neighbour, 'who knows everything about dogs' is heeded.

The selling of puppies, is a legal mine field and a moral battleground. I am particularly careful about not selling puppies to people who, rightly or wrongly, I believe will not look after a puppy, but I have made so many mistakes. I have learned not to equate opulence with a good home for a dog for many times I have had families of very scruffy children and adults who return to show me the happiest of dogs, animals gleaming with health and radiating happiness without a single psychological problem. I have also seen similarly bred puppies whose owners fetched them in immaculate brand new Mercedes cars brought back as physical and mental wrecks, their lives made hellish simply because they shed their coats. A good home for a dog is a happy one not necessarily a rich one. Love not wealth constitutes the vital ingredient of a good home. Some of the happiest dogs I've ever seen were reared on a cheap diet, supplemented with kitchen scraps and tender loving care. I have also seen dogs reared on the most expensive food which were returned in bad condition simply because their owners had no real affection for them.

# 13

# Hand Rearing a Litter

JUST NOW AND again a bitch is unable to rear her litter and the puppies have to be hand reared. Reader, think long and hard before on embarking on such a project, and then set three weeks of your life aside – three weeks, twenty-four hours a day and make no plans for any other venture for that period. The process of hand rearing a litter is one of the most time consuming, mentally taxing process known to man. The self same process may also destroy your morale as for no reason in particular, puppy after puppy seems to die – and this alas is quite frequently the case.

Firstly let us examine why a bitch is unable to rear her own puppies, and there are many reasons for this inability. Some bitches just do not have any maternal instincts and will, on the appearance of puppies emerging from their bodies, attack them with gusto killing and maiming them with an unwholesome ferocity. I have sometimes seen this behaviour in terrier bitches which are mated during their first seasons and are bewildered by the appearance of puppies emerging from their vaginas. Some will recoil in horror at the sight of these newcomers and abandon them, moving away from the litter and scattering them around the box. Some of them will be very resentful of these intruders and after examining them carefully nip and kill them. This peculiarity usually corrects itself when the bitch is mature enough to breed – in her second or third season perhaps, and parturition is followed by a very normal rearing programme.

Forgive the following digression but this behaviour pattern rather begs the question just how instinctive is the maternal instinct. If the disposition were innate as Mr McDougal would have us believe then surely the quality would manifest itself during the first whelping no matter how young the bitch is at the time of parturition. When I consider this problem I cannot but question current thinking concerning instinctive behaviour. Only once have I encountered a mature bitch which displayed no mothering instinct and was savagely hostile to any puppy she produced. During the period when I was endeavouring to produce a distinctive new breed, the Plummer Terrier, I sought out a variety of excellent terrier types to refine the breed I was creating. At that time one of the best breed types was bred by Eric Taylor of Etwall, Derby whose stock produced animals of excellent confirmation and fine working ability although these Russell types were a shade short on nose. I bought a bitch from this strain in 1968, a fine black and white bitch Eric called Badger whose only cosmetic defect was that her ears lifted slightly but not to the extent that they were pricked but lifted just enough not to be showable in top class working terrier shows. I mated her to Rupert one of my foundation studs who was homozygous for tan and white factor so I expected a fine litter. I sat with Badger as she whelped – she was three years old at the time – and was horrified to see the puzzled look on her face as the puppies emerged from her body. A telephone call, a knock at the door, I cannot remember which attracted my attention away from the bitch and I returned to find her litter torn and bloody. She produced her last puppy while I supervised the whelping and she didn't wait for it to escape the foetal sac but shook it savagely, killing it instantly. She whelped easily and had plenty of milk yet she was decidedly hostile to her puppies. Next year I mated her again and took the puppies from her as soon as she produced and showed hostility to them and laboriously reared them by hand, although one was fostered by a sycophantic bitch appropriately named Creepy because of her grovelling attitude when I appeared in the run. I gave Creepy's foster child away to an old girl friend, and she later bred from the animal who reared the puppies as well as any bitch I've known, but two of Badger's grandchildren, the daughters of Creepy's foster child, displayed the same lack of mothering instinct as did their grandmother. This rather begs the question as to whether or not man should allow or encourage the continuance of blood lines which are patently unsuitable for breeding. Animals such as bulldogs etc. which are physically incapable of normal births are clearly unsuitable for continuing a bloodline as are bitches which manifest no maternal instinct. This however is a hobby horse I've ridden far too long so I shall desist from discussing this subject further.

Sometimes a bad mistake on the part of the breeder can cause a bitch to abandon or savage her litter – another tale I am afraid.

One night I received a telephone call from a fellow breeder whose cairn terrier bitch had refused to give milk despite veterinary treatment and the breeder was at his wits end to find a way of rearing the puppies. It was the time of the summer holidays at a time in my life I had quite a run of luck at the Hall Green dog training track backing pedigrees rather than form – it was to cost me dearly during the next season. Hence I did not get my customary summer job to tide me over the holidays – I once worked part-time as a septic tank emptier – for I have no pride where money is concerned. The fact that my win at the track (I was to repay it ten times over later, what a misspent life you've had, Plummer) meant that I had the holidays to myself and my cairn breeding friend knew this. Hence I was more or less tricked into the daunting prospect of hand rearing a litter of cairn puppies for a man who was decidedly ungrateful and would have vilified me had a single puppy died during the long tedious hand-rearing process. I cursed my ill luck for, for the first time in ten years I had no intention of working through the summer holidays and had intended to spend my time rebuilding my tumbled down cottage.

However I remembered a friend of mine whose greyhound bitch was about to whelp a litter of lurcher puppies to a half bred collie dog and as luck would have it whelped a small litter of only three puppies. I immediately passed the telephone number of the friend to the cairn breeder and suggested that he contacted the man with a view to fostering the cairn puppies on the greyhound bitch, who was easily capable of rearing both litters. I believe the process of fostering proceeded in a ham-handed fashion for the greyhound bitch not only refused to accept the cairn puppies but also rejected her own puppies once tainted with the scent of the newcomers. I've explained the process of fostering in an earlier chapter. The outcome of the matter was that I was pressured into rearing both the cairn and lurcher puppies by hand and I returned to school exhausted and sleep shotten. Truly the saying that there is one born every minute is correct, but after my birth there must have been a five hour lapse before the next sucker entered the world. Moses Aaron Smith, the Romany savant, once described my curious lifestyle as 'Gullible's travels'!

Sometimes a bitch will die during the process of whelping, at one time a fairly common occurrence but rare today due to advances in veterinary science, but just now and again a bitch will not survive the birth of her puppies. Hence the puppies must be reared by hand if they are to survive. Likewise a bitch may refuse to let down milk despite oxytocsin injections which facilitate the process and once again it is necessary to rear the litter by hand though if the bitch is willing to allow the puppies to suckle, even though they gain no sustenance, it is wise to leave the puppies with her, to hand feed them but allowing the dam to clean the whelps. I've reared many litters by hand – far too many litters as it happens – and I believe the worst foster mother, providing she doesn't harm the foster whelps, does a much better job of rearing puppies than the most efficient human being armed with the most modern equipment. I've known two bitches, both GSD's, which refused to give milk yet cleaned the puppies and cared for them until weaning, while I fed them every two or three hours until they were capable of eating solid food. The bitches both vomited partly digested food for the puppies from the time the puppies were roughly seventeen days old as if to apologise for the fact I had to hand feed them. I once engaged in the daunting prospect of rearing premature puppies fully formed but born to a bitch when she was only fifty four days pregnant, and the bitch while she didn't produce milk, attempted to clean and nurse the whelps. I confess I lost the entire litter and I freely admit I have had little success rearing premature puppies of any breed though I believe there are professional puppy rearers who specialise in rearing even premature toy breed puppies.

The hand rearing of orphaned puppies or rejected puppies has progressed so much since the days when Metcalf advertised his fleet of foster bitches in 1921, although I repeat that if a foster bitch can be obtained, for Heaven's sake use the animal rather than hand rear the whelps. In the 1920s breeders suddenly realised that cows milk was really not suitable for rearing a puppy, for a bitch's milk is roughly five times as nutritious as milk obtained from a cow. Hence the process of 'reducing' cows milk by boiling and evaporation to concentrate the milk was adopted. Yet as late as the 1930s breeders advocated watering down cow's milk (cows are bigger than dogs ergo the milk must be stronger!) and this nonsense was still publicised in reputable doggy magazines at the time. How these breeders reared a single puppy on watered down cow's milk is mystifying and the death rate amongst orphaned and rejected puppies was distressing, even amongst those who used cows milk by boiling it down to a fifth of its volume. Some of the advice offered in many 'dog books' clearly indicates that the writers have had little experience of kennel management and gleaned their research by copying from other books. Indeed even a win at Crufts seldom qualifies a person to write a book about breeding and rearing puppies.

Today proprietary dog milks are so readily available that it is foolish to attempt to reduce cows milk to hand rear puppies. There are several proprietary brands of puppy rearing milk, including a variety of American products available. Such milks are carefully balanced to have the correct nutrients and it is wrong to add anything to them. The makers instructions should be obeyed to the letter and no attempt to concentrate or dilute the feed must be attempted.

The temperature at which hand reared puppies are kept is all-important. Readers may remember that J.M. Evan's paper on neonatal deaths and the effect of hypothermia on puppies. Evans reports that a temperature of 70°F will produce hypothermia very quickly in isolated new-born puppies, so it is imperative that a temperature of 80°F plus is maintained in the rearing box for at least six or seven days after the birth of the puppy. A thermometer is fairly essential if a litter is reared under somewhat Heath Robinson conditions – a hot water bottle etc., but too high a temperature is just as damaging as too little heat. It is important to watch and listen to the puppies to ascertain whether the whelps are happy in the condition in which they are kept. Cold puppies will bleat with a characteristic cry, and puppies which are too warm tend to wriggle to get away from the source of heat. America is so far in front of Britain where dog welfare is concerned and produces small incubator kits which facilitate the rearing of puppies. These kits are thermostatically controlled and have the same moisture regulating devices (to prevent dehydration) that are fitted to high class pheasant egg incubators. These kits are usually made of some sort of clear plastic so that the whelps can be observed without disturbing them, and are excellent value for anyone who owns a large kennel and wishes to take on the onerous task of hand rearing puppies. In 1996 I adapted a cheap chicken egg incubator – a metal device – to rear puppies, but with limited success for the puppies became damp because of the condensation within the metal incubator, and I am presently engaged in importing a purpose built puppy incubator from Chicago – an incubator which received excellent reports in the American dog press. There can only be a limited market for such devices so it is hoped that the firm which manufactures this equipment stays in business if only to supply me with parts! I attempted to keep my home-made puppy rearer at 84°F for the first few days after the birth of the puppies and then reduced the temperature to 80°F after that time until the puppies were three weeks old after which they lived at the temperature in my kitchen where the whelps are reared

The puppies milk supply must be warmed to the temperature of the lactating bitch, 100°F approximately will suffice and the whelps must be fed every two hours day and night. Three complete weeks must be set aside if the litter is to be reared by hand and no commitment, shopping trip or day out must be considered during that time. It is likely that the person rearing these puppies will feel physically exhausted and mentally jaded long before the first week of the venture, and the inevitable sense of despondency increases out of proportion if the whelps start to die after three or four days of hand feeding. This sense of despondency will be increased tenfold if a person really gets to know the whelps that are being reared, and worst still gives the litter names and forms attachments to each individual puppy. The combination of sleeplessness, physical exhaustion and despair when the puppies start to die can have a terrible effect on the health of any person, and I have nothing but praise for the odd few who attempt to a sort of living by hand rearing other peoples puppies – cue for tale.

I hate to harp on about farmers and the meanness that characterises some of these people, but I have seldom encountered even a rich farmer who was generous with his praise or money. Some time ago in 1981 a local farmer bought a Great Dane bitch with a view to selling puppies, which he was assured would sell for £450 each, as indeed good quality Great Dane puppies will. So he travelled south and bought a quite good quality blue bitch which he told me with some delight he 'bid' the owner down from £450 to £200 and hence was delighted at his acumen and almost contemptuous of the breeder who sold him such a bargain. He referred to the lady who had sold him this paragon as the Old Biddie, and related how he had haggled over the price for two hours before the breeder had relented and agreed to the price this man offered for the animal. Now perhaps I am too cautious but I cannot but wonder why someone would want to sell such an adult bitch (ready for breeding as my farmer associate put it) when there was a market for good class puppies at the price the whelps were said to fetch, and my suspicions deepened when the farmer produced a large number of championship show rosettes the bitch had supposedly won. When I mentioned the sort of class of dog that won in these shows my associate's pride and his haggling technique increased tenfold, and he now spoke of the Old Biddie as the Old Sucker. Sucker the good lady certainly wasn't and as I went over the animal remarking on her fine structure and condition, I noticed two scars which indicated that the bitch had undergone at least two caesarean sections. I mentioned this to the farmer who ridiculed my lack of knowledge of dogs and matters canine, for according to him the bitch had never produced a registered puppy. I know my job however, and sat by as he went deeper and deeper into the quagmire that awaits any foolhardy avaricious dog breeder. A month passed and the bitch came into season, though she was not the picture of health and condition she was when he bought her, for I suspect the farmer was a little sparing with food.

So he ventured south again to see the breeder and to use the stud dog of her selection which was owned by a nearby neighbour of the breeder. My associate promptly haggled over the stud fee for two hours thereby reducing the fee by nearly ten pounds and the bitch returned mated.

Her condition was quite obvious by the time she was five weeks pregnant for I saw her frequently when her owner came to beg free of charge raw meat from my freezer. 'You've got such a lot Brian, you won't miss a few pieces' and so saying he loaded up the boot of his BMW to the gunwails with the inevitable utterance 'I'll give you a drink later'. I hate this expression, particularly when it was patently obvious he did not intend to pay for the twenty pounds worth of flesh he had taken at one sitting, but I am by nature a coward and gritted my teeth in impotent rage.

The bitch went into labour on time and she was obviously experiencing difficulties when he brought her to me for 'veterinary treatment costs money', I quote. It was patently obvious that the bitch needed a caesarean section to allow her puppies to be born, and the farmer reluctantly agreed to the operation which cost £60 if I remember correctly – and I do. The bitch produced a dozen puppies all of which were sound but despite injections of oxytocsin she failed to produce milk so once again the now weary farmer brought them to my house. 'Is there a chance of your rearing them', he muttered adding 'I'm a bit busy at the moment'. Now 1981 was a tumultuous year for as far as I was concerned for I wrote three books that year and featured in the TV documentary '*A Hunting Man*', a costly time consuming stab at my fifteen minutes of fame, so I declined to agree to rear the puppies for the man. However I mentioned that I knew a lady who made pin money, nothing more, by performing the service of hand rearing puppies from a day old.

The old lady lived in one of those unpleasant cottages which are typical of someone whose dogs had taken over the lives of the house, for a house can soon become a hovel if dogs take over the place – I know, it has happened to me. Yet despite the smell of her living room, a stench that resembled a knacker's yard flesh bin, and the lady's dirty appearance, she was a genius at hand rearing puppies. Hence I passed her name to the farmer and allowed him to telephone from my house, 'telephone calls are costly aren't they Bri'. He telephoned and spoke to the lady but after a moments conversation I saw him recoil in horror as though someone had hit him hard in the solar plexus so I gathered she had mentioned a price for her services, and ashen white he replaced the receiver. 'The old swindler wanted £150 to rear the litter to eight weeks of age' he gasped. 'I told her I would rather give you a tenner or so – he meant me – and chanced my luck'. One hundred and fifty pounds was a pitiful sum to ask to hand rear a litter of Great Danes to eight weeks of age and as I watched my associate's face I made a mental calculation how much food alone would cost and I suspected she had some connections with the local foxhound kennels to obtain offal to rear the puppies so cheaply. I was amazed at the tiny cost of the lady's three weeks sleepless labour and convinced the good woman was some form of financial anachronism in pricing her labour at Victorian wages. I was snapped back to reality by the enraged hiss of my farmer friend 'I'll never pay that price', he almost squealed and repeated 'I'd rather slip you a tenner for your troubles'. Of course I declined his generous offer and he set out trying to rear the litter himself begging his first two cans of milk powder from me. 'Milk costs money doesn't it Bri?'. I watched rather dispassionately as he arrived to announce the death of each and every puppy until the last whelp squeaked and squawked into the hereafter. His bitterness at dogdom and doggy people knew no bounds and I believe he blamed me for his financial losses. 'I'd have given you a drink for your troubles but I'm not paying the old skinflint £150', he repeated each day as another puppy expired. The good lady would have possibly reared the entire litter for Danes are lusty dogs and if my calculations were correct my associate would have sold his twelve puppies for £5400. As a result of his refusal to pay a pathetic sum of money he failed to rear a single puppy.

Quite as important as the quality of the food ingested by puppies and the temperature at which they are kept, is the cleaning action of the bitch's tongue. Bitches repeatedly lick puppies not merely to clean them but to stimulate the actions of the bowels and the bladder. The ancients were fairly convinced this licking action determined the shape of the adult animal so different was the shape of the foetus from the mature creature, hence the expression 'licking someone into shape'. The action however is vital to the puppy's body functions. To imitate the action of the bitch's tongue, moistened paper tissue can be used to clean the belly and the anus of the whelp after every meal, an action which usually causes the puppy to both urinate and defecate. In some ways I am quite lucky about the choice of dogs I keep, for I own some very maternal bitches which will not only lactate mid season at the merest sight or sound of a puppy but will readily clean up the hand-reared whelps. I keep one bitch, a white headed bearded collie bitch called Tilly, (she is a colour not liked by farmers for the white head is said not to engender the respect of sheep – bunkum, Tilly would terrorise a lion), who really enjoys the role of foster mother despite the fact that her age now denies her motherhood. However she stands by tail wagging while I feed the puppies and 'tops and tails' the whelps with her tongue after they are fed. Such an animal is a treasure in any kennels for the more natural the art of rearing a puppy is, the better the whelp thrives.

The first week of the hand-reared puppy's life is the most critical, and when the puppy is over that period its chances of survival improves dramatically. As with naturally reared puppies the highest death rate occurs when the puppies are only three days old, a time when dehydration takes its greatest toll in the litter. Of course the survival rate of hand-reared litters is less than what would be expected if the same litter was to be reared by a dam and there are many reasons for this. First, although the whelps receive some antibody protection across the placenta the vast majority of antibodies are donated by the colostrum or first milk and this of course is denied the hand-reared puppy. To compensate for this lack of antibody conferred protection, it is important to sterilise all equipment used in puppy rearing. The puppy bottle and its rubber or plastic teats cannot be boiled for the rubber teat perishes when heated but there are mild non poisonous disinfectants such as Milton in which the bottles can be left between meals. Bedding which is regularly wetted with puppy urine should be changed equally regularly for urine and faecal matter provide a rich substitute for bacterial growth. Bitches ingest puppy faeces to keep the lair or nest clean so faecal matter and urine must also be removed twice a day or the puppy's fur becomes soiled. It is worth noting that penises and vulvas of the hand-reared whelps are often rendered red raw by the sucking action of fellow puppies and thus the genitalia of the puppies needs to be cleaned so as to prevent infection. A bitch's saliva contains a powerful disinfectant called lysozyme and this too offers the whelps some protection against bacterial infection but the hand reared puppy is denied the bitch's saliva, so extra care about puppy hygiene needs to be taken when raising a hand reared litter.

Thus the practical aspects of hand rearing a litter, now to the economics of such a practise. At the age of eight weeks, no matter how well the litter has been reared and how much care has been taken over the rearing of the litter, the puppies will not be sufficiently mature or attractive to sell. Most will be bloated, ugly with misshapen legs and a shape designed by Heronymous Bosch and it will be weeks before they regain their proper shape and attain their proper size – but they will eventually catch up with puppies which have been naturally reared with their dams. Here however, as Shakespeare put it, is 'the rub'. Puppies are most saleable at eight weeks of age and lose some of their infantile appeal at twelve weeks. Hence an orphan hand reared litter may not only be expensive and tedious to rear but also quite difficult to sell. I have reared a great many orphaned puppies and I am aware that with the correct food and attention the whelps will catch up with naturally reared puppies, but I would be reluctant to take on an eight week old hand reared whelp simply because at that age the puppy is invariably unsightly.

As has been my custom, I have garnered opinions from both ends of the spectrum of dog breeding, namely the highly successful Toy Box toy breeder Eve Smail and at the other pole the worlds most successful lurcher breeder David Hancock. They have this to say on the subject of hand rearing puppies.

Eve Smail interviewed 11th April, 1998.

> Because of the problems which attend breeding toy dogs (there is a tendency to breed smaller and smaller toy dogs) there are many difficulties whelping. Indeed I have always regarded breeding Pomeranians, the breed for which the Toy Box kennel is famous, as being a financial black hole that sucks up all my money and gives little or no return for my investment. As breeding problems are by no means uncommon, hand-reared litters are common, and hence I employ a professional hand rearer to do this work for me. I am quite capable of hand rearing puppies myself but I will concede that this lady is better at the job and I do not begrudge the nominal price she charges for her services. I am not concerned about the misshapen puppies which arrive back with me at eight weeks of age for I know they will grow into quite shapely adults – besides which much of my trade in Pomeranians is for older dogs of show quality and there is usually a market for good class adult toy dogs anyway.

David Hancock interviewed 4th June 1998.

> It just isn't worth my while rearing puppies by hand, though God knows I've done enough of it, and Joan (David's wife) is quite good at it. I own a large kennel of lurcher breeding grey hounds and seldom do I have a single bitch whelp more than a few days before or after another. Hence I foster puppies if I can and painlessly destroy those I can't. I don't believe hand reared puppies fare as well in the tough life a lurcher has to lead and many naturally reared puppies don't come up to some people's standards so what chance has a hand-reared whelp. The cost of running on these whelps until they are saleable is also prohibitive. Most sensible trainers want puppies of eight weeks old and hand-reared whelps aren't ready to sell at that age. I foster if I can if not I put the puppies down – fortunately most greyhounds are easy whelpers and I get little trouble with orphaned litters.

Might I now refer to Eve Smail's professional hand-rearer mentioned earlier in this chapter, a lady who is possibly one of the best in the trade in Britain. In August 1997 I attended a seminar given by this lady and organised by the Scottish Pomeranian Club and spent a most interesting afternoon. Heather Ridley views are heretical by any standards yet her success rate at rearing even premature toy dog puppies (an incredible feat by any standards for I have only succeeded in rearing one premature litter, a litter of very hardy working bearded collies).

As Mrs Ridley receives puppies from some distance away which have not suckled in transit, she assumes them to be dehydrated and therefore gives them a drink of electrolyte solution rather than milk as a first feed. For those not au fait with the subject of electrolytes I'll explain. Mammalian body fluids are composed of weak solutions of salts, sodium potassium and magnesium chlorides and other substances including glucose. When an animal loses water via urine or by dint of scouring these salts are lost and as the salts facilitate most body functions they need to be replaced by subcutaneous injection or orally as in the case of lamb dehydration kits. Most electrolytes were once contained in two sachets, one of glucose which was mixed with the body salt sachet and added to water before use. That which was not used was thrown away for there is a tendency for glucose to ferment particularly if given nutrients to facilitate the actions of wild yeast and certain bacteria. These days ready to use solutions of electrolytes can be purchased and frankly, no kennel should be without a supply of these useful compounds,

The puppies thus re-hydrated are then fed on Carnation Evaporated milk for Mrs Ridley has had better results with this feed than with proprietary puppy rearing milk. Mrs Ridley has achieved phenomenal results at rearing puppies this way.

## 14

# An Idiots Guide to Genetics

I QUITE LIKED Stephen Hawkins erudite book *A Short History of Time* though I can't say I understood it. Apparently even Bernard Levin read to page twenty-nine before throwing in the intellectual towel and I'm not at Bernard Levin's academic standard. I simply liked the book because of its absence of baffling algebraic formulae – the only formula Hawkins uses is Einstein's $E{=}MC^2$, which I also don't understand. The fact is that the layman attempting to understand genetics and faced with a muddle of algebraic letters and symbols promptly shuts the book and pushes any data he has gleaned to the back of his mind. Hence I shall try to make this chapter as simple as possible, eschewing the use of symbols and formulae where possible, for I've written this book to entertain as well as to edify.

In true Dylan Thomas fashion – to begin at the beginning and the beginning must include a reference to one of life's enigmas, the son of an Moravian farmer, one Johann Gregor Mendel. According to Thoreau, an American naturalist cum philosopher, some people march to the beat of a different drum and this could describe Mendel's formative years. Mendel's academic life was a muddle and to quote Hermann Wendt, his teachers voted him a 'hopeless clodhopper' – he even failed his teacher's certificate – a feat in itself if my own teacher training days were anything to go by. He retreated from society, joining a monastery run by a perspicacious abbot, one Cyrillius Napp, who allowed Mendel to gravitate to the role of monastery gardener. Mendel soon began breeding plants, experimenting firstly on bean breeding and noticed that if he crossed a white flowering bean with a red flowering bean he produced beans which bore pink flowers. However when he mated two pink flowering beans together, inserting the pollen from one pistil to the other, he produced a quarter of the progeny with red flowers, one half with pink and one quarter with white flowers. To his surprise the white flowering beans mated to other white flowering beans produced only white flowering beans, and likewise the red flowering beans, while the pink flowering beans mated together still produced a quarter white, half white and a quarter red. Mendel, then turned his attentions to the breeding of peas, comparing the results of mating tall and short varieties and smooth and wrinkled skin varieties, with similar results to those he obtained from breeding beans. In short, Mendel and his successors found that the characteristics of the parents were passed on to posterity in certain numerical proportions. So just how does this research into beans and peas apply to dog breeding? Here dear reader I shall introduce you to the terms recessive, which means hidden, and dominant, which masks recessive qualities – stay with me reader, matters won't get any more complicated than this I promise.

Let us take as an example the mating of a pure-bred black and tan GSD with a white GSD where white is recessive to the black and tan pigmentation. The puppies born to the union are black and tan (BW) but carry white 'genes'. Now a dog and bitch from the union are mated together – I'll explain with a diagram.

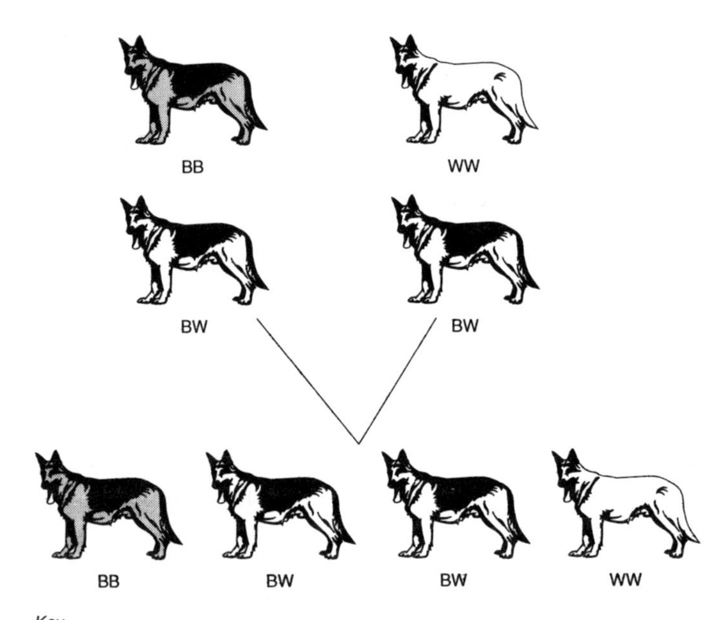

A white dog mated to another white dog will only breed white puppies. While the pure breeding black and tan dogs mated to the same colour will only produce black and tan puppies. The black and tan puppies carry white genes and when mated together will breed a litter of quarter white pure breeds, half black and tan carrying white genes and a quarter pure-breeding black and tans.

Let us take this breeding pattern one stage further. At the time of writing the overall quality of white GSD's is generally inferior to the quality and conformation of black and tan GSD's, particularly in the top class German imports which are regularly brought into Britain. So how can the breeder improve his or her white GSD's? Firstly the breeder seeks out the very best black and tan German Shepherd dog and if the owner is willing, and some won't be, mates this dog to his white GSD bitch. The resulting puppies will be all black and tan – check the previous diagram. When mated together the black and tan animals which carry the white gene (BW) will produce a litter one quarter of which will be white, which when mated to other whites will breed only white puppies which in theory at least will improve the quality of the white GSD's in ones kennels. A few generations of mating these now improved whites to superlative black and tan males will, in theory at least, produce a strain of white GSD's which is equal in confirmation etc. to the very best black and tan GSD's.

A hot potato now, namely the subject of the Parson Jack Russell terrier which when the breed received Kennel Club recognition was a very mixed breed type, with very poor quality coats, heads and toplines. Ken Bownden once described them as resembling 'a variety class at a pet show'. At that time, Gary Middleton of Kendal was breeding very typey fell terriers (an unregistered Lakeland Terrier), which regularly produced a white puppy or so in a litter of coloured whelps. This was due in part to the fact that in the late 1920's the huntsman, Fred Barker of Ousby, brought in a fine pair of white terriers from the Ilfracombe Badger Digging Club. So let us assume Middleton's dogs, superb as they are, are not pure fell terriers, and hence the genetic formulae of BW (black and tan). Thus when two fell terriers of the strain are mated together they produce at least a quarter white puppies.

There is no doubt that some of Middleton's white fell terriers were registered as Parson Jack Russell terriers and entered the common gene pool improving the type greatly, although producing a rather undesirable, untypical coat perhaps. When I published this fact in *Countryman's Weekly* my letter produced an outcry from the Parson Jack

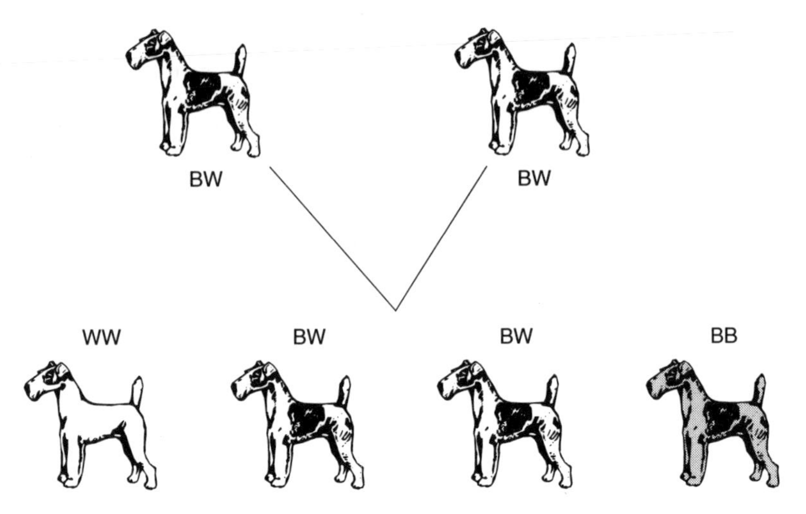


Russell Club and the almost inevitable threat of a civil action for libel. Seemingly one can question the paternity of a terrier man's children but not the origin of his terriers. In fact the improvement in head size wrought by introducing the blood of Middleton's white Lakeland terriers was tremendous.

Meanwhile back at the rank the ill-fated Cinderella terrier club, The Jack Russell Club of Great Britain did not appreciate the value conferred by the introduction of this fell Lakeland terrier bloodline. Eddie Chapman in his self-published book, *The Real Jack Russell Terrier,* comments that because of this introduction of fell or Lakeland terrier blood into the Jack Russell terrier gene pool people should not be surprised to find a black and tan puppy being born to a pair of white Jack Russell terriers. In 1976 I gave a seminar concerning the use of Mendel's law in the improvement of terrier types explaining why this could not happen. Long, long ago, even before I was born, Cassandra the daughter of Priam, Prince of Troy, was cursed by the gods to always to be able to predict the future, but never to be believed. '*Timeo danaios et donna ferentis*' if my Latin still serves me well. I now know how the poor girl must have felt! The WW terrier produced by mating two black and white terriers together could not possibly carry black and tan genes.

Certain defective characteristics are also carried in this manner, take for instance the defect known as the undershot mouth, a condition where the bottom jaw protrudes beyond the top jaw. This is acceptable though not desirable in mastiffs, and commonly found amongst English bulldogs but is considered a serious defect in most other breeds. Just a few days ago I received the following letter via the pages of

*Countryman's Weekly*, which illustrated just how little the dog owning public understand about the genetics behind dog breeding.

> I mated my fell terrier bitch to a friend's dog and bred a perfectly sound litter with good mouths. In order to breed a better class of show dog I then took my bitch to be mated to one of the best fell Lakeland terriers in Britain – two puppies out of this litter of four had terribly undershot mouths which proves this top class show dog carries this defect.

My reply would be that the bitch also carries the defect because undershot mouths are recessive to good mouths, and the dog you used for the first litter did not carry the abnormality.

At one time the ancestors of the Plummer terrier were plagued by the terrible defect called cleft palate, the absence of a roof to the mouth. This defect prevents puppies suckling and hence the whelps die about the third day after birth from dehydration. To rid the breed of the problem was a nightmare but rid the breed of the defect I did. I kept a young defective bitch puppy alive by dint of feeding it with an eye dropper  and reared her to maturity. I failed with five other cleft palate puppies I must add. I then mated her to every available male within the breed and only if the bitch produced an entire litter with good palates did I continue to breed from the male. If the dog produced a litter with a single cleft palate in the nest, I castrated the male and gave him away. His puppies, the ones that survived, were also given away as non-breeders.

I will conclude this chapter with a tale that indicates how inflexible and plain daft the world of dog breeders can be. In 1976 I was elected as the first chairman of the newly formed Jack Russell Terrier Club of Great Britain, a dubious distinction as I am not a confident, forceful man, and the clubs members warred incessantly. One day the subject of the use of Lakeland terrier blood to improve Jack Russell terriers was discussed and I stopped to explain that white puppies born to black and tan fell terriers could not carry the colour gene. 'Who says?' shouted one angry member. 'A man called Mendel' I replied, only to see the questioner bang his head on the table. 'That's with peas' uttered the exasperated head-banger, amazed at my stupidity. I tendered my resignation to Muriel Jones the next day. ' No man is an island', says John Donne, but never have I felt such terrible insularity.

# 15

# Breeding for Vivisection

I MUST ADMIT I am cringing as I put pen to paper about this subject, but write I must for puppies are an important source of income for some breeders. While I could not possibly dispassionately rear a litter of puppies to weaning age, feeding them each day and, God forbid, making friends with the mites, before shipping them out to be destroyed, as most vivisection breed puppies are I am afraid, I am aware that such a trade is essential to future canine welfare.

Readers may think on reading this book that my two main phobias, and I confess that I have many, are dealing with dog buying farmers and the dreaded parvovirus, for I mention the subject of these entities repeatedly throughout the book. However I freely admit that such was the trauma I experienced when parvovirus broke out in 1979, that I sat on the edge of my seat following the progress of scientific research while Smith Kline and Nobivac produced a suitable vaccine to protect stock against the ravages of the disease. Yet I was aware that to produce and perfect the vaccine a great many young dogs would die of the infection and a great many more would be put to sleep after testing was carried out on them. I was also aware that these dogs and puppies did not materialise out of thin air and some breeders must have been involved in producing them. Yet I was prepared to accept this research and the death of sundry puppies in order that certain laboratories would be able to produce a suitable vaccine to protect my own stock.

The subject of vivisection, which simply means the experimentation on living creatures, always conjures up the image of laboratory beagles inhaling clouds of carcinogenous nicotine smoke in otherwise sterile conditions, or of sad looking puppies, living out a caged existence in an equally sterilised laboratory, with electrodes protruding from their heads. The image extends to include strange wide-eyed

Frankensteinous lab technicians dispassionately feeding and watching the condemned, oblivious to the agonies these animals will suffer before death brings a merciful end to their sad little lives.

I am sure many animals are reared in these conditions, but veterinary tests must also be made in the field, and fieldwork is conducted in breeders' kennels under normal kennel conditions, and contrary to popular beliefs many caring breeders produce stock for vivisection. For instance one of the many breeders who produce puppies for vivisection has just completed a study on *toxicarva carnus*, the round worm, a serious pest in kennels a creature that has existed hand in hand with the wolf, the wild dog and the domesticated canine for many thousands of years. Certain litters are scheduled for research on roundworm long before they are born and, in certain cases, while the bitches are about to be mated. Both bitches and puppies are then dosed with certain chemicals to test antihelmintic qualities and side effects and at ten weeks of age the puppies are destroyed and dissected so that the scientists can test how effective these drugs actually are. The puppies are destroyed humanely and no suffering is involved. Indeed before test can be conducted on live animals of any sort, even wild rats, a licence must be obtained from the Home Office and an assurance given that no unnecessary cruelty will be practised on the recipients of the research, although the expression 'unnecessary' is open to interpretation.

Not all research animals are put to sleep once research has been terminated. A friend opened his kennels to researchers concerned with the dog flea and the far more common cat flea. Animals are injected with systemic insecticide and the fleas are later combed from the fur for testing. No further harm is perpetrated on the animals involved in the experiment.

At the time of writing, certain kennels in the USA, where licences to perform test and experiments on animals are equally difficult to obtain, are producing strains of border collies which are extremely susceptible to avemectides, such as the popular antihelmintic and insecticide Ivomec to which most strains of border collie are susceptible. Some of these strains show obvious adverse reactions to even the slightest trace of toxic avemectide. Reports of another strain of border collie which is very susceptible to any of the corona viruses (corona – a crown shaped organism) have been published. At the time of writing there is little evidence to suggest that this type of virus has an economic importance among dog breeders in Britain, yet I regularly correspond with a breeder from the mid-west who says that he has the same terror of some strains of corona virus as I have of parvo virus.

By far the most popular breed of dog for use in research is the beagle and there are obvious reasons for this choice of dog. The breed's willingness to live in pack conditions without displaying much of an inclination to fight must have something to do with it, though when beagles do fight they can be devils. I once whipped-in for a small private pack that was so impoverished that I wore jeans and sweater as my hunt uniform. So fierce were the members of this pack that new hounds could only be draughted in with some difficulty. Beagles are also extremely tough little dogs, indeed the pursuit of a hare with these dogs becomes a grinding act of attrition rather than a straightforward hunt, for hares are often run to a state of exhaustion before they are captured. However I suspect one of the main reasons for the use of beagles is their general uniformity. Though this was not always the case. In Norman and Angelin times the hounds were seldom encountered but were simply smaller editions of the more powerful staghounds, foxhounds and harriers. Today beagles breed very true to type though there is a dichotomy between the show and working strains appearing, breeders of the latter preferring much larger beagles for few hounds of less that 14 inches at the shoulder will show sport.

The lot of most dogs bred to used for vivisection is seldom as bad the antivivisectionists depict in their posters. Not only must the breeder run the gauntlet of the 1973 Breeders Act which allows environmental officers to inspect and regulate any breeder's kennel, but those who perform the various experiments on dogs are subject to even more careful scrutiny by the licensing authority. It is wise however for the breeder who specialises in producing animals of any sort for vivisection or research to keep his business pursuits private and discreet. Indeed to be a proprietor of an establishment that produces dogs for scientific research is to court danger. I am not pro vivisection, I believe I have explained my moral dilemma about the subject, but there are groups who are decidedly antipathetic to the production of any animals, particularly dogs, for vivisection or experimentation. I can understand the attitude of these people, indeed I share some of their distaste, yet I cannot condone attacks on laboratories and breeding establishments that so often hurt the very creatures the perpetrators are attempting to protect. Might I conclude this chapter with a quote from a breeder who produces dogs for vivisection, and who, for obvious reasons, wishes to remain anonymous? 'My living, or at least a good proportion of my living, depends on the production of puppies and growing dogs for licensed scientific experimentation (vivisection). My kennels are kept scrupulously clean and my stock is well fed and cared for, far better in fact that the show breeder who lives near my home and who is so vehement in his condemnation of me. Yet I receive considerable criticism, condemnation and even verbal abuse from those living near my premises. I no longer seek to explain my conduct. I have long since stopped doing so, for people will listen to my reasons. As a result of this attitude I live in a state of security which resembles that of Fort Knox, and yet attacks on my premises are not infrequent and I find the press handle reports of such attacks with sympathy for the perpetrators. The public are decidedly anthropomorphic in their treatment of anyone who breeds dogs for licensed scientific experiment.'

# 16

# Disposing of Elderly Stock

AT THE TIME OF writing, my kennels, a very large kennels, is experiencing a crisis. It would be policy to bring in new stock, possible new and different breeds, for there is a glut in the market where German Shepherd dogs are concerned and we are unable to sell even good, sound, tested puppies. However I certainly don't have kennel space for additions to the kennels for we are woefully overstocked with elderly, non-breeding dogs.

So numerous are the elderly occupants of the kennels that it has been necessary to set aside a wing of the kennels to cater for the geriatrics, or the pensioners as my kennel help rather euphemistically refers to them. Cher, a daughter of Old Dotty the twenty three year old bearded collie matriarch who died within months of our arrival at the kennels, is now twenty two and still hale and hearty, as is her litter brother, who despite his venerable age, still becomes excited at the appearance of a new bitch. His enthusiasm is however deceptive, for such is his age that he would find mating difficult and a 'tie' something akin to the thirteenth labour of Hercules.

My lurchers are also antique. Mereb, my oldest bitch, a daughter of Old Fathom, who died at the age of twenty seven, is a doddery twenty one and her movements are restricted by scar tissue, the result of an operation for the removal of a tumour some years ago. Her granddaughter Phaidra is still fit and well, but no longer capable of the acrobatic feats that characterised her childhood, youth and middle age. Old Finn, another bearded collie from a different line will probably die this winter once the first frosts of November arrive. However I believed she would die some five years ago when she showed obvious signs of declining vigour. The winter of 1993 was a harsh one and saw off the elderly Fathom and her grandson Ilan, a twenty year old, but somehow Old Finn survived. I could relate tales of each and every oldster in the kennels, each of which finds a soft spot in my heart and will cause grief when they die. However, delightfully sentimental as these passages may seem, the policy I have adopted is financially ruinous, and hence the following pages of advice may smack of hypocrisy for I must suggest that the reader does as I advise, not do as I have done.

Kennel Club rules suggest that no bitch above the age of eight should be considered as a brood, and also disapproves of breeding more that six litters from a bitch unless a special dispensation is granted to the breeder. Such regulations are both fair and just. A bitch that has bred six litters in her lifetime has produced enough puppies to guarantee that her bloodline has a fine chance of surviving, and by this time her reproductive tracts will have become less efficient. There is a fair, or more that fair chance that she will experience a problem during parturition and the birth of the puppies will need to be assisted by a shot of Calcium Oleate or Oxytocsin. There is an even more likely chance of any delivery being marred by uterine inertia, tired womb syndrome, as one of my veterinary friends so aptly refers to the problem. Smaller than usual litters is also often the lot of elderly bitches as are problems during parturition.

Hancock, who is superbly analytical about kennel costings, states that after six litters, greyhound bitches usually produce less than five puppies which makes their continued use as commercially viable brood bitches unprofitable. Stud dogs enjoy a considerably longer breeding life and while their fertility declines slightly, a male mammal can usually sire offspring into its dotage. There is a tale of an Arab sheikh, a tale I believe to be questionable, who produced 105 children and who sired his last child when he was 98. Indeed there seems to be quite a lot said for the benefits of enduring an alcohol free, halal meat diet and low humidity conditions. Some of my own stud dogs have proved to be equally fecund however. During my elderly bearded collie stud's tenth year he failed to fertilise four visiting bitches from members of the Working Bearded Collie Association, so I withdrew him from stud as I considered that despite his eagerness to mate, some condition, or disease perhaps had rendered him infertile. My opinion was confirmed when I ran him with a team of eager young working bitches for four seasons, and not one of them conceived. Yet in his sixteenth year he produced a litter to the best bitch in the kennels who had been recuperating from injuries in the geriatric dog wing.

However interesting as such homespun anecdotes may appear, keeping elderly animals in a kennel is a financially ruinous practice, as I know to my cost. An old animal, no matter how much you love them and how useful it has been in its youth, is a liability in any kennels. Not only could a younger, more financially worthwhile animal occupy its space, but also elderly animals often need special diets to maintain their body weight and general condition. Ilan, my antique lurcher stud dog who died aged twenty in 1993, developed an inability to digest raw animal protein during his seventeenth year and lived on a diet of cooked meat and meat juices for the rest of his life. Fathom, his grand dam fasted two days in every three during her last years and on the third day engaged in a gluttonous feast of cooked rabbit. If I changed her lifestyle, adopting a different diet, her body weight fell dramatically and nothing looks worse than a skeleton-thin elderly dog.

So what is to be done with elderly dogs that are no longer capable of earning their keep? I have explained the practice of running a geriatric wing is financially ruinous venture, indeed I confess I have been forced into penning books in order to keep old canine friends, a terrible admission for an author, who according to tradition 'writes because he must, not because he can'.

Once more I shall resort to interviewing my two kennel owners who represent different poles in the world of dog keeping, namely Eve Smail who runs the very successful Toy Box Kennels which specialises in producing show quality Pomaranians, and David Hancock who runs an equally successful lurcher kennels.

Mrs Smail interviewed 20th October 1997 said:

> I don't find much difficulty rehoming my elderly Pomeranians if I have to, but I admit I often keep old favourites until they die. They occupy little space but often need special food when they get old, but then I need to experiment to find what is the best food to keep any Pomeranian. Breeding Poms is such a financial black hole that it devours any spare money I have. I make many contacts around the shows, and I show regularly and judge abroad frequently and so I am able to home all my elderly stock with little difficulty. Some years I have had a waiting list of clients wanting to rehome old dogs and stock which hasn't lived up to its early show potential. I homed some in Iceland just recently, but I am careful where I do place my oldies. They need special treatment and special diets in order to survive, for Poms are often quite delicate even when they are young and healthy. No, I don't have much trouble homing my oldsters, though I've known some stud dogs that are dirty devils about the home until they settle in.

David Hancock interviewed August 1997 by Peter Mayor:

> My position is different from most other dog breeders, its unique actually. My breeding stock bitches are always greyhounds which usually come to me after retirement, for hounds are of little use as competitive animals after six or seven years of age. Some of the younger hounds I get are superbly bred but are reluctant to chase a mechanical hare so I am given them when they are eighteen months old; the alternative is that breeders will destroy them rather that retrain and reprogramme them to being rehoused with other live-stock. (A greyhound, which has not been reprogrammed to live amongst other livestock, can be a nightmare to own, for many cannot differentiate between cats, chickens etc. and legitimate quarry. Some greyhound societies perform sterling work training these hounds so their behaviour is modified or sublimated so that they can be kept as family pets).
>
> I know something about the Kennel Club rules of not allowing more than six litters from a bitch although this regulation does not affect me as I breed unregistered lurchers, but I seldom breed from a bitch beyond her eighth year and I can't remember when I bred six or more litters from a bitch. It just isn't financially worth while keeping and breeding from older stock as the litter size drops dramatically once animals start to age. I make it a policy not to breed from a bitch once it has whelping problems (these are rare among grey-hounds) or if the bitches produce two successive litters of less than five puppies. I would willingly give away the ageing greyhound bitches to pet owners, I sometimes have, but there is really no possibility of rehoming the majority of elderly bitches I keep. Hence I destroy them quickly and painlessly. I salve my conscience by saying that for at least four years I have extended their life span, for they would have been destroyed once their speed waned anyway. Of course I have favourites, who doesn't, and of course I experience some regrets about putting these down, but there really is no alternative, is there? Perhaps it would be better if I prepared myself by not making friends with partic-ular dogs. I suppose I have dual values for I tend to keep my stud dogs until their dotage, or to the time when I believe that life becomes painful for them.

Clearly it is difficult to rehome elderly dogs and bitches, particularly stud dogs which may, because of the nature of the stud dog, have developed antisocial habits such as spraying to mark territory. Castration usually does little to quench their enthusiasm for this habit though there is some slight evidence to suggest that the urine is slightly less pungent than that passed by an entire animal. Personally I detest the practice of castrating a dog. I find it alters their antisocial behaviour little if at all, and a castrate in kennels causes havoc. Males attempt to mount it, as the dog, deprived of its gonads, starts to secrete female hormones. A castrated male, particularly a territorial castrate, who has perhaps served bitches during his spell as an entire male, will react with great fury when another dog tries to ride him. It is however best to at least try to home elderly dogs and bitches rather than to simply destroy them. An advertisement in the local papers stating exactly what is offered and perhaps a small price or free of charge will attract some customers.

Example:

*Golden Retriever bitch 8 years old (not for breeding) free to a good home. This bitch is not house-trained but makes a loving pet.*

An advertisement of this type will attract quite a few people, who will be prepared to rehome the bitch. Elderly people are often looking for a dog which is also past its prime and therefore requires less exercise than would a younger dog.

It is always wise to make sure the pedigree is given away with the dog, but the registration forms are withheld. I will illustrate my point. When my dogs were kennelled in Caithness I experienced a time when I needed to rehome several bitches, which while they were not old, were genetically unsound and had produced quite a few puppies which had unacceptably high hip scores. So it was I advertised in the local papers thus:

*Adult German Shepherd Dog bitches – not for breeding. Free to good homes*

As I expected I received quite a few phone calls. Some were made after pub closing times, and I would not place dogs with such people. Another caller decided she would home the entire kennel provided I delivered them the three hundred miles away free of charge. The good lady claimed she had ponies, which prevented her making the trip north to collect the dogs. I finally managed to rehome the bitches, which were delightful animals and in perfect health, but carried genetic qualities that were undesirable. One bitch, a real sweetie, went to a woman who ran a dog training school and I believed the animal had a home for life. Months later the woman contacted me for the bitch's registration forms as she said she had joined the PATDOG group, a group of dogs which are taken around hospitals to visit the elderly and the infirm. The group required proof of ownership of the animal before the bitch could be considered for the service. Rather foolishly I gave the woman the registration certificate and weeks later I heard she had mated the bitch to a very poor, unregistered dog with defective hips, and had produced a litter from her. A month after whelping that the bitch died of some liver disease – not a happy ending to a sad tale.

One man who wished to rehome a bitch and asked if I had one with an antisocial disposition, he used the expression 'savage bastard', I believe he wanted to keep it chained up to guard his scrap yard. I could not sentence an animal to this fate so I rather tactfully avoided giving him an animal. Another exitinerant wished to mate a bitch to a greyhound to breed lurchers, and then return the animal to me, and of course I avoided placing a bitch with him too. As a point of interest the fact that the bitch carried genes which produced hip dysplasia wouldn't matter in the slightest if the animal was mated to a greyhound, for greyhounds are so genetically sound that they seem to absorb and neutralise any defects in the first generation greyhound cross. However I did not like the look of the client and once again made some excuses, but continued to advertise until I had homed the entire collection of bitches in good, and I believe permanent homes. I have so many mistakes where people and dogs are concerned that in my declining years I make doubly certain that my dogs are placed with suitable people.

# 17

# Kennel Staff

IF YOU ARE ABLE to manage your kennels by yourself, or with the help of a friend or partner, do so. The employment of kennel staff is a nightmare, particularly if the situation of the kennels requires one's employee to 'live in'. Just now and again one finds an employee who is only a little short of ideal, please, please hold on to such a person for he or she is as valuable as fine gold. The majority of kennel staff are usually ill-suited to the work, and those who stay and are good at the job are rare, very rare indeed.

At first sight a young school leaver, someone who has never before had a job, may seem a good prospect as a kennel person. The young person has not been spoilt by a previous employer and can be trained to the ways of the kennel owner. However there is a caveat. Most young people are aware that dogs need cuddling, feeding and walking, but seem totally unaware that dogs also urinate and defecate. In short, kennel work is often messy, unpleasant and in winter, cold and wet. Hence many youngsters who were previously delighted at the prospect of 'working with animals' quit after a few days of cleaning out kennels as they discover kennel work is not what they thought it was. It is often good policy to try to employ a person who has a history of part-time farm work or kennel work, perhaps the child of another kennel owner who wishes to work at a different establishment. These people are only too aware of the work involved and will not suffer the disillusionment of those from a more urban background. Sadly the services of such people are seldom obtainable.

Homesickness of young staff is invariably a problem if they have to live as a member of the family or occupy rooms in the grounds. They will not easily find friends close at hand, as most kennels by dint of the nature of the business are often situated in remote districts, far from a town and its social life. I have several times taken on young people, only to find them in tears at the prospect of living in a village amongst people they didn't know. One instance comes to mind, and will always be remembered. In an emergency I requested an agency to send me someone to help in the kennels and eventually a girl with a blank face but a cheerful disposition arrived. I thought the girl, who seemed to have a below average intelligence, was unsuitable but I needed help fairly desperately, so I took her on, on what was to prove to be an extremely short trial. As I set off to take her to the kennels she uttered, 'Can I phone my mother?' – a lady who lived twenty-five miles away – and of course I agreed. She returned from the telephone with her face bathed in smiles and set off at last to the kennels. As I was introducing her to the dogs, a good policy as staff need to know each dog by name, she again asked 'Can I phone my mother'? Puzzled, I asked 'Didn't you get through when you phoned five minutes ago?' and rather tearfully she agreed she had. I am quite a gentle person despite my reputation for being coarse and worldly, and so I agreed to nine telephone calls home that day, but as evening approached I noticed that tears now accompanied the agitation. I therefore phoned her mother myself, and the girl returned home. Two other kennels had the same problem with the child, despite the fact that one of the kennels was situated only half a mile from her home.

If one takes on a youngster straight from school it is a good idea to see their last school report. Personally I am not the slightest bit interested in whether the child has mastered why the square on the hypotenuse is equal to the sum of the squares on the other two sides, but I am interested in the child's attendance record, for nothing is more habit forming than persistent absenteeism. When I had the misfortune to be a teacher, I was given the task of being form master to the worst truants in the school, thieves and prostitutes, for the school was in a very rough area. To get my children to school, I fetched them myself, sometimes from amusement arcades and in the case of the girls, from lorry drivers' car parks. I did this simply because I believe that children need to be taught the habit of coming to school regularly and on time before they leave school and start work. Those who believe that children suddenly start to attend work regularly once they are given full employment, despite a record of truancy, are deluding themselves. A truant allowed to develop the habit of not coming to school regularly finds the habit hard to ditch once he starts work. The slightest weariness, the merest sniffle, or the first indication of a taxing day ahead usually means the youngster does not turn up for work. In kennels where routine is essential, more essential perhaps than in a factory, absenteeism has a devastating effect. In short, avoid employing anyone who has a record of poor attendance or truancy.

Beware of employing thieves, and forget the hooey of the do-gooder and the people who seek to prove that man is capable of reform; thieves seldom mend their ways and are a liability to employ. If I can, I try to check up on a future employee's background, though this is difficult, for members of the teaching profession are reluctant to mention a child's criminal record on a school reference, despite an assurance that a report will be treated with the strictest confidence. Very few youngsters with a tendency to steal, reform, and because of my teaching career I claim to be an expert on larceny, having taught many of what the police refer to as A thieves, people who only steal objects beginning with A – a bike, a car, a wallet, etc. Many of the thieves I taught, I really liked; some asked me to be godfather to their children, but to employ them, no matter how likeable they were, would have been madness. There is a huge labour market in Britain and one can afford to be selective and should be especially if the young person is required to live in. This can be difficult however because of the low wages paid to kennel staff, and many employment agencies will suggest many unsuitable people.

Clients often decide to buy a puppy long before they examine whelp, simply because of the appearance of the house, the kennels and the owners of the kennels. I once interviewed a youth with a vulgar tattoo on his lower lip, and even though he would have been employed to cart barrow loads of manure, he would hardly have given the potential buyers confidence. I did not employ him, but it would be interesting to trace the boy and find out if anyone else decided to employ him, but I digress.

On the subject of tracing the future career of anyone who had taken up employment with a kennels, or even attended an interview, I cannot resist telling the following tale. Some years ago when I was teaching in Walsall I kept a large kennel of terriers and was plagued by thieves, who visited my kennels so often that they would break-in to check when puppies were ready for selling and return when the whelps were six weeks of age. I therefore needed someone to look after the kennels while I was out at work. I advertised, and my advertisement brought a flood of applicants, some reasonable, some ridiculous and some I would have paid to stay away from my home. The most likely candidate was a smart, good-looking boy, the son of a gamekeeper, who lived thirty miles away in the sort of family T. H. White was want to describe as ' good, solid yeomanry', but then looks can be decidedly deceptive. The boy fitted in quite well for the first week, but on the eight day I returned home from school to find my house unlocked and the boy gone, leaving no note to explain his departure. I locked up my premises, checked my dogs, and raced over to the gamekeeper's house, to find the youth there at home. Apparently something trivial had upset him and so he returned home. He travelled back to the kennels with me, but two days later he did exactly the same thing. This time his father brought him back, apologising for his son's conduct, and both father and son seemed decidedly sorry about what the boy had done. However, two days later he had gone again. I did not bother to fetch him this time.

Some eight years later I received a letter from a kennel owner, a man who bred and trained gundogs, stating that the youth had given my name as a referee. I was amazed and now believe that his stay with me had been less turbulent than his stay with other employers. I am not a malicious person, but I declined to give the young man a reference, for to allow someone like this the chance of working with animals would be morally wrong.

A new scheme involving the training of kennel help has been adopted by some agencies. This is an in-service scheme for people under twenty five years old, working for an NVQ certificate in kennel management. This form of training has proven far more successful in producing good class kennel staff than a purely academic qualification with no practical experience of the job. It involves trainees serving some sort of apprenticeship coupled with correspondence course training. There have been good reports of kennel hands trained in this way.

A young person straight from school needs gentle but firm handling if he or she is to become a useful member of the kennel staff and it is important to start as one intends to go on, by being firm at the beginning of their time at the kennels. My mother had a very Jewish saying 'If a boy isn't doing something, he's doing something'. A sort of Semitic way of saying, 'Satan provides work for idle hands'. It is good to treat young kennel staff in a kindly, avuncular manner, but one should also ensure that they are kept gainfully employed all day. Nothing destroys a youngster's morale more than boredom. If there is a lull in the day's normal activities, find a job for the employee, be it painting kennels or doing minor repair work, and there is always plenty of this to be done in any breeding kennels. Someone standing around doing nothing will soon become disenchanted with kennel life and consider leaving the job. Someone who is almost run off his or her feet however, finds the day passes so quickly that there is little time to contemplate unhappiness.

Not all potential kennel staff will be school leavers who are malleable, ductile and capable of being shaped in a manner the kennel owner requires. Some will be experienced and have had a number of other jobs, and it is wise to find out from the previous employer why they left their last job. Dishonesty makes an applicant undesirable, and so does a fractious disposition. Someone who loses their temper at every turn, or every time he or she is corrected will seldom find the often menial side of kennel work very appealing and I would be reluctant to take on anyone who had left their previous job because of a nervous disposition, or someone who had severe psychiatric disorders. If this statement brands me as a heartless brute, so be it, for my dogs must come first in my priorities, not the possible frailties of kennel staff. Cue for yet another tale I am afraid.

In 1978 I took on a young woman of about twenty-eight simply because she was the best of a bad batch of applicants, but rather wisely, as it happens, I gave her a week's trial period before she began permanent employment with me. On her first morning I took her to watch me dock some puppies tails. ( Incidentally, it is illegal for a person other than a veterinary surgeon or a qualified person to dock tails today; I have included afterwords from the Council of Docked Breeds at the end of the book.) As I docked the first tail I glanced up and found the young woman in a state of shock, shaking violently and nearly speechless with terror. I rushed her into the house, sat her down and plied her with strong, sweet tea, and it was some minutes before she was capable of speaking. Clearly the rough and tumble life of a working dog kennels was unsuitable for someone of this disposition, so I telephoned her sister to come and fetch her and she was still shaking and ashen when her sister arrived from thirty miles away. The sister did not appear surprised however, and stated that the young woman had left a cake shop on her first day under similar circumstances. I would be fascinated to what incident in the day to day running of a cake shop could have produced such a reaction.

It was, I believe, the American social reformer and criminologist Homer Lane who said ' there is a place in this world for everyone' – but not in my kennels! However the tale does much to explain why many American kennels insist on what is known as a 'hello, goodbye', no contract trial period for potential employees. This will not prevent unpleasantries and acrimony if an employee is found to be unsuitable, but it will go some way to alleviate bad feeling. American kennel owners tend to be more ruthless that their British equivalents and their kennels are more efficiently run. When I boxed in the United States, (my record will be hard to beat, I fought eleven bouts and lost eleven bouts) I once stayed with a breeder of scent hounds. Most American hounds are descended from 'foul running' foxhounds, imported from England and France and put out to farmers, hunters and ranchers when these hounds decided to run game other than foxes. I learned much from my stay, particularly about the employment of staff and how to deal with the acrimony which followed the dismissal of an employee. This kennel owner, on dismissal of an employee, would pay the person their 'notice money', up to a month or more, and ask them to leave immediately. He told me a sickening tale of a young Hispanic boy, who while working his notice mutilated several hounds.

At the time of writing a Labour government has set itself the goal of creating work for all – a magnificent aim, albeit an unlikely one – and have given employers incentives to take on long-term unemployed people. One of the incentive schemes is the New Deal, a system, which gives the employer £60 a week for six months towards the wages of a hitherto long-term unemployed person. My advice to employers, has I am afraid, taken on the nature of Pandora's box, with references to all manner of evil and near lunatic future employees. Employers must be so careful about the people they take on to work with animals. I am not exactly in agreement with Carlysle (who lived only a few miles from my present kennels), who believed that hard physical labour was character forming, but there is every indication that many of the long-term unemployed are in this category simply because they have little inclination to seek work.

During the bad times when the chill wind of penury caused me to seek work in the school holidays, I found work with a company which specialised in the fitting and unblocking of drains, perhaps suitable employment for a man with my surname, but extremely hard and messy work. One day when the boss foolishly left me in sole charge of the yard, I was approached by three long-term unemployed people who had been sent to the yard by the Department of Social Security to seek work. Not one of them seemed to want an interview but all of them asked if I would sign their forms stating that they were unsuitable for work. It would seem that life on the dole was preferable to a life of hard physical labour. Such people are virtually impossible to settle in full-time work, and life in a breeding kennels is always hard and taxing. The New Deal, with its sixty pounds a week grant might seem an incentive to any employer, but I would advise him or her to think about the possible staff that will be sent, and remember that the welfare of one's dogs must always come first, and no kennel help is preferable to bad kennel help. I could write an entire book about the mixture of people the DSS have sent to me to be interviewed for jobs in the kennels. Thoreau describes misfits, such as myself, as marching to the beat of a different drum, but some of the people I have been sent must have written their own music in order to be able to march! One interviewee said that he found the presence of the birds fluttering around my house distressing. This was puzzling as we do not keep birds, but all was revealed when his CV showed that he had been in an institution where he was treated for his delusions about birds fluttering around his bed-sitting room. A sad person, but totally unemployable. Another candidate, Frank, arrived at midnight after a three hundred mile trip, courtesy of a DSS train pass. He elaborated on his rich and varied career, and as he spoke I made a mental calculation of his age, if his tales were correct, and found that his lifestyle did not tally with his chronological age. He admitted to being twenty nine, his DSS card said he was thirty three but his CV indicated that he was a little less that three hundred and fifty years old, that is if he left school at fifteen as he said he had. Frank, a hybrid mixture of Walter Mitty and Marco Polo, was clearly unemployable, and after marking his card 'unsuitable' I sent him on his way south to the Midlands again.

Yet even Frank paled into insignificance when I was faced with Adrian, who again arrived courtesy of the DSS train pass. Adrian was a hale, healthy, strong twenty-five year-old who, because of circumstances, had somehow never managed to find work of any sort. Within minutes of meeting him I was to realise what those 'circumstances' were. He had scarcely stepped inside the house when I realised that a Marxist, Leninist, Trotskyist was about to interview us with a view to considering a job. I have always prided myself on the bloodlines of the livestock I keep as much as the way in which they are kept, but Adrian gasped in horror when he heard how much my initial bloodstock had cost. 'Do you realise that family of Albanians could live for two years on that money you have spent buying a single German Shepherd Dog' he snarled, and for the rest of the day his conversation resembled Garbo's script from Nanotchka. I should like to have had the termerity to say that I wasn't really interested in breeding Albanians for sale, but his furious attitude and athletic build dissuaded me. I should also like to have said that his own work-free lifestyle would have done little for the hoi poloi in any country, but as usual discretion became the better part of valour, and I said nothing. That night I slept with my best German Shepherd Dog in my bedroom and with the door wedged by a chair lest Adrian struck a blow for the Revolution and attempted to dispose of what he obviously saw as a neofascist, neocapitalist dog breeder. Never have I been more delighted to sign 'unsuitable' on a DSS form and escort someone to the railway station. Of course not all applicants will be liars, lunatics or villians. Some will be ideal, but you will undoubtedly see a lot of frogs before you discover your handsome prince or princess. Once you have found the right person, treasure this person, and do all you can to keep them even if this means paying a higher than normal wage.

Kennel regime must be fairly strict and regimented to be successful. Cleaning out and feeding must be done at the same time each and every day, and every allowance must be given for the idiosyncrasies found in the dogs. This does not apply to the kennel staff however, for each member must be allotted his or her work each day and never allowed to look around to find something to do. I do not allow smoking on the premises and will not employ anyone who smokes. I have seen a cattery fire and have no wish to see another similar fire. It is easier to say that smoking bans a person from a job than to restrict the practice when a person comes to work for you. I dislike the sight of pedestrians dodging traffic while harnessed up to a Walkman, and will not allow such a contraption in the kennels. If a person is tuned into the sound of a pop group it is highly unlikely that he or she will hear a kennel fight or a dog screaming in pain. If a person is paid to do a job he or she must give the job one hundred percent of his or her attention. Kennel work requires lightening responses and immediate interpretation of unusual or warring sounds. A person dancing around to the music of a Walkman is unable to give the dogs the required attention.

I am not a prude in any sense of the word, indeed my bizarre lifestyle indicates the opposite, but I will not allow live-in kennel staff to sleep with boyfriends or girlfriends on my premises. I never question the morality of any person above the age of sixteen engaging in any sexual practice, but I will not allow it to happen under my roof simply because it smacks of lax kennel discipline which may cause harm or hurt to my dogs. A partner wandering aimlessly around the kennels, getting in the way of the morning's activity and distracting the worker for their job can result in the kennels help not listening to warning sounds in the kennels. So many problems can be detected just by listening to the sounds made by the dogs, and one needs to be very vigilant to these sounds, and I expect my kennel staff to be alert at all times.

Kennel staff will invariably ask to bring a pet with them when they come to work and have to live in. My answer to this is 'by all means – once you have passed your probationary period and I know you are going to stay and work with us'. It is extraordinarily bad practice to have a succession of dogs enjoying a brief spell in the kennels due to a peculiarity known as intra-specific inter-family aggression, which causes the regular inmates of an otherwise peaceful kennels to fight each other even after the new dog has left the kennels. A constant run of new dogs in an established breeding kennels causes untold problems.

Such is the ephemeral nature of kennel staff that many times I have been left with what I had believed to be a beloved pet when the magic of kennel work has died and the youngster moved on. I have been left with a tarantula, white mice, hamsters and once, and only once, a German Shepherd Dog who was so fixated upon the girl who owned him that he refused to eat and was the very devil to rehome. One part-time useless dropout, a would-be hippy of thirty-five, who came to work for us in Caithness not only borrowed my van (I had to fetch it from Brighton six months later, for the drop-out had lived in the vehicle), but left me with two vicious terriers and two very badly trained lurchers, which were nearly impossible to rehome. Personally I would endure some fairly bad conditions rather than part with my dogs, (I once lived in a tin shed next to a cemetery for this reason), but seemingly my views are not shared by everyone. When some people tire of kennel work, they simply move on to premises where it is not practical to keep a dog and leave the dog at the kennels. The man who went to Brighton left me to feed and house his dogs for an entire year free of charge, before he decided to part with them. It was only when I put his dogs in a nearby boarding kennels which would have cost him over £30 a week, that he decided to ask me to rehouse the dogs for him.

I shall conclude by saying that no kennel staff should be taken on unless the kennel owner takes out employer liability insurance. Injuries sustained in kennels are by no means unknown and these circumstances need to be covered by insurance. A bad injury to kennel staff can be extremely costly to the kennel owner unless he has adequate insurance to cover such an eventuality.

# 18

# Bedding and the Disposal of Kennel Waste

AT A TIME WHEN eco-friendly systems, designed to prevent the almost inevitable destruction of the planet through the agencies of man, are in vogue, the disposal of kennel waste, bedding plus faecal matter, is a controversial one, particularly in the light of the 1990 Waste Disposal Act and the amendments which are almost certain to follow. The general public is enthusiastic about using excrement from herbivors as fertilizer. Horse and cow manure find a ready market with gardeners and commercial horticulturist, however to find anyone who is prepared to take compost and dog faeces and bedding liberally soaked in dog urine can be a problem. While pedestrians find the presence of horse dung in the road quaint and countrified, the stools of dogs seldom evoke the same feelings. Of course the dung and urine of any creature has its attendant problems. At the time of writing there is a scientific study concerning the build up of BSE prion protiens in fields where infected cattle have grazed being conducted, and horse droppings are known to be a rich source of the bacillus that causes tetanus. However it is the faeces of dogs that seems to infuriate the general public, this is largely due to the publicity concerning the presence of roundworm eggs and larvae in dog faeces, parasites which can and do cause an unpleasant disorder, viceral larval migrans. This is rarely found, but there are reports of children reared at hound kennels who have gone blind as a result of infection with roundworms. In 1968 while I was in America, I read of a survey conducted in Central Park that indicated that soil of samples taken for this popular dog walking spot yielded a high level of roundworms. A similar sample taken from my garden in Lichfield yielded a sample with eleven times the number of roundworm eggs supposedly found in a sample taken from Central Park, New York, as a result of regularly using dog faeces as compost.

Mention needs to be made of the types of bedding used in kennels and way these can be disposed of. Sawdust is readily available and cheap, but not liked by dogs. It tends to get into food and into the eyes of the animals that are bedded on it, so it has questionable use as bedding material. However, it does absorb a large volume of dog urine and is easily cleaned up. Disposing of soiled sawdust can however be rather a problem, one I shall deal with later.

Shavings made from the pine type conifers are often used as bedding. It is surprisingly expensive, one third of my kennel bill is spent in the purchase of bales of shavings, although some large woodyards will allow kennel owners to fetch quantities of shavings free of charge. Shavings too, absorb large quantities of dog urine, but is also difficult to dispose of, however it does not cause problems when it gets into dogs' food.

Peat moss, the upper reaches of peat beds, the result of the partial decay of sedges and mosses is an excellent absorber of dog urine and is only slightly more expensive than pine shavings. It is easier to dispose of and can be dug into the garden as a conditioner/fertilizer, for the faecal matter of dogs has a fairly high nitrogen phosphorus and potash content. It has the disadvantage that some samples will, when wet, stain a dog's fur a rather messy brown colour. When I lived in Caithness I knew of a house where the water was drawn from a peat loch. The water was quite pure but was the colour of weak tea, which often dissuaded newcomers to the area from drinking it.

Straw of all sorts is readily available and quite reasonably priced. Wheat straw is perhaps the best as it is free from the irritating spiked awns found in barley straw. It is not as absorbent as shavings, sawdust or peat, but as David Hancock expressed it in a journal article, urine sinks to the bottom-most layer of the bedding, allowing the dogs to 'sleep dry'. Barley straw is not well liked by dog breeders simply because of the barley awns. These often break and puncture the dog's skin, causing a irritation. Oat straw is more expensive and is more often than not sold as a cheap stock feed to supplement good quality hay rather than as bedding.

Shredded paper has become popular lately and is a good, easy to obtain, fairly cheap form of bedding. It is more absorbent than any of the straws, and will absorb many times its own mass of urine, but when wet it is difficult to dispose of by incineration. One minor disadvantage is the fact that sometimes the print on the shredded paper is partly dissolved by urine and this may stain the dogs' fur.

The disposal of bedding is difficult in zones where fires are prohibited, and these smoke-free zones are becoming more numerous. Sawdust burns with some difficulty and is normally only combustible on a fire made of other materials or in specifically constructed incinerators, which allow the passage of air through them. Wood shavings are also difficult to burn unless the fire is properly constructed with twigs and other loose material at the base of the fire. Once a shavings fire is mouldering however, it is difficult to put out and can be fed fresh shavings daily, providing that the new bedding material is carefully placed so that it does not extinguish the smouldering mass. I once kept a shavings fire burning for two years and fifty days until the continuance of the fire became nearly an obsession. At the time I employed a kennel boy called John Derry who was fourteen at the time, and the best kennel help I ever had. John shared my enthusiasm for the maintenance of what we both called the 'Forever Fire'. Each night, we would race home from school to put fresh bedding on the fire, and such was our enthusiasm for the 'Forever Fire' that one day when a torrential rain storm soaked the district, John came into my classroom, his face wearing a worried looked, convinced that the rain had extinguished it!

Local councils will often collect rubbish at a special rate, although these rates are often quite expensive. If one's kennels merit the hire of a skip this is by far the best value for money. Most of the plastic bags sold by local councils are suitable only for the transport of cardboard and allied materials. They are usually far too flimsy to contain wet dog bedding and will split, and most refuse men will refuse to handle them.

I am greatly indebted to Mr Charles Denham of Wonderworms UK for his help in compiling the following information. Early in 1998 I contact Mr Denham after seeing an article about how he had devised a method of reducing organic rubbish to compost and raw protein by dint of the use of worms. Subsequently I attended a course run by him and am now fairly convinced that his methods are the way ahead in a world that is destined to be a lot more ecologically friendly.

Denham experimented with kennel waste and cardboard and found that the blue nosed worm, not the common earth worm or the night crawler, is highly omnivorous and is easily capable of devouring the faecal matter from kennels together with its accompanying bedding, providing that the shavings or sawdust are given a month or so to decompose before it becomes worm feed. A pile of soiled bedding and faeces is started in a container, and covered with a tarpaulin to conserve the heat generated by decomposition. The pile is turned every week to prevent aerobic decomposition or fungal growth, and is then spread in bays so that it cools. Worms and worm eggs are added to an eighteen inch layer of waste and the bays are again covered with a tarpaulin, this time to prevent the rain making the compost material too wet for the worms to thrive. If the worms are sufficiently numerous and the conditions ideal for vermiculture, the bedding is reduced to a serviceable compost in two or three months in summer and perhaps a little longer in winter. The worms and worm eggs are found in the top six inches of the soil and compost and can be transferred to another freshly prepared bay to continue their work. Denham states that he sells worm cast compost for £3 a half hundred-weight and worms for up to £80 a thousand, which could mean that the faecal matter produced by breeding dogs could be as valuable as the puppies they produce. This seemingly absurd paradox is endorsed by Denham who says that providing the worms are sold directly to fishermen as bait, a bed of compost 8ft by 4ft is capable of earning the worm breeder an income of £100 per week.

The venture is not cheap to start though it is possible to build up one's stock of worms over a period of years. One pound of blue nosed worms will devour one pound of partly composted faecal matter and bedding each day. As I produce roughly one hundred weight of waste material each day, I would need about 100 pounds of worms to cope with the waste my kennels produces. Worms multiply rapidly once mature and if conditions are right, produce fifty times their number in a single year. A single pound of worms could therefore produce upwards of 2500 pounds of worms in a two year period, more than enough to devour all my kennel waste, providing I use straw and paper rather than shavings as bedding. Paper soaked in dog urine and allowed a fortnight to compost apparently produces excellent worm feed. I am however, uncertain as to whether a compost worm is capable of devouring, digesting and rendering harmless the eggs of the roundworm, or whether the roundworm eggs pass undigested and undamaged through the compost worms digestive tracts.

This method for using kennel waste effectively and possibly profitably is well worth considering, providing the kennel owner has a suitable place away from the kennels, for the kennel waste, for the sight of a pile of decaying bedding might be disconcerting to some clients.

# 19

# The Future of Dog Breeding

THE BREEDING OF Dogs Bill was introduced in 1973 by Mr Gordon Oaks, then the Member of Parliament for Widness. He stated: 'It has been said that the degree of civilisation of a country can be measured by the way it treats its animals. If the House gives me leave, the Bill would protect our dogs, man's so called 'best friend' from the exploitation of those who sole motive is greed'. He added, 'My Bill would be aimed at curtailing the cruel activities of those whose greed has totally overcome any humanity that they may have had'. The Bill which eventually became the Breeding of Dogs Act 1973, one of the most fair and reasonable 'animal acts' passed since the Production of Animals Act 1911 (1912 Scotland), and had the Act been properly implemented, further Breeding of Dogs bills would have been superfluous. Needless to say the Act was not properly implemented for many authorities clearly turned a blind eye to legislation and allowed unlicenced dog kennels to continue in business. For a while many environmental health officers in certain authorities perused the newspapers for indications of those who sought to flout the Act and not register under the title Dog Breeders. Then a spate of prosecutions were brought by authorities only to see the magistrates court treat the conviction of unlicenced dog breeders as something of a joke and fine the miscreants nominal sums. It is therefore not surprising that the early vigilance of local government officers declined a little until it was not uncommon to see large numbers of puppies advertised from kennels which are so badly organised that there would be little chance of any environmental health officer granting them a licence. A glance at the field sport press will show a great many litters advertised from council houses, where the nature of the premises prohibits the running of a business. One breeder in the Midlands advertised sixteen litters of lurchers from his council house in 1997, and so far not action had been taken against him.

So it was that in 1998 another Breeding of Dogs Bill was introduced but without time to debate it the document did not become an Act of Parliament, but I feel it will, indeed it must. In addition to the implementation of the Dog Breeders Act 1973 there will be other measures to curb the avarice of insensitive dog breeders. I would be willing to wager that in the future it will be illegal to breed two litters a year from any bitch, and that dog dealers along with other anachronisms, such as cock fighters, will be a thing of the past. A future Act of Parliament will certainly make provisions that no person other than the breeder, or the owner of the sire of the dog will be allowed to sell puppies, which will close up the gaps in the Pet Traders Act 1951, a singularly badly thought out piece of legislature.

However man is an ingenious sort of creature, indeed his ingenuity alone facilitated his passage from the trees to the hostile savannah beneath them. I suspect this Bill, should it become an Act of Parliament in the future, will contain certain clauses that will be difficult, if not impossible to implement. For instance I cannot see the unscrupulous heeding the proposed regulation that no bitch produces a litter more than once year. To circumvent this clause I suspect unscrupulous breeders will register 'ghosts', bitches that exist on paper only, thus allowing breeders to produce two litters a year from bitches that do exist. Lurcher and working terrier breeders will be exempt from the regulations, for neither lurchers, long dogs nor fell and unregistered Jack Russell type working terriers are usually registered with the Kennel Club. It will therefore be impossible to regulate the activities of breeders of these types of dogs, particularly in view of the fact that very few of them registered when the Dog Breeders Act 1973 was passed. The proposed clause advocating that only breeders and owners of the stud dog are able to sell the litter will also be difficult to implement. All breeders have to do is to register his stock as being owned by the dealer to whom he has agreed to sell the litter. The dealer will then officially be the breeder of the litter and will be able to sell the puppies. It can be argued that local government officers will be able to track the progress of a litter from nest to buyer but it should be remembered that lack of manpower in some authorities has prevented the implementation of the regulations of the 1973 Act.

What I believe will have a more catastrophic effect on dog breeding today is the pressure exerted by certain animal welfare groups on the continent. These groups work somewhat differently from British Animal Rights activists and achieve greater and more lasting results as a result of carefully controlled parliamentary lobbying. Already there are moves afoot to outlaw the breeding of breeds of dogs that because of the cranial structure of their puppies, are usually unable to whelp without the aid of a Caesarean section. This legislation will see the end of certain bulldog- type breeds, including the English and French bulldogs as well as the Boston terrier. It will also see the end of the miniature bull terrier, which is no longer, a self-whelper, a great tragedy. It would be possible to save these breeds from extinction, but only if breeders would refrain from breeding-in aberant characteristics which make it difficult, if not impossible for the breed to whelp naturally. A selection programme which totally disregards the finer aesthetic points of the standard but concentrates on producing self-whelping animals would save these breeds in the nick of time. Breeders of bulldogs claim that the loss of the modern bulldog would be a tragedy because of the breed's supposed antiquity, but this is nonsense. The modern bulldog, described as a wheezing asthmatic, bears little resemblance to the Crib and Rosa type bulldogs painted by Abraham Cooper in 1813. These were a pair of sporting bulldogs, which were athletic, free from exaggeration and probably of a self-whelping strain.

The continental animal welfare groups are also lobbying to outlaw dogs which display an innate disposition to produce offspring in which entropia, a painful affliction of the eyes, is common. This is curious for the very worst sufferers form this affliction seems to be the Neopolitain mastiff, a continental breed. However there are apparently moves afoot in the appropriate breed clubs to breed out this affliction, which invariably needs a surgical operation to correct.

The bloodhound, a once useful breed of working dog, is now bred with such heavy jowls that eye problems are also inevitable. Some of the working strain of bloodhounds of this type once bred by Eric Furness, did not suffer from the eye disorder, a form of bloat which killed many bloodhounds immediately after World War II. Furness obviously used allied breed types such as Dumfreeshire otter hounds for example, to correct this defect. The continental animal welfare groups also wish to outlaw the breeding of merle coloured animals. Merle is a strange dappling of the fur which apparently continues into the very liver of the merle coloured animal. It is found in three basic colours brown, black/blue and tricolour and is an acceptable colour in dachsunds where it is referred to as 'dapple', collies and certain strains of Great Dane. Merle coloured animals are not a bit inferior to their self-coloured littermates, but the danger lies when two merle coloured animals are mated together, a genetic peculiarity first explored by Punnet and Bateson in 1908.

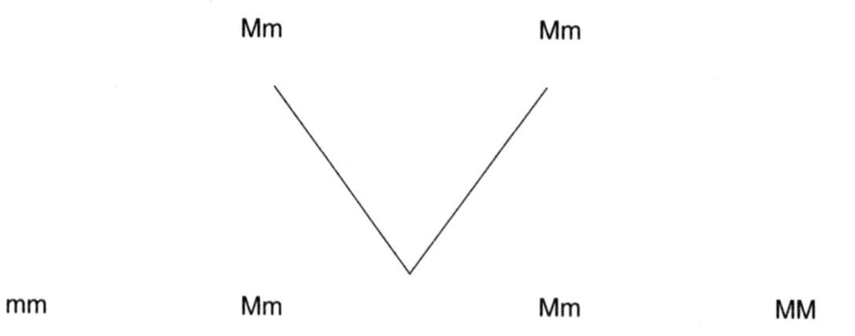


*Key*

Mm = Merle coloured
mm = White, sometimes deaf and blind
MM = Self-coloured

Breeders of merles are only too aware of this peculiarity and it is a very foolish breeder who deliberately mates two merle coloured animals.

I possess no special powers of seerdom but I do have my finger on the pulse of public opinion, and I see an end to the highly profitable process of 'shuttle breeding', and for those not conversant with the practice I will explain. Germany has a justifiable reputation for the production of excellent specimens of its native breeds, the German Shepherd Dog, Rottweilers, Dobermans, German short and wire-haired pointers and Schnauzers of all sizes and the best specimens of these breeds are still bred in Germany. Good class bitches are therefore brought in from Germany in whelp to top winning dogs of the day. These bitches whelp and rear their puppies in Britain in quarantine kennels. Stock from top German males are then sold at a high price and when the bitch comes into season again she is shipped back to Germany to be mated to yet another top German stud dog, thus spending her life in the restrictive environment of a quarantine kennels.

An end to this practice seems in sight, not because of legislation, but simply because the success of modern rabies vaccines will eventually bring an end to the quarantine laws which result in dogs entering this country, spending six months in quarantine kennels. I am a little apprehensive about abolishing quarantine regulations as rabies is a horrendous disease, and at the time of writing, an incurable one. Indeed, the English word, rage, a blind ferocious temper, is derived from the French word for rabies. I am aware of how damaging the six month quarantine period is to a much loved pet, and how the period in kennels puts a strain on the relationship between the animal and its owner, but England has been rabies free for many years simply because we have rigorously enforced the quarantine regulations. No doubt further legislation will follow the publication of this book.

# *Appendix 1*

# Breeding of Dogs Act 1973

### 4. Breeding of Dogs
### Breeding of Dogs Act 1973
(1973 c 60)

**4-2552 1. Licensing of breeding establishments for dogs.**—(1) No person shall keep a breeding establishment for dogs except under the authority of a licence granted in accordance with the provisions of this Act.

(2) Every local authority may, on application being made to them for that purpose by a person who is not for the time being disqualified—

(*a*) under this Act, from keeping a breeding establishment for dogs; or
(*b*) under the Pet Animals Act 1951, from keeping a pet shop; or
(*c*) under the Protection of Animals (Cruelty to Dogs) Act 1933, from keeping a dog; or
(*d*) under the Protection of Animals (Cruelty to Dogs) (Scotland) Act 1934, from keeping a dog; or
(*e*) under the Protection of Animals (Amendment) Act 1954, from having the custody of animals; or
(*f*) under the Animal Boarding Establishments Act 1963, from the boarding of animals,

and on payment of a fee of two pounds or such reasonable sum as the authority may determine, grant a licence to that person to keep a breeding establishment for dogs at such premises in their area as may be specified in the application and subject to compliance with such conditions as may be specified in the licence.

(3) *Repealed.*

(4) In determining whether to grant a licence for the keeping of a breeding establishment for dogs by any person at any premises, a local authority shall in particular (but without prejudice to their discretion to withhold a licence on other grounds) have regard to the need for securing—

(*a*) that the dogs will at all times be kept in accommodation suitable as respects construction, size of quarters, number of occupants, exercising facilities, temperature, lighting, ventilation and cleanliness;
(*b*) that the dogs will be adequately supplied with suitable food, drink and bedding material, adequately exercised, and (so far as necessary) visited at suitable intervals;
(*c*) that all reasonable precautions will be taken to prevent and control the spread among dogs of infectious or contagious diseases;
(*d*) that appropriate steps will be taken for the protection of the dogs in case of fire or other emergency;
(*e*) that all appropriate steps will be taken to secure that the dogs will be provided with suitable food, drink and bedding material and adequately exercised when being transported to or from the breeding establishment;

and shall specify such conditions in the licence, if granted by them, as appear to the local authority necessary or expedient in the particular case for securing all the objects specified in paragraphs (*a*) to (*e*) of this subsection.

(5) Any person aggrieved by the refusal of a local authority to grant such a licence, or by any condition subject to which sucha licence is proposed to be granted, may appeal to a magistrates' court; and the court may on such an appeal give such directions with respect to the issue of a licence or, as the case may be, with respect to the conditions subject to which a licence is to be granted as it thinks proper.

(6)–(8) *Duration of licence.*

(9) Any person who contravenes the provisions of subsection (1) of this section shall be guilty of an offence; and if any condition subject to which a licence is granted in accordance with the provisions of this Act is contravened or not complied with, the person to whom the licence was granted shall be guilty of an offence.

[Breeding of Dogs Act 1973, s 1, as amended by the Local Government, Planning and Land Act 1980, Schs 6 and 34.]

**4–2553 2. Inspection of breeding establishments for dogs.**—(1) A local authority may authorise in writing any of its officers or any veterinary surgeon or veterinary practitioner to inspect (subject to compliance with such precautions as the authority may specify to prevent the spread among animals of infectious or contagious diseases) any premises in their area as respects which a licence granted in accordance with the provisions of this Act is for the time being in force, and any person authorised under this section may, on producing his authority if so required, enter any such premises at all reasonable times and inspect them and any animals found thereon or any thing therein, for the purpose of ascertaining whether an offence has been or is being committed against this Act.

(2) Any person who wilfully obstructs or delays any person in the exercise of his powers of entry or inspection under this section shall be guilty of an offence.
[Breeding of Dogs Act 1973, s 2.]

**4–2554 3. Offences and disqualifications.**—(1) Any person guilty of an offence under any provision of this Act other than the last foregoing section shall be liable on summary conviction to a fine not exceeding **level 4** on the standard scale.

(2) Any person guilty of an offence under the last foregoing section shall be liable on summary conviction to a fine not exceeding **level 3** on the standard scale.

(3) Where a person is convicted of any offence under this Act or of any offence under the Protection of Animals Act 1911 or the Protection of Animals (Scotland) Act 1912, the Pet Animals Act 1951 or the Animal Boarding Establishments Act 1963, the court by which he is convicted may cancel any licence held by him under this Act, and may, whether or not he is the holder of such a licence, disqualify (**a**) him from keeping a breeding establishment for dogs for such a period as the court thinks fit.

(4) A court which has ordered the cancellation of a person's licence, or his disqualification, in pursuance of the last foregoing subsection may, if it thinks fit, suspend the operation of the order pending an appeal.
[Breeding of Dogs Act 1973, s 3 as amended by the Criminal Justice Act 1982, ss 38 and 46.]

(**a**) He may also be disqualified from keeping any dangerous wild animals (Dangerous Wild Animals Act 1976, s 6(2), title ANIMALS (Control), ante). A magistrates' court shall not in a person's absence impose any disqualification on him except after an adjournment after convicting and before sentencing him, see Magistrates' Courts Act 1980, s 11(4), ante.

**4–2555 5. Interpretation.**—(1) References in this Act to the keeping by any person of a breeding establishment for dogs shall be construed as references to the carrying on by that person at premises of any nature (including a private dwelling) of a business of breeding dogs, with a view to their being sold in the course of such business, whether by the keeper thereof or by any other person.

Provided that nothing in this Act shall apply to the keeping of a dog at any premises in pursuance of a requirement imposed under, or having effect by virtue of, the Diseases of Animals Act 1950.

(2) In this Act, unless the context otherwise requires, the following expressions have the meanings hereby respectively assigned to them, that is to say—

"breeding establishment" means any premises (including a private swelling) where more than two bitches are kept for the purposes of breeding for sale;

"local authority" means in England and Wales the council of a London borough, the council of a district or the Common Council of the City of London; and in Scotland means the council of any county or burgh;

"veterinary practitioner" means a person who is for the time being registered in the supplementary veterinary register;

"veterinary surgeon" means a person who is for the time being registered in the register of veterinary surgeons.

[Breeding of Dogs Act 1973, s 5, as amended by the Local Government Act 1974, Sch 7.]

# *Appendix 2*

**SOUTH LANARKSHIRE COUNCIL**

**BREEDING OF DOGS ACT, 1973**

## Licence for Keeping a Breeding Establishment for Dogs

SOUTH LANARKSHIRE COUNCIL, under the provisions of the Breeding of Dogs Act, 1973, hereby authorise **Mr D.B. Plummer**

to keep a dog breeding establishment at the premises **Raggengill Cottage, Abington**
to keep an animal boarding establishment at the premises **Raggenhill Cottage, Abington**
in South Lanarkshire for the period from the date hereof to the Thirty-first day of December, 1997 unless sooner suspended or revoked, on the conditions specified overleaf.

GRANTED in the name and by the authority of the South Lanarkshire Council as the Local Authority under the Aforesaid Act, this **Twenty Forth** day of **December 1996**

Clydesdale Area Offices
South Vennel,
Lanark ML11 7JT.

..........................................................
Area Manager (Environmental Health)

# Appendix 2 cont. . .

BREEDING OF DOGS ACT, 1973

**Provisions Relative to Above Act**

2.--(1) A local authority may authorise in writing any of its officers or any veterinary surgeon or veterinary practitioner to inspect (subject to compliance with such precautions as the authority may specify to prevent the spread among animals of infectious or contagious diseases) any premises in their area as respects which a licence granted in accordance with the provisions of this Act is for the time being in force, and any person authorised under this section may, on producing his authority if so required, enter any such premises at all reasonable times and inspect them and any animals found thereon or anything therein, for the purpose of ascertaining whether an offence has been or is being committed against this Act.

(2) Any person who wilfully obstructs or delays any person in the exercise of his powers of entry or inspection under this section shall be guilty of an offence.

3.--(1) Any person guilty of an offence under any provision of this Act other than the last foregoing section shall be liable on summary of conviction to a fine.

(2) Any person guilty of an offence under the last foregoing section shall be liable on summary of conviction to a fine.

(3) Where a person is convicted of any offence under this Act or of any offence under the Protection of Animals Act, 1911, or the Protection of Animals (Scotland) Act, 1912, the Pet Animals Act, 1951, or the Animal Boarding Establishments Act, 1963, the court by which he is convicted may cancel any licence held by him under this Act, and may, whether or not he is the holder of such licence, disqualify him from keeping a boarding establishment for animals for such a period as the court thinks fit.

## CONDITIONS APPLICABLE TO THE FOREGOING LICENCE

1. Animals will at all times be kept in accommodation suitable as respects construction, size, number of occupants, exercise facilities, temperature, lighting, ventilation and cleanliness.
2. Animals will be adequately supplied with suitable food, drink and bedding material, adequately exercised and (so far as necessary) visited at suitable intervals.
3. All reasonable precautions will be taken to prevent and control the spread among animals of infectious or contagious diseases, including the provision of adequate isolation facilities.
4. Appropriate steps will be taken in case of fire or other emergency.
5. All appropriate steps will be taken to secure that the dogs will be provided with suitable food, drink and bedding material and adequately exercised when being transported to or from the breeding establishment.
6. A register shall be kept of all bitches in the establishment, their ages, dates of heat periods, mating and whelping; such register to be available for inspection at all times by an officer of the Local Authority or other authorised officer under Section 2 (1) of this Act.
7. The licensee will carry into effect any requirements by the authorised officer of the South Lanarkshire Council or any veterinary surgeon or veterinary practitioner after referred to regarding precautions and steps to be taken under conditions 3 and 4 hereof respectively.
8. South Lanarkshire Council may at any time alter, amend or add to the foregoing conditions.
9. Without predjudice to the foregoing conditions the establishment shall comply with the Chartered Institute of Environmental Health Model Council Consitions as adopted by South Lanarkshire Council.

# *Appendix 3*
# Tail Docking

## Council of Docked Breeds

PRESS RELEASE

Tail docking is a practice which has been carried out for centuries as a normal part of dog breeding and management. It is a procedure which until recently has excited little interest or concern, but with the heightening of the debate surrounding animal welfare, docking has become caught up in a bitter argument between dog owners and breeders on the one hand and the veterinary establishment on the other.

In Britain some 50 recognised dog breeds are customarily docked, including gun dogs, terriers and working breeds, and docking is undertaken for a number of very specific reasons. The most obvious is the prevention of tail damage. Working gundogs, such as spaniels and the hunt-point-retrieve breeds are expected to hunt eagerly through heavy cover in a way that leaves their tails at risk from abrasion against brambles, thorns and other vegetation. The simple removal of the end of the tail prevents such abrasion, and enables the dog to work without injury. Likewise terriers are expected to work below ground, often in confined spaces, and the removal of the end of the tail greatly assists the dog, again preventing risk of injury.

Nor is the risk of tail damage confined to dogs which hunt in the field. Recent experience with breeds such as the boxer has shown that long, thin, whippy tails can easily be damaged in the home through contact with furniture, door jambs and other hard objects.

*Continued on next page . . .*

PROTECTING THE FUTURE WELFARE OF ALL DOCKED BREEDS

*. . . Continued*

Long-coated breeds such as the Old English sheepdog are docked for reasons of hygiene, to avoid the hair around the base of the tail becoming fouled by faeces. Even with constant grooming and washing, such fouling is unpleasant. If allowed to get out of hand it can lead to severe problems of hygiene or even flystrike and subsequent infestation by maggots. Such problems are greatly reduced or eliminated by docking.

In addition, breeds which have been docked over many generations have been selected for specific qualities of build and conformation, but not for tail length, shape and carriage. If left undocked it is unlikely that the best dogs would carry good tails. In seeking to maintain the quality of their breeds, breeders would therefore be left with a diminished number of suitable sires and dams. The genetic pool would be reduced, greatly increasing the risk of hereditary disease, and some breeds could even disappear altogether.

Docking is carried out when puppies are between 24 and 96 hours old and before the eyes are open. There are two methods. Either a ligature, normally an orthodontic band, is placed over the end of the tail, effectively cutting off the blood supply so that the tail comes away within 3 days, or the tail is simply removed with scissors. The majority of pro-docking vets prefer the latter method, and find that there is normally no need for stitches. However, these may sometimes be used, especially with larger breeds.

The charge of cruelty is often levelled at docking. However, long experience indicates that, correctly carried out, the procedure causes no pain or discomfort. Indeed, some puppies which are docked while they are sleeping do not even wake up. After docking, puppies will immediately return to their dam to feed, and there is no evidence that docking arrests development or weight gain.

Though anti-docking campaigners might wish it otherwise, the fact remains that docking continues to be popular amongst the great bulk of committed dog owners and breeders. Even five years after an important restriction in the law regarding docking, in the shooting field most spaniel and HPR owners continue to work docked dogs, while in the show ring docked exhibits continue to dominate the classes for traditionally docked breeds.

It was during the 1980s that a serious threat of prohibition of tail docking developed and a committee, the Council *for* Docked Breeds, was formed to defend the docking position. The Government was keen to prevent unqualified breeders from docking tails and in 1989

Home Office Minister Douglas Hogg offered a compromise position whereby an amendment to the 1966 Veterinary Surgeons Act would be passed, prohibiting docking by lay breeders, but leaving it open to qualified vets to continue docking. The Council accepted the arrangement and was disbanded shortly afterwards.

However, in 1991 a new and disturbing announcement was made by the Royal College of Veterinary Surgeons (RCVS) to the effect that following the passage of the new legislation it would proceed to declare docking both unethical and prima facie evidence of disgraceful professional conduct. Effectively, Government was saying that it was all right for vets to dock, but vets were told by their ruling body that if they did so, then they risked being struck off.

Dog breeders were incensed at the way in which they had been misled, and in 1991 at a packed meeting in the midlands they formed a new membership organisation, the Council *of* Docked Breeds (CDB), to campaign for the maintenance of the docking option. Two years later, in July 1993, the amendment to the Veterinary Surgeons Act cam into force, and the CDB found itself at the eye of a storm which spread throughout the dog world and the veterinary profession.

The CDB quickly identified three principal aims. Its first objective was to ensure that breeders could continue having their litters docked by sympathetic veterinary surgeons, and to do so it set up a helpline whereby members could be put in touch with local pro-docking vets. Secondly it mounted a campaign of media and public relations activity which ensured that the docking issue remained firmly in the spotlight and could be conveniently 'buried' by Government or the RCVS. Thirdly it elected to defend any of its members against unfair charges brought against them as a result of the new legislation and, crucially, to defend any veterinary surgeon who fell foul of the RCVS disciplinary process by continuing to dock.

The CDB had itself conducted a survey amongst vets, the results of which mirrored a survey by the RCVS itself and indicated that around 10% of the profession were favourably inclined towards docking. However, the intense pressure placed on vets by their professional body meant that very few were prepared openly to risk the sever sanctions with which the RCVS threatened those undertaking 'unethical' procedures. Matters came to a head within months, when Essex vet Marshall Dale was brought before a full disciplinary hearing at RCVS headquarters in London. The four day hearing amounted to a trial in court, complete with barristers in wig and gown. The CDB, at a cost of many thousands of pounds, conducted Marshal

Dale's defence, and it did a good job because to the dismay of the RCVS, the disciplinary committee found that Mr Dale had no case to answer. Sympathetic vets throughout the country who had been observing the case with great interest realised that the RCVS had proved powerless to stop its members taking their own professional decisions in relation to the issue of tail docking.

This, however, did not satisfy the animal protection bodies. The RSPCA had long declared its opposition to docking, and with the implementation of the new legislation it stepped up the pressure against dog owners and breeders who were thought to be in possession of docked litters. A string of incidents followed in which RSPCA officers interviewed breeders, sometimes in oppressive and high-handed manner, alleging that tails had been removed illegally. Again the CDB took action, defending its members, providing expert legal assistance and advising all breeders on the approach to be taken with the RSPCA. It soon became clear that neither the threat of disciplinary action against veterinary surgeons nor the bullying of breeders would prevent a practice which most dog breeders and a substantial minority of vets felt to be both legitimate and in the best interests of their dogs.

There followed a period in which the CDB developed its strength as a membership organisation and forged close links with field sports organisations such as the British Association for Shooting and Conservation and the British field Sports Society (now the Countryside Alliance). With a membership in excess of 10,000 the CDB became a member of FACE, the European federation of field sports associations, and started a programme of attendance at country sports fairs, gundog working tests and major dog shows. It also worked hard to win acceptance from the Kennel Club, where an equivocal attitude to docking remained entrenched. Such acceptance, however, remains elusive and while the CDB is welcomed at the prestigious CLA Game Fair, it has consistently been excluded from Crufts.

Meanwhile both the RCVS and the RSPCA persisted with legal and disciplinary moves against docking. To some extent these fell apart in November 1997 when the RCVS Council finally admitted that it would not refer to the Disciplinary Committee two cases in which it was alleged that a veterinary surgeon had docked puppies' tails for reasons that were neither therapeutic nor prophylactic – in effect admitting that it could not discipline vets who docked. A few days later a court dismissed charges of cruelty brought against a breeder by the RSPCA. The breeder had been defended by the CDB.

Overseas, however, the clouds have gathered. The Council of Europe Convention for the Protection of Pet Animals, which opposes docking and imposes draconian restraints upon the breeding of many old-established dog breeds, has been signed and ratified by a growing number of European states, and prohibitions on docking have swept through northern Europe, with bans imposed in Scandinavia, Germany, Holland and Austria. These moves are viewed with concern by the CDB, which has assisted overseas pro-docking groups with advice and assistance, and has strengthened its political monitoring and lobbying at European level in response.

Nevertheless, the threat of UK signing and ratification of the Council of Europe Convention must be take very seriously, for this would give the anti-docking lobby the opportunity to press the British Government for outright abolition of non-therapeutic docking.

And what of the dogs? Since 1993, when a number of breeders experimented briefly with long tailed litters, the vast majority of traditionally docked breeds have remained docked. However, where tails have been left on, a succession of tail damage cases has emerged. Not surprisingly, many of these relate to the use of dogs in the shooting field, and English springer and cocker spaniels have been hardest hit. Typically, young dogs are introduced to the beating line and very quickly end up with lacerated tails which, despite the employment of every possible remedy by the owner, fail to heal. In these circumstances a dog may finish a day's shooting literally covered in blood, and although the tail soon stops bleeding, subsequent shooting trips or even exercise in the field causes the wounds to reopen. The pain experienced by the dog is liable to put it off entering thick cover, and owners who have encountered the problem unanimously vow never to have another undocked dog.

The only remedy in these cases, and in the cases of other breeds – notably boxers – which have suffered tail damage, is amputation of the injured tail by a veterinary surgeon. This is a serious and costly operation which has to be conducted in a veterinary clinic under general anaesthetic. The healing process is long and painful, and if insufficient tail is removed, the damage may recur, requiring further surgery.

Unfortunately dogs cannot speak – at least in the conventional sense – but if anyone were to ask those dogs which have to undergo amputation of injured or diseases tails, there is little doubt that they would vote for docking, a tiny and insignificant procedure conducted a few hours after birth, which most caring and responsible breeders believe to be in the best interests of the dog.

Further information about tail docking or about membership of the Council of Docked Breeds can be obtained by calling the CDB helpline on **07000 781262** or visiting the CDB website on **http://www.cdb.org**

Graham Downing 14 July 1998